CRIMINAL
INVESTIGATION
A PRACTITIONER APPROACH

knowledge
question
experimental topic matte
fact hypothesis collecti
tests prediction interpretation alternat
subject
conclusion
investigation
testing
sample
discuss structural support developmer
answer
practical work issue advanc
purpose expansion information ste
understanding standard ide

ERNIE DORLING

Kendall Hunt
publishing company

Kendall Hunt
publishing company

www.kendallhunt.com
Send all inquiries to:
4050 Westmark Drive
Dubuque, IA 52004-1840

ISBN 978-1-4652-8485-3

DEDICATION

To my many colleagues and students who have been part of my life during both my law enforcement and academic careers. Your friendship and counsel have proven to be invaluable. You cannot imagine how many of you have enriched my life.

To my former Dean, the late Richard H. Ward, who passed away in February 2015. Your encouragement to write this book will never be forgotten. The study of all things related to criminal justice will not be the same without your daily presence.

To my current Dean, Mario Gaboury, who has talked me off the ledge of leaving teaching on more than one occasion. Thank you for the lifeline when I needed one.

To Lynn Monahan, Ph. D., Professor Emeritus, Department of Criminal Justice, Henry C. Lee College of Criminal Justice and Forensic Sciences, University of New Haven. Your painstaking review of each chapter has helped make this book possible.

To my good friends John Sherry, Carlos Sanchez, and Alan Pinette. Three of the best golf partners anyone can hope to have. Thank you for agreeing to let me use your fictitious alter ego in this textbook. I hope that you're happy with the outcome.

To John Wiener, former Lieutenant, Nassau County Police Department. You were very generous with your time and giving of your vast knowledge of police work. Nobody can review a document better than you can.

To my wife Linda. My sincere appreciation and love for the many editorial suggestions and understanding of the long hours spent in the den pursuing this project. Thank you.

CONTENTS

PREFACE

For the last two decades at least, television has inundated us with shows about the adventures of police work. With the exception, in this author's view, of the award-winning HBO series *The Wire* and the original *Law & Order* series, most shows seek primarily to entertain and often leave the viewers, and potential jurors in criminal cases, with the belief that most all crimes are solved with someone's DNA pointing to the unrealistic guilty party. Of course, those who actually practice the profession are well aware of just how false this is.

In reality, before one runs, one must learn to walk. Before putting a roof on a house, one must build a foundation. A major difference between this introductory book on criminal investigation and many of the other fine textbooks on this subject is that this book aims to aid the student in walking and building the foundation of basic knowledge necessary to pursue a more advanced study of this topic. And hopefully, doing so in a manner that encourages them to read, communicate and think analytically.

With this in mind, I've attempted to create a very different kind of textbook. To be clear, this book is not of the traditional kind most often found and used in this type of course. Written in quasi-novel format, with a brief academic discussion at the end of each chapter, the text introduces the reader to a number of fictional investigators who find themselves tasked with investigating a crime that evolves into a variety of other crimes as more evidence is uncovered during their investigation. Based on 25 years of experience in the field, and 15 years of teaching the subject, along with the information contained in a number of textbooks on the subject, I've taken, what I believe to be many of the basic principles of criminal investigation that serve as the foundation of information necessary to understand the basic concepts of this topic. This book is designed with the intent of creating a fun-learning process where students follow fictional characters and learn the most basic concepts of criminal investigation through dialogue and the personal interaction of its characters. In the process, I also hope to help the student of this subject to demystify the process of criminal investigation. Students must also understand the many legal considerations that investigators must be aware of while operating within those same legal boundaries. Throughout the text, there are various references to a number of legal cases with which students will want to be familiar.

Finally, one of the many traits good investigators exhibit is the ability to think analytically. This textbook attempts to guide the student through an analytical thinking process both through the dialogue of its characters and through the Discussion Questions and Exercises found at the end of each chapter. In most cases, these discussion questions allow the student and instructor to delve more deeply into the evidence and the case being presented. The exercises, in a number of instances, allow the student to actually inject themselves into the investigative process in order to move the investigation along. Hopefully, the students, and instructors, will find this approach to be one that makes learning fun.

ACKNOWLEDGMENTS

The author would like to thank the following individuals for reviewing all or parts of this text and providing valuable advice and comments in the writing of the book. I am very fortunate to have had the support and expertise from such a stellar group of professionals in both academia and law enforcement.

Cathryn Addy, Ph.D.	President, Tunxis Community College, Farmington, Connecticut
Anthony Arico	Assistant Special Agent in Charge, Department of Homeland Security, Immigration and Customs Enforcement (retired)
Michael Bouchard	Assistant Director, Bureau of Alcohol, Tobacco and Firearms (retired)
Leonard Boyle	Attorney, Chief State's Attorney's Office, Connecticut
Michael Clark	Federal Bureau of Investigation (retired); Instructor, University of New Haven
Steve Carmen	Senior Agent, Bureau of Alcohol, Tobacco and Firearms (retired); Certified Fire Investigator
Richard Cole	Assistant Professor, University of Connecticut
Howard Cox	Former federal prosecutor (retired)
Mark Davison	Sergeant, Connecticut State Police
Linda Dorling	Special Agent, Defense Investigative Service and OPM (retired)
Darren Gil	Professor, Southern University at New Orleans
Brian Havens	Defense Criminal Investigative Service, retired special agent

Bruce Jordon	Former Detective Sergeant, Dalton, GA Police Department
Donald R. Kincaid	SAC, Bureau of Alcohol, Tobacco and Firearms (retired)
Erin King	Senior Environmental Scientist and world's greatest daughter-in-law
Peter Massey	Lecturer, University of New Haven, Connecticut
Lynn Monahan	Ph.D.; Professor Emeritus, Department of Criminal Justice, Henry C. Lee College of Criminal Justice and Forensic Sciences, University of New Haven
Paul Murray	Deputy Chief State's Attorney for Operations, Connecticut (retired)
David Olson	P.E. (retired)
Jennifer Roberts	Office of the Chief Medical Examiners in CT
James Thomas	Attorney, Defense Logistics Agency (retired)
Joseph Toscano	Senior Fire Consultant; Jack Ward Fire Consultants, LLC
Joseph Vince	Director of Criminal Justice Programs, Mount St. Mary's University
Richard D. Walter, M.A.	Scholar-in-Residence, OSU-Graduate School of Forensic Sciences. Co-founder of the Vidocq Society
John Wiener	Lieutenant, Nassau County Police Department (retired)
Martin Wright	Environmental Protection Agency (retired)
Bernard Zapor	Special Agent in Charge, Bureau of Alcohol, Tobacco and Firearms (retired); Adjunct Professor, Arizona State University.

INTRODUCTION

"Blackstone's Police Operational Handbook recommends the ABC of serious investigation: Assume nothing, Believe nothing, and Check everything."

Ben Aaronovitch, Moon Over Soho

THE INVESTIGATOR

No one would dispute that the role and responsibilities of an investigator have changed significantly in recent years. Since retiring in 2001, I have seen dramatic changes and advancements in technology that simply did not exist during my 25 plus years in this profession. There was no social networking then. No smart phones either. iPads were only a figment of someone's imagination. Specialists trained in computer searches were just coming into being. The field of science, along with advances in technology, is changing and developing so fast that even the most vigilant investigators face challenges keeping up with all the new developments. Today, investigators are required to be far better educated as they deal with not only these changes, but an array of societal differences in this country, along with the ever-growing threat of international terrorism.

Many textbooks on the subject of criminal investigation begin with a chapter dedicated to the history of law enforcement and criminal investigation. This is certainly an important component of this topic of study, and students should certainly be aware of a few of the more significant events associated with the origins of criminal investigation. For instance, paid investigators can be traced back to England, where in the late 1700s, a staff of trained detectives was established. These men (women were not part of this development) did not wear uniforms and co-existed with local constables until the passage of the Metropolitan Police Act in 1829.

New York City later adopted a system of law enforcement similar to the one found in London. In 1880, Thomas Byrnes, after rising through the ranks as a patrolman and later a sergeant, was appointed as what we would refer to today, as the chief of detectives in the New York City Police Department. He gained renown through solving the Manhattan Savings Bank robbery of 1878. In 1886, Byrnes instituted the "Mulberry Street Morning Parade" whereby arrested suspects would be paraded before the assembled detectives in the hope that they would recognize suspects and link them to more crimes.

Byrnes' brutal questioning of suspected criminals popularized the term "the third degree," which was apparently coined by Byrnes.(1) The third degree, as practiced by Byrnes, included a combination of physical and psychological torture.(2)

In his autobiography, *The Making of an American*, Jacob A Riis, a police reporter for the New York Tribune, describes Byrnes "as tough, effective, unscrupulous, autocratic, and utterly ruthless. He believed that thieves had no rights a police officer was bound to respect. Above all, he was a ferocious and imaginative interrogator. Byrnes coined the phrase "third degree" to describe his methods of eliciting useful information from criminal suspects. He had no scruples about torture and did anything necessary to make suspects confess. Anything."(3)

Today, Byrnes' methods are not only outdated, they are illegal. Investigators employing Byrnes' tactics will, at a minimum, be fired, and worse, could end up in prison. As noted earlier, today's investigators must be far more educated and trained than ever before. Moreover, it is imperative that they make every effort to keep up with the many changes and advancements in both technology and science in order to better utilize those changes to help solve the crimes they are tasked with investigating.

Some things, however, have remained constant since Byrnes led New York's finest as they investigated criminal activity in the city. Investigators then, and now, look to successfully reconstruct past events, especially in cases related to homicide. In doing so, they have a number of responsibilities including the following:

1. Determine whether a crime has been committed.
2. Decide if the crime was committed within the investigator's jurisdiction.
3. Discover all the facts pertaining to the complaint or incident. This includes preserving all physical evidence.
4. Recover stolen property, if applicable.
5. Eliminate suspects.
6. Identify, locate, and apprehend/arrest the perpetrator.
7. Aid in the prosecution of the offender.
8. Testify effectively as a witness in court.

Determining if a crime has been committed relies on an investigator knowing the elements of a criminal act. Years ago, long before the availability of online texts and digital references, investigators carried, or had available, a book with the various elements to the offenses they investigated. Today, these elements are readily available to everyone. It has been this author's belief that a good investigator can investigate virtually anything as long as he/she knows the elements to the offense. While there are certainly some crimes that will benefit the investigator who has a high degree of specialized training in that area, such as computer forensics, it still holds true, given that the facts and evidence and knowing the elements to a particular offense should guide the investigator accordingly.

Discovering the facts in a case still relies on the tried and proven concept of asking:

- Who
- What
- When
- Where
- How
- Why

Far too often, young investigators fail to ascertain the answers to these questions. Failing to do so leaves too many questions unanswered. What you don't want is the answers to the questions you failed to ask, coming to light by a defense attorney that is doing his or her job better than you're doing yours.

There are many opinions as to what the most desirable traits are with regard to what one needs to be a good investigator. Some of these traits include but are certainly not limited to:

1. The ability to think analytically. This would, of course, include a high degree of intelligence and reasoning ability. This is a form of visual thinking. It involves a methodical step-by-step approach to thinking designed to break down complex problems into single and manageable components. Learn to weigh the information. Ask yourself, what is the main argument or line of reasoning?
2. Curiosity and imagination. This would include being skeptical, suspicious of people, and having a sense of awareness.
3. Having good observations skills. Being alert at all times.
4. Knowledge of life and people. With the societal changes in our world, this is more prevalent than ever. This would include good common sense, and in the case of interviewing people and/or working undercover, some acting ability and role playing.
5. The ability to control bias and prejudice. If interrogating a child molester is something you can't do without demonstrating your total disgust for the subject during the interview or interrogation, you have no business in the room with them. Leave your prejudices and biases at home. Don't bring them to the job. Those biases will take you where they want to go; not where the evidence should take you.
6. Sensitivity to others. Keeping people's confidence and treating people with respect.
7. The ability to express oneself both orally and in writing. This is often found to be a critical element in yearly evaluations of investigators and federal agents. There is no substitute for accurate report writing. Failure to do so can quickly destroy your case even before it reaches the prosecution stage. If you can't write effectively, take steps to remedy that now.

Investigators must also understand that no two crimes are exactly alike. They may indeed appear quite similar in nature, but there is always something different about them. Humans may appear to be similar in nature; however, there is always something that makes one standout from the other. So it is with crimes.

Many investigators, if they are being painfully honest, will admit that many crimes are solved by guesswork and luck. But I've found that good investigators have a tendency to "make their own luck" based on being tenacious, hard working, and relying on experience and the assistance of others. They know too that criminals always make mistakes. It's up to you to find those mistakes and capitalize on them. Evidence is always present. It's there. Sometimes, it's more glaring than others. But it's there.

Good investigators should also keep in mind that everyone lies. People lie. You've lied. You've lied to your parents, your friends, your teachers, etc. Everybody lies. Unfortunately, it's a natural part of life.

Good investigators should learn how to work with others. In today's complex society and areas of specialization, you can't be expected to know everything. You have to rely on others. It never ceases to amaze me that when professors give group assignments, there is always the complaint that this one or that one is not cooperating or doing their share. While I was a young agent at the Bureau of Alcohol, Tobacco and Firearms, a wise supervisor once reminded me that the work I did for him did not count as much as the work I did with and for other agents, especially those outside of our field office's jurisdiction. Reputations are often made, or destroyed, by one's ability to work successfully with others. Pull your weight. And when a member of the team doesn't, let them know. But be professional about it.

Investigators should understand that there is never enough time to do everything you need to do. Time is your most valuable commodity. We'll discuss this more later in the book. Realizing that time is valuable, investigators should know when to give up. You only have so much time. Sometimes, one must cut their losses and move on.

This book will demonstrate, in most cases, that criminal investigators rely on six basic investigative techniques to solve crimes:

1. Informants
2. Use of undercover agents
3. Laboratory results of physical evidence
4. Physical and electronic surveillance
5. Interviews and interrogation
6. Wiretapping, when and where permitted.

This book takes a unique approach to teaching the subject of criminal investigation. Written in quasi-novel format, students will learn the basic principles of criminal investigation through character dialogue. At the end of each chapter, there are, in most cases, questions for discussion and exercises. The exercises are designed to have the students inject themselves into the investigation by completing certain tasks that may or may not further the investigation.

The first chapter begins with the arson/bombing of an aircraft and the attempted bombing/arson of a business. Most textbooks on this subject include this type of crime late in the book. We start with it to demonstrate that investigations can:

1. Stand alone and be investigated for the crime they are.
2. Branch off into a number of other areas, many criminal in nature.

During the course of reading this text, students will see the emergence of other crimes take shape and the addition of a variety of actors and characters from other agencies that have jurisdiction in the crimes being uncovered. Hopefully, this will demonstrate the absolute necessity for working together with any number of agencies at the local, state, and federal levels. Also, this should demonstrate that outside agencies and individuals not having arrest authority can often provide a valuable service as part of the investigative process.

Students should take note as they read through the book to make notes of the evidence and facts being developed. You will no doubt be tasked with presenting what you believe to be the evidence of several different crimes aimed at any number of defendants as you reach the end of our fictional story.

Questions for Discussion

1. What are some additional traits, not mentioned in this Introduction, that you think good investigators must have?
2. Why do you think that analytical thinking is important to being a good investigator?
3. Discuss if you believe the statement, "everyone lies." What are your thoughts on this statement? Can you describe a time when you lied and it proved to be a huge problem for you?

Work Sheet

Exercise

1. Contact a local law enforcement agency (any agency including your hometown), and interview a detective or federal law enforcement agent about his or her impression of the future of law enforcement and criminal investigation. Try to do it in person. If you do it by phone, so indicate in your narrative. Ask this person the following questions:

   a. What are their thoughts about the impact technology and the advances in science that are having on the field of investigation.
   b. What are the skill sets needed to make a good investigator?
   c. What are the biggest challenges police administrators face today. How would "they" (the person you're interviewing) solve this problem?
   d. What issues cause police officers the most problems that result in discipline, including possible termination?
   e. What is that YOU must do to make yourself competitive for an entry-level position with the agency of the person you're interviewing? That is, if you're interviewing someone from Secret Service, imagine yourself applying for that agency and find out what you need to do to become competitive for a job with them.

   Prepare a 3–4-page, double-spaced paper on your interview. Be sure to identify whom you interviewed, their department, and area of specialization. Feel free to ask any additional follow-up questions you and/or your professor deem appropriate.

   Note to students: I've always found that after this exercise, a personal (not an email or text) handwritten note to the person you interviewed goes a long way. Think about how this person might display this note/card on his or her desk and show it to others. Then, when you graduate, send this person a follow-up note letting him or her know you've finished your degree. You never know that this person, who is now a contact for you, might have some thoughts as to where you might actually apply for a job.

Work Sheet

Notes

1. Byrnes, Thomas. (1886). *Professional Criminals of America*. Vol. 3. New York: Cassell and Company.
2. Riis, Jacob A. (1901). Chapter XIII, Roosevelt comes—Mulberry street's Golden Age. *The Making of America*.
3. ibid.

Supplemental Reading

Osterburg, James W. and Richard H. Ward. (2014). *Criminal Investigation: A Method for Reconstructing the Past*. 7th Edition. Anderson Publishing.

CHARACTERS

1. Special Agent Mike Cook, Bureau of Alcohol, Tobacco and Firearms
2. Detective Tony Martin—local police department
3. Carlos Sanchez—Assistant U.S. Attorney (AUSA)
   Courtesy of Carlos Sanchez. Copyright © Kendall Hunt Publishing Company
4. Lt. Tom Gonzalez—Fire Department
5. Lisa Swanson—Supervisor, ATF
6. Latrelle Jackson—Special Agent, Environmental Protection Agency
7. Angela Lyle—Office Manager, D & B Environmental
8. Sara Howard—Supervisor, Crime Lab
9. Alan Thompson—Co-owner, D & B Environmental
10. Eric Mann—Co-owner, D & B Environmental
11. Amber Fox—Special Agent, Defense Criminal Investigative Service (DCIS)
12. John Thomas—Foreman, D & B Environmental
13. Ed Van Pelt—Lt. Local PD
14. John Sherry—Insurance Investigator
    Courtesy of John Sherry. Copyright © Kendall Hunt Publishing Company
15. Alan Pinette—Auditor/Accountant
    Courtesy of Alan Pinette. Copyright © Kendall Hunt Publishing Company
16. Kimiko Matsui—Medical Examiner
17. Ralph Browning—Owner, Crane Environmental
18. Sammy Collins—Driver, D & B Environmental
19. Rachael Flynn—Scientist, EPA
20. Pamela Sullivan—Local Prosecutor

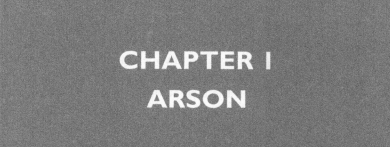

CHAPTER I
ARSON

"Those you trust the most, can steal the most."

Lawrence Lief, Industrial security analyst

There's a simple way to solve the crime problem: obey the law; punish those who do not.

Rush Limbaugh

Chapter Objectives

1. Gain an understanding of what constitutes an arson.
2. Obtain a good idea as to what investigative steps are necessary in conducting an arson investigation.
3. Be able to identify the types of people who commit arson.
4. Gain an understanding of the various motives for arson.
5. Understand the four classifications of fire causation.

Recommended Reading

1. Wambaugh, J. (2002). *Fire Lover*. New York: Avon Books.

THE CRIME

© Fer Gregory/Shutterstock.com

No one heard the explosion at 3:00 a.m. It was clear it happened, but it wasn't heard or seen by anyone. At least as far as it was known. The Twin Engine King Air exploded on the tarmac of the small private airport. Within seconds, the cockpit was engulfed in flames. It was only due to luck that the local zone car happened by and saw the flames. A quick radio call made sure that the fire department was dispatched without delay. As the first responder, she made sure to record the exact time she first observed the fire. While waiting for the fire department, she checked to see if there were any injuries or anyone requiring medical attention. The officer found no such persons. Nor, did she find any witnesses. She did take a photo of the fire knowing that the detectives would need to see that.

By 3:20 a.m., the local fire department were on the scene, and within minutes, had the fire under control. In fact, by 3:45 that morning, the fire had been extinguished. The fire commander, Lt. Tom Gonzalez, wasted no time securing the fire and the scene. The officer who called in the fire also remained on the scene. But his efforts to save the plane were all in vain. The plane would never fly again. At first glance, Lt. Gonzalez could only wonder what had caused the plane to blow up and burn the way it did. As soon as it was safe (his priority of course being to protect life and then, to save further property damage), he did his walk-around of the ravaged airplane. He was looking for the point of origin. And when he looked inside what was left of the cockpit, he found it. It was then, that he knew immediately what had caused the fire. It was an explosive device. Crude and simplistic, yes. But effective nonetheless. The fire had been intentionally set. He was sure of it. He had quickly pinpointed the point of origin; could see that the fire had been intentionally set, and, could smell the remnants of what appeared to be gasoline. The fact that there were pieces of what looked like a five-gallon gas can inside the cockpit helped confirm his suspicions. Gonzalez knew that he was at the scene of a crime and ordered his firefighters to stand back. He didn't want anything touched. Gonzalez motioned the patrol officer to join him in order to show her what he'd discovered. "Call your department and tell them a plane has just been intentionally set on fire here at the airport," Gonzalez said. "They need to send a detective out here right away."

Tony Martin had been a police officer for almost seven years, but he'd only been a detective for about six months. He was still learning the ropes. Tony was also realizing that being an investigator required a different skill set than the one required for being a uniformed patrolman. In fact, Tony was discovering that being a criminal investigator was not something easily taught. Instead, it was something he was going to have to learn over years of experience. But the department was small, and having someone spoon feed him through the process, was a luxury the agency could not afford. Tony would have to learn most of what he'd have to know to be a good investigator on his own. And he was smart enough to realize that this meant a lot of trial and error along the way. What he didn't know was that as soon as he received the call to meet the fire department at the local airport, that he was about to embark on a journey that would challenge all of his skills as investigator.

"Take a look at this," Lt. Gonzalez said to Tony as he exited his car just a few yards from the burnt aircraft.

"What am I looking at?" Tony asked.

"See this burnt gas can. It was inside the cockpit. This is what caused the plane to explode and burn so quickly," Gonzalez said.

"I do see it," Tony replied. "I also see these batteries, and, what looks like a time clock of some sort."

"I'm no bomb expert," Gonzalez said. "But someone placed this device onto this gas can with some sort of ignition device. When it was triggered, it set the gas can on fire."

"In other words, a simple time bomb," Tony suggested.

"That would be my guess," Gonzalez replied. "But I don't see, or, have any idea as to what the detonator might have been. It could have been something simple but I don't think we're going to find it here in this rubble. My guess, it was something simple or crude and burned up in the fire. This is going to be your most important piece of evidence as far as the fire scene goes. And, this is your point of origin."

Detective Tony Martin started to take notes. He wanted to make sure that he recorded the time the fire department had been notified; the time they arrived; what they saw; and what they did. He also had a patrol car cordon off the area so that no one entered the crime scene. Protecting the evidence against damage or contamination would be critical. He called for assistance from the department's forensic crime scene unit to help in ensuring that the evidence was collected correctly and in accordance with department policy and procedures. Detective Martin also made a record of the weather conditions at the time of the fire. Normally, he would have asked the first responder several additional questions about the fire such as the color of the flames, and anything she may have smelled. In this case, he didn't ask those questions.

By 5:15 a.m., Tony Martin knew that he was going to need more help than his small department could provide regarding the destruction of this airplane. Someone had deliberately blown up this plane; that he was sure of. But he had no idea why. Nor, did he know anything about the plane or its owners. All he knew was that this aircraft had been burnt and that a small crude device had been deliberately set to make sure that happened. Tony's first call that morning was to Bureau of Alcohol, Tobacco, Firearms and Explosives (BATF) Special Agent Michael Cook. Tony had met Michael just once before. It was a short introduction when Michael Cook stopped by the department for a routine criminal history check. Michael too was new to BATF. It was only recently that he began working his own cases after spending almost a year tagging along with a senior training officer. Michael had handed Tony his business card with the usual comment, "call me if there is anything I can do for you." Tony had heard a few of the older cops talk disparagingly about the feds. But he'd also been told that, "one can't have enough friends in this business." So Tony kept the card. And now, he called the number.

"Did I wake you up?" Tony asked.

"Of course you did," Mike replied. "Who is this?"

"It's Tony Martin. We met two weeks ago when you stopped by the department. Is your offer to do anything you can to help me still good?"

"Of course. But it better be good to call me at this hour of the morning."

"Just had a plane blow up on the tarmac at our private airport here. Fire department found a five-gallon gas can in the cockpit and what looks like the remnants of a timing device. Interested?"

"Absolutely. Anybody hurt? Witnesses."

"No on both accounts," Tony replied. "No one in the plane and no one saw anything as far as we can tell. Airport was closed. No security either. Fire department got the call about 3:20 a.m."

"Who called it in?"

"Patrol officer working her zone. Saw the fire and called it in. She's still here."

"Okay. What are you doing with regard to the crime scene?"

Figure 1.1 Twin Engine King Air.

"We have it secured. I've started documenting it. We're taking videos and photographs. We'll diagram it when you get here."

"Any witnesses?"

"None that we know of."

"Give me an hour or so. I'm on my way," Mike said.

Michael Cook wasted no time getting ready. He dressed quickly, and by 6:30 a.m., he was on his way to meet Detective Tony Martin. Cook knew that this case might require a more seasoned agent. But first, he'd access the scene and see what might be needed on behalf of BATF to assist a local agency in this investigation.

At 7:00 that same morning, while Special Agent Michael Cook was driving to meet Detective Tony Martin, a man named John Thomas arrived for work at the D & B Environmental Waste Facility. D & B was located just six miles from the airport where the Twin Engine King Air had just blown up. John Thomas was the company foreman. Around 7:00 each morning, he unlocks the gates to the truck parking lot and opens the warehouse by lifting a huge bay door in the back of the company. On this morning, as John Thomas opened the bay door, he froze dead in his tracks, like a deer in headlights. Thomas came face to face with what he believed to be a ticking time bomb.

Thomas stood there for what seemed like an eternity. In reality, it was only for a few seconds. He slowly backed away and took a picture of the device with his cell phone. As soon as he walked back outside the gate, he called the police.

The first officer on the scene looked at the photograph Thomas had taken with his cell phone. What he saw in the picture was what looked like a small windup clock connected to some batteries and matches. Nothing elaborate at all. But the small crude device was placed on top of what appeared to be an extremely large pile of papers.

"Did you notice anything else?" the officer asked Thomas.

"That's it. Just like in the picture. But there is a strong smell of gasoline in there too."

The responding officer called the department and requested a detective on the scene as quickly as possible. It was 7:15 a.m. and the one detective already working that morning was Tony Martin. Fifteen minutes later, Detective Martin was looking at the cell photo John Thomas had taken. A minute later, Martin was calling Special Agent Mike Cook for the second time that morning.

"Tony, I'm on my way. Should be there in about 20 minutes. What's up?" Mike asked without first saying hello.

"Don't go to the airport Mike. I want you to come straight over to D & B Environmental, it's just a few miles from the airport. I'll text you the address."

"Why there?"

"We have another bomb. Only this one hasn't gone off," Tony said.

"Don't do anything until I get there," Mike instructed.

"Don't worry, I'm not. We've got the place sealed off with the fire department here. I'll also text you a picture of the device. Doesn't look like much. But we'll wait on you."

The place looked something out of a Hollywood movie scene, when, 20 minutes later, Special Agent Michael Cook arrived. Police cars and fire trucks had surrounded the plant. The police had kept the employees from entering the plant. Even the local newspaper, always monitoring the police scanner, had sent a reporter to the scene in an effort to get a scoop on what was happening.

"It doesn't look like much of a bomb to me," Tony said.

"Me either," Mike replied. "I still want to talk to the foreman again. I want to hear what he saw, heard, smelled, and so forth before we do anything."

John Thomas told Cook and Martin what he'd told the officer who first arrived on the scene. He opened the plant most every morning around 7:00 a.m. His daily ritual was virtually the same every morning; unlock the gates to the parking area around seven, then open the loading door and enter the bay area through the back of the facility. This morning, he saw the device on top of a pile of papers and noticed a very strong odor of gasoline.

"That's when I called the police," Thomas said.

"How long have you worked here?" Mike Cook asked.

"About two years."

"Any sign of a break-in when you came in this morning?"

"None that I saw," Thomas replied.

"Any idea who might want to do something like this?" Cook asked.

"No idea whatsoever," Thomas replied.

Fire commander Lt. Tom Gonzalez told Martin and Cook that his department could easily remove the timing device from the gasoline-saturated papers and did so without incident. Once the crude device was safely away from the papers, Cook could tell from his training that the clock had malfunctioned. It was clear that the device was set to go off at 3:00 a.m. But it failed, stopping short of the time it was set to go off. A large quantity of matches were supposed to ignite from a spark which in turn would have, hopefully, set the papers saturated in what smelled like gasoline, on fire and potentially destroying the facility. It was a simple and normally effective ignition and timing device. But in this case, it failed.

"This clock looks exactly like the one, or the remnants of the device we recovered at the airport," Lt. Gonzalez told Martin and Cook. "Even the batteries look exactly alike."

Martin and Cook looked at the device along with a couple of cell phone photos of the burnt device Martin had taken at the airport.

"What do you think Mike," Martin asked.

"I think that I don't believe in coincidences. Do you Tony?"

"In this business; no, I do not. I don't think there is any such thing as coincidences."

What Tony Martin and Mike Cook didn't realize was that there is a trend in the insurance industry where insurers are saying enough is enough and are starting to take a tougher stance against fraud.

"Fraudulent fire losses have always been a problem, not only for us, but for

© Gregory Smith/Contributor/Getty Images

Figure 1.2 ATF Agents Searching Arson Crime Scene.

the insurance industry as well," Lt. Gonzalez told the two investigators. "Along with all the other types of fraudulent claims faced by the industry federal statistics issued in 2010, suggest that arsons involving structures, both residential, storage and public, accounted for almost 45.5% of the total number of arson offenses. By far the most common crime involving fire is the illegal burning of buildings. Owners burn their own property in order to make fraudulent insurance claims. But you'll hear more about that from the insurance investigator whenever they hear about this and show up."

"Insurance investigator?" Detective Martin asked.

"Yeah," Mike Cook replied. "Most all of the insurance companies have established special investigation units, referred to as Special Investigative Unit (SIU) to work with law enforcement in an attempt to help combat these bogus claims. I haven't worked with them yet but I know several of the agents have. Most of them are pretty good. Many are even retired feds or local state fire marshals, so they know the system. But we don't know if this is a bogus claim or not. We have no idea what's going on here but the insurance investigator will be a big help. We need to find out the name of the company that holds the policy on this plane as well as on the facility."

"We'll get that soon enough," Tony Martin said.

Many insurance adjusters have been involved in some sort of fire investigation training, and are aware of the basic fire science, characterized by the fire triangle that includes fuel, oxygen, and heat which, when combined, form a chemical reaction that we call fire. Depending on the circumstances, each particular fire will grow and develop differently.

Experienced adjusters are normally proficient at locating the origin of fire, and identifying potential ignition sources. It is critical to locate the point of origin. There could also be multiple points of origin. Once located, the point of origin must be examined for sources of ignition and traces of accelerants. Experienced adjusters also recognize the potential for subrogation due to fires caused by equipment failures, or tenant negligence. Similarly, they recognize potential arson fires, and understand the potential to deny payment on the claim. This is often where the adjuster will bring in an expert to look into the causation issues for future litigation. Fire causation is obviously a critical issue, and the first question that has to be answered when investigating a fire. Having a fire adjuster or investigator from the insurance company can prove invaluable when putting an investigative team together.

"I'm not trying tell you guys how to do your job," Gonzalez added. "But keep in mind, that at some point, you're going to have to prove this was an arson."

"What exactly do you mean?" Detective Martin asked.

"Fire causes can be viewed in terms of three categories," Gonzalez said. "Natural, accidental, and incendiary. Sometimes, we are unable to determine the reason for a fire. The crime of arson has basically three elements. First, you have to prove that there has been a burning of property. Second, you have to show that the burning was started with malice, that is, with the specific intent of destroying property."

"How do we do that?" Martin asked.

"We can do that by establishing a motive," Cook interjected.

"That's right," Gonzalez replied. "Figuring out the motive to all of this is going to be crucial."

"Yeah," Cook responded. "We need to get that insurance investigator here sooner than later."

"One more thing," Gonzalez said. "You'll have to prove that the burning was incendiary in nature. There must be proof of the existence of an effective incendiary device. I'll be able to testify to that easily enough for the plane. And, it's going to be easy enough to prove that the plane fire was not natural or accidental. We know that by far the most common arson fires that are set is the direct result of the pouring of a flammable liquid with ignition by match, which is found in almost two-thirds of all cases. The plane that was destroyed is a clear example of this. As for the attempted arson of the company, you'd normally have to prove that all possible natural or accidental causes have been considered and ruled out. But since the bomb malfunctioned, and, it appears to have been the same type of device that destroyed the plane, you shouldn't have to worry too much about that."

"We'll certainly run that by the prosecutor when the time comes," Mike Cook said.

"But as you said Mike, we have no idea what's going on here. Why would anyone want to blow up this plane and try to blow up the company?" Tony Martin asked.

"There are a number of reasons that we're going to have to explore," Cook replied. "People commit arson for a variety of reasons. They might be trying to conceal another crime. Maybe they're trying to eliminate some business competition. It's also possible that someone is trying to intimidate someone or scare them or their family. Maybe it was just for insurance money. I don't know. We're going to have to figure this all out. And we're not going to do it anytime soon. We're just getting started. We're going to have to look at all these records that were saturated in gasoline."

"Will we need a warrant for that?"

"No. Investigating a fire scene or in this case, the attempted bombing of this company, allows us to search without a warrant under the rules of exigent circumstances, as long as we do so within a reasonable period of time. Since we're going to take these records today, I'm sure that will be interpreted as a reasonable period of time."

A Brief Conversation about Arson Investigation

Fire investigation: where does it stop?

While fire cause is important, equally important is fire spread after origin. As a rule, fire moves or travels upward through a heat-transfer process. And, fire travels the path of least resistance. As it hits a surface, or a wall, or ceiling, it spreads out in V pattern. Often, accidental fires grow much larger than they should, thereby creating much more financial damage than might be expected. It is always necessary to determine how the fire started, but it is equally important to consider such matters as,

1. Was the building properly constructed?
2. Was the fire protection equipment properly installed and maintained?
3. Were fire stops in place, and did they work?
4. Did all the people involved do their job properly, whether they be a maintenance contractor, an equipment inspector, or a fire suppression crew?

For example, if a smoke detector had no batteries, and the tenants in the building perished as a result of a fire, could they have been awakened and escaped if the batteries had been in place: Further, who removed the batteries, and who is responsible for maintenance of the equipment? In this situation, it is not sufficient to determine that the fire had started in the living room couch by careless smoking without answering the questions of fire spread.

Where there's smoke, there's fire

Most people have a pretty good idea of what fire is. However, when investigating a fire, trying to interpret the wording on an insurance policy fighting a civil or criminal action in the courts, a more definitive definition is required. One of the most accepted definitions of fire is put forward by the National Fire Protection Association as . . . "a rapid oxidation process with the evolution [generation] of light and heat in varying intensities."[1] In short, if a fuel is being oxidized at a fast rate and there is heat and light or a glow being generated by the reaction, it is a fire.

So, what is oxidation? It's a chemical process. And for our purposes here, it's a process whereby a material or fuel, say, gasoline, combines with oxygen and produces something such as a fire.

The financial motive for arson

"In general, two primary factors influence the insured person's decision to commit arson fraud: (1) the desire for financial relief and (2) greed—the desire for easily obtained financial assistance."[2] These two reasons apply to cases dealing with arson-for-profit. Arson is committed for a variety of other reasons to include, murder, revenge, excitement, and covering up other crimes. In order to deny insurance coverage in a case of suspected arson, the insurer must establish motive, opportunity, and incendiary origin. The first criterion may conjure up pictures of extreme financial stress driving an owner to burn down his or her own property. This note simply points out that financial stress need not be a factor in establishing the financial motive for arson. All that one needs to motivate arson is a sufficiently large net benefit from a fire.

There is one class of benefits from arson that is fairly easily measured: the potential for financial gain. In many cases, there may be the opportunity for outright profit if properties are over-insured. The potential arsonist may also recognize that insurance payments following a fire can relieve him or her of a heavy debt burden, improving his or her cash flow. Thus one might turn to arson as a means of backing out of a contract gone sour. A businessperson's hopes that he or she would turn a profit have not materialized. Insufficient profits, or actual losses, may not warrant a continuation of the project. The owner would just close up shop if it were not for the cost of mortgage payments.

A fire in a building fairly insured might free up the funds to pay down the mortgage and allow the producer to move on to another project. If arson is perceived as being more profitable than not turning to arson, there is a financial incentive to burn. Once these potential financial gains have been measured, they must be compared to the less easily quantifiable perception of potential for detection (and the associated financial loss due to the insurance denial and even jail) and the personal cost of doing what is wrong. In general, the greater the potential financial gain is, the greater will be the net benefits of arson.

As James W. Osterburg and Richard H. Ward (2014) state in their book, *Criminal Investigation, a method for reconstructing the past*, "the investigation of arson—especially arson-for-profit—is a demanding task. The technical assistance of auditors, tax lawyers, real estate agents, and credit and financial managers will often be needed to get past the roadblocks set up to hide ownership of the property and the identity of the individual responsible. In some cases, circumstantial evidence may provide the basis upon which prosecution is possible."[3] Forensic auditors should also have knowledge of business and asset valuation for determining the dollar amount of fraud, should fraud be the reason for the crime.

It is generally believed that the most important interview that the investigators will conduct with regard to any suspected arson investigation is the interview of the owner or owners. With this in mind, it is important to ask some very key questions. Some of these questions include, but are not limited to:

a. Who was the last person on the premises?
b. Is the business a corporation, partnership, or proprietorship?
c. What year was the business organized?
d. Any other locations used in conjunction with business for storage?
e. Who has a financial interest in the business?
f. What is the companies commodity, i.e. what do they make?
g. Name/addresses of suppliers.

   h. How many persons employed? (Get names, address, etc. of employees.)
   i. Any judgments, liens, or suits against business?
   j. Do you think someone set the fire?
   k. Of those you know here, who do you feel is NOT involved?
   l. Has anything like this ever happened to you before?

I always liked to add the question of whether or not one might be receptive to taking a polygraph test. I often found that initially, the answer was yes. Later, after reflection, or on advice from counsel, that answer would very often be changed to NO.

The primary purpose of this introductory chapter is to familiarize the student with the very basic aspects of investigating an arson or bombing case. Becoming a seasoned arson investigator requires extensive training and experience; not something any introductory course in criminal investigation is going to provide. More advanced courses on this subject will deal with issues related to multiple points of origin; the importance of smoke coloring; and the subject of alligatoring of wood, which is charring that produces blisters on wood and provides an indication that, perhaps, the fire moved quickly. Advanced courses on this topic, which are best served for students in a more advanced course in criminal investigation and/or in arson investigation, will also include the study of arsonist profiles, vehicle bombings, and reconstructing explosive crime scenes. An excellent example of this was the Bureau of Alcohol, Tobacco and Firearms reconstruction of the device used in the Boston marathon bombing in 2013. The device, a simple pressure cooker, was reconstructed from parts recovered at the crime scene and the point of the blast site and recreated by ATF crime scene and arson specialists.

This textbook, and our fictional story, begins with crimes associated with arson, attempted arson, and the bombing of an aircraft. Students, and investigators, will learn that these types of crimes usually require incorporating virtually every type of investigative technique available. Investigating such crimes usually involves laboratory analysis; financial analysis; the use of sources/informants; extensive witness interviews; the coordination with multiple agencies and outside entities such as insurance companies and their investigators; and employing various types of surveillance activity. Personally, I found them

Figure 1.3 BATF agents examining crime scene of Boston Marathon Bombing.

to be the most challenging and rewarding of all the various types of investigations I've ever been involved with. In time, I believe that many of you will also find this to be true.

Key Terms

Accelerant

Pyromania

Flashover

Fire patterns

Questions for Discussion

1. Discuss the complexities of investigating an arson case.
2. Identify five people, other than the principle owners, foreman, and office manager, that Detective Martin and SA Cook should interview next with regard to this investigation? Why? What question(s) should they ask and why?
3. What do you think the reason for the arson/destruction of the aircraft is?
4. What do you think the motive for the attempted arson of the environmental waste facility is?
5. What questions should the first officer on the scene be asked? Why?
6. What are some of the most common reasons for arson?
7. What types of collateral crimes might arson be used to cover up?
8. What is the purpose of the National Insurance Crime Bureau? Do some research.
9. Do some research and identify who, in your home town, has primary jurisdiction in arson investigations.
10. What are the four classifications of fire causation?

Work Sheet

Websites

1. https://www.nicb.org/
2. https://www.atf.gov/

Notes

1. Walters Forensic Engineering, | 277 Wellington Street West, Suite 800 | Toronto, ON M5V 3H2. http://www.waltersforensic.com/articles/fire_investigation/vol6-no1.htm.
2. Swanson, C., N. Chamelin, L. Territo, and R. W. Taylor. (2009). *Criminal Investigation*. 10th Edition, 603. McGraw Hill Publishing.
3. Osterburg, James W. and Richard H. Ward. (2014). *Criminal Investigation: A Method for Reconstructing the Past*, 7th Edition, 529. Anderson Publishing.

Supplemental Reading

ATF Arson for Profit Manual.

Campbell, Richard. (2014). *Intentional Fires*, National Fire Protection Association, April.

Fraud Examiners Manual, 3rd Edition.

Lasley, James R., Nikos R. Guskos, and Randy A. Seymour. *Criminal Investigation: An Illustrated Case Study Approach*. Pearson Publishing.

Osterburg, James W. and Richard H. Ward. (2014). *Criminal Investigation: A Method for Reconstructing the Past*, 7th Edition, 529. Anderson Publishing.

Rossotti, Hazel. (1993). *Fire: Servant, Scourge and Enigma*. New York: Dover Publications, Inc.

Swanson, C., N. Chamelin, L. Territo, and R. W. Taylor. (2009). *Criminal Investigation*, 10th Edition, 603. McGraw Hill Publishing.

U.S. Department of Justice. (2010). FBI, Crime in the U.S.

CHAPTER 2
THE CRIME SCENE

© Loren Rodgers/Shutterstock.com

"A crime scene investigator has to have a positive attitude. You've got to believe you're going to find the evidence."[1]

Dr. Henry C. Lee
Professor Emeritus
Henry Lee College of Criminal
Justice and Forensic Sciences
University of New Haven, New
Haven, Connecticut

Chapter Objectives

1. Define a crime scene.
2. Be familiar with the major considerations that dominate a crime scene search.
3. Understand the types of crime scenes.
4. Understand the various types of evidence.
5. Understand the purposes of a crime scene search.

Tony Martin and Mike Cook had two separate and distinct crime scenes to process; the one at the airport where the plane was destroyed, and, the one at D & B Environmental. Neither scene was all that large. And because the crime scenes were so small and isolated, it allowed the two investigators to work together closely to process the scene with the help of a single forensic investigator from Tony Martin's department. They knew that before their investigation could start, both crime scenes needed to be explored for evidence. And then, they'd have to get the evidence to the crime lab without destroying it. "Let's start here at the plant," Tony Martin said. "We can gather up all these records and place them in plastic bags. We'll have to dry them out and look at them later."

Detective Tony Martin assigned a patrol officer at the airport to protect the crime scene until he and Cook got there. The patrol officer would create and maintain a log of anyone who came into the crime scene. The *chain of evidence* would start with both Tony Martin and Mike Cook.

"No plastic bags," Mike Cook said. "We want to make sure that we identify the accelerant as quickly as possible. I'm sure this is gas, and if so, it's a petroleum-based hydrocarbon. The vapors will dissipate over time, how much exactly, I'm not sure. Plastic can react with the hydrocarbons. By putting them in plastic bags, we're running the risk of having the gases escape through the damaged material."

"How did you know that?" Martin asked.

"Just got back last month from some advanced arson training at FLETC. Trust me, until a month ago, I had no idea either. What we need are some large metal cans, maybe even a large trash can."

"I'm not sure we have any large metal trash cans at the department," Martin replied.

"Can you send someone down to the local hardware store right now and buy some. Bring me the receipt. I'll voucher this off."

"Sounds good," Tony said. "While we're waiting, let's grab that printer that was put next to this pile of paper."

The crime scene at D & B Environmental was small. The office was relatively close in proximity to where the papers had been stacked in a pile. It was clear that someone had rifled through the file cabinets and dumped the papers into a pile. As they began to place the papers into a large aluminum garbage can that had been purchased by a local officer, they were met by Angela Lyle, D & B's office manager.

"Ms Lyle, I'm special agent Mike Cook with the Bureau of Alcohol, Tobacco, Firearms and Explosives. This is Detective Martin. What can you tell us about this?"

The last thing Angela Lyle thought she'd be doing this morning was learning that her office had been ransacked and that someone had tried to blow up the place where she worked. She was visibly shaken. Seeing her files torn to pieces and stacked in a pile the way they were, Lyle thought, was like seeing a part of herself violated. She was stricken with fear.

"I don't know anything about this," Angela said. "I just got to work and saw the police cars and fire trucks. Can you tell me what happened?"

"It appears someone broke in, although we don't know how just yet, and tried to blow the business up," Cook replied.

"But why?" Angela asked.

"We were hoping you could tell us," Tony Martin responded.

"I have no idea."

"We're going to want to talk to you a bit later if that's alright," Mike Cook said. It wasn't a request; it was simply a polite way of putting Angela Lyle on notice that they'd be back soon to talk to her more in depth. For now, they simply wanted to know who owned the business and where they were at present.

"The company is owned by two people, Mr. Alan Thompson and Mr. Eric Mann."

"Do you know where Mr. Thompson and Mann are right now?" Special Agent Cook asked.

"No, but I can call them."

"Please do. And please let me know when you might expect them here," Cook instructed her.

"Do we have your consent to search the office and the facility in connection with this attempt to destroy it?" Special Agent Cook asked.

"Sure," Angela Lyle replied. "Anything we can do to help."

"Thank you," Cook replied. "And after you call the owners, would you please go with this officer and see if you notice anything else missing from your office."

Angela Lyle went with a crime scene specialist who worked with Detective Tony Martin to watch as her office was checked for fingerprints, photographed and searched. Cook and Martin would speak with her in more detail later. For now, they concentrated on securing the documents and the crude explosive device that failed to start a fire. Cook also asked Angela Lyle to sign a "Consent-to-search form" allowing him and Detective Martin to search the offices of D & B Environmental. Agent Cook knew that a consent to search had to be given voluntarily by a person reasonably believed to have control and legal access to the D & B. Cook was confident that Angela had such control and legal access. Cook and Martin were also confident that searching and seizing the records stacked in a pile and the odor of what they believed to be gasoline, along with the timing device, did not require a warrant. Cook was confident that he had obtained the all physical evidence available to identify the method of operation used by whoever committed this act. Later, it would help him reduce the number of suspects and hopefully, help identify the perpetrator.

As soon as Cook and Martin had all the records carefully placed in a garbage can, the two investigators immediately went to the local airport to collect whatever evidence was available.

"If you look here inside the cockpit, you'll see what looks like a five-gallon gas can," Lt. Tom Johnson said. "And here, is what looks like some batteries, and what's left of what looks like a wind up alarm clock."

"It's all pretty charred," Special agent Cook said. "But we're going to take it to the lab anyway. Who knows what they might find. Those people are amazing sometimes."

Cook and Martin gathered what appeared to be the remnants of the crude explosive device that was suspected of starting the fire that destroyed the aircraft. They also gathered what remained of the five-gallon gas can they suspected of having contained the fuel that ignited the fire.

"What's this?" Cook asked, pointing to a book.

"Let me see that," Detective Martin replied.

It only took the detective a moment to realize what the book Cook was pointing to was. "It's the flight log," Martin said. "We're going to want to look at this. Might contain some helpful information for us."

Martin knew that a flight log would contain information from the recent history of the airplane to the destination and purpose of its flights. It would also include out/in operating time, the destination and purpose of flight; adding oil, and inspections performed.

"That we'll put in a paper bag and seal it," Cook said.

After photographing and sketching the crime scene associated with the burnt aircraft, Tony and Mike found themselves with a van full of evidence gathered from the scene of the airplane fire and from D & B Environmental. They had quickly realized that the work involved in gathering the evidence was not as romantic as it is portrayed on a variety of television shows where everyone looks like a Hollywood movie star dressed in perfectly matching outfits that fit snuggly on their thin frames. In this case, they were both filthy dirty from searching both crime scenes. And, they were exhausted from rummaging through the debris left behind by the explosion of the aircraft as well as from the attempted bombing of the environmental plant. Each piece of evidence was carefully photographed and tagged in order to later recreate the exact location where it was found. At some point, if they were successful in identifying those responsible for participating in either of these crimes, this evidence could very well find its way into a court of law. If that happened, the rules of evidentiary procedure would require a careful presentation to the jurors. Any contamination of the evidence could, and would no doubt, result in that evidence being excluded for the trial. Two hours later, they arrived at the regional ATF crime lab.

Sara Helms had been with the crime lab for over 10 years, and, had been the director of the lab for the past two years. Sara was an expert witness in more courts than he could imagine. And, she had appeared on more news shows than she cared to remember, often explaining the pain-staking process involved in gathering and analyzing evidence. Sara never ceased to be amazed at the number of jurors who still wanted to see the DNA evidence in a case, even when none existed. It was one of the unfortunate results of the many television shows that had clearly poisoned much of the general public into believing that crimes could be solved and guilt established by simply presenting the DNA evidence. And, she never ceased to be amazed at the times when jurors acquitted someone because there was no DNA in the case. Still, she loved her work, no matter how often she had to explain to jurors the fact that no DNA was present, or when she had to mentor young investigators through the process of exactly what it was her lab did. Simply put, Sara's lab dealt in criminalistics. She and her staff were, first and foremost, scientists. They were concerned with the scientific examination of minute details found in physical evidence for the purpose of trying to identify substances, objects, and instruments, and to establish a connection between the physical evidence and suspects; in some cases, even between the victim and between crime scenes themselves. Sara's lab had come a long way from the one first established by August Vollmer in 1923. But the concept was the same; link the evidence to the suspects and/or victims. Sara had not worked with either Tony or Mike in the past. What she did know about them was little other than they were young and were working what seemed to be a very difficult case indeed.

"Nice to meet you," Sara said, extending her hand to Mike first and Tony second. "What have you got for me?"

"A van full of evidence," Tony said. Not exactly the specific answer Sara Helms was looking for.

"Can you be a bit more specific?" Helms asked.

"We have a van full of burnt debris from an airplane that was blown up," Mike replied. "We have some parts we think are from the explosive device that blew up the plane, and, the device that malfunctioned at the environmental plant. The records we recovered are in two large aluminum garbage cans. I think that they're saturated in gasoline but need to be sure, if that's possible."

"It's certainly possible," Helms replied. "We'll try to extract the chemical accelerants from the paper and other debris to single out what the compounds are."

"I'm curious," Detective Martin said. "How do you do that?"

"There are several ways," Helms replied. "Since you guys put the papers in an aluminum container, a good call by the way, we can try something called a solvent extraction. What we'll do, in essence, is take a sample from the can and place it in another container with a solvent. The solvent dissolves the sample separating the hydrocarbons. Then we can analyze it using a technique known as gas chromatography."

Tony Martin and Mike Cook's eyes met briefly. Each man could sense what the other was thinking; *"what would we do without these lab guys."*

An hour later, Mike and Tony had unloaded the van full of evidence and carefully laid everything out in a large room Sara Helms had designated for them. Everyone involved was careful to maintain an accurate chain of custody; often the source of many procedural errors identified by the courts. Each piece of evidence was logged in and assigned an identification number. It would be placed in storage so as to not be intermingled with other evidence. Sara Helms personally supervised this operation so that the evidence would not be successfully attacked in court on issues dealing with tampering, contamination, or substitution.

Once the evidence was in a position for it to be examined, Sara told the young investigators that she doubted she would be able to get any fingerprints from the physical evidence the two of them had brought him because of the intense charring of the pieces associated with the airplane. Sara did offer some limited hope that she would do her best to get a latent print from the rudimentary device that failed to explode inside the facility.

"Why do you think that's going to be a problem?" Tony asked.

"Because there are a variety of conditions that affect the quality of fingerprints," Sara said. "Fingerprints are impressions of the friction fridges on the skin of the fingers. They leave an impression or outline of the ridges when transferred to some object. For instance, the surface on which the print is found can affect this. Latent prints on smooth surfaces such as glass can last for years. Latent prints on documents such as paper vary as they tend to fade or deteriorate over time. In this case, latent prints resulting from contamination such as the fire debris or soot are quickly destroyed. That's what you have on the burnt parts from the airplane. The parts of the so-called timing device or bomb as you call it have rough ridges, except for maybe the batteries."

"So you think that getting a print is out of the question?" Mike asked.

"Don't be discouraged. It's important that we maintain a positive attitude about this. Sure, a latent print usually requires a smooth surface for us to recover it. In other words, it can't have a lot of ridges, although we've had some success with leather products. But that's not the case here. Rough surfaces create problems for us because the ridge lines in the finger tips are not always present. But that won't stop us from trying. Remember from your basic school training, something called the Locard Principle."

"Sure," Tony replied. "Every contact leaves a trace."

"That's right," Sara replied. Even if we can't find a print, maybe we can find something else. French criminologist Edmond Locard developed this theory, which still holds true today. This theory, that every contact leaves a trace, is the foundation to all of forensic science."

"Okay, but what do you mean by ridge lines?" Tony Martin asked.

"Ridge lines are found on the tips of fingers," Sara replied. "Human fingerprints are unique, and very difficult at best to alter. Everyone has their own set of prints; even identical twins. The prints you're born with are the prints you die with. And remember, even if a person tries to burn their prints off, they'll usually only succeed for a short period of time. As the skin grows back, the print reappears. Once we have the ridge lines, we can classify the prints and run a check through IAFIS, the Integrated Automated Fingerprint Identification System, for you."

"Yes, we've used IAFIS before," Tony replied. "I've heard stories from the old-timers who had to wait weeks and sometimes months for the FBI to check a set of prints on a case."

"Yes," Sara replied. "I heard the same stories. Some of those old-timers still work here, so be careful. The old-timers, as you say, had to wait for the FBI to check prints and get back to us, back in the day that is. Things can move much quicker now. IAFIS is now commonplace and takes a matter of minutes sometimes to get a hit. And yes, while IAFIS can search hundreds of thousands of prints in less than a second, once it establishes a match, a trained agent, or specialist in fingerprint examination, still has to personally check the file. The human element is still an integral part of the process. So don't simply rely on fingerprints and DNA to make your case. You're still going to have to interview people. And there is not an app on your smart phone, or computer, or any other scientific advancement that I'm aware of that will negate that step in the investigation for you."

"What about all of the records we recovered from the company?" Tony asked. "They were doused in what we think was gasoline."

"Documents pose a number of challenges," Helms told the investigators. "Why do you think that the records were saturated in gasoline and thrown into a big pile?"

"It's obvious who ever wanted to blow up the building, wanted the records destroyed," Tony replied. "Or, they simply thought that it was the easiest way to set the building on fire. Either way, we're going to have to examine the records once you've finished testing them for any evidence of gasoline being present and, when we dry them out."

"Let's look at this from two angles," Helms suggested. "First, once the records are tested and dried, we'll see if we can get prints from them. However, I imagine that there will be a lot of prints on those records, especially those belonging to people who work at the company. But let's also look for documents that might have been photocopied and spliced together. We'll also try and match some of the documents to the printer you brought in. Perhaps some of the documents were printed away from the business."

"That's going to take some time," Mike replied. "We're going to want to review them all ourselves. And as soon as we can."

"That's right," Tony added. "We're not exactly sure what we're looking for. Not yet anyway."

"I noticed that there isn't anything here from the business itself that might tell us how anyone might have gotten inside the company to grab all those records and place this device on top of it," Helms said.

"There wasn't any sign of a break-in," Tony replied. "Nothing. When the foreman opened the back garage door in the morning, he came face to face with this device. It almost scared him to death."

"Well, whoever did this had to have had access to the business somehow. If they didn't break-in, then they had access to the building."

"That would appear so," Mike replied. "But it has to have something to do with the plane blowing up. It's either an inside job, or, someone has it out for the owners of the company. That's our early thinking."

"Probably a good thought at this early stage," Helms replied.

Sara Helms didn't know either, exactly what the records might yield, that is. They were part of the administration of the company. These records, which she had yet to see, were not questioned documents in the sense that there was an instant suspicion that they had been altered or that their authenticity might be in question such as if someone had forged a signature. But that remained to be determined. For now, Helms had a lot of work to do, and not just on the evidence Tony and Mike had brought them. This wasn't television; she had cases backed up and would not be providing any answers to the young investigators within the next hour or two.

Mike and Tony shook hands with Sara Helms and said good-bye.

"Let's make a quick stop by the office," SA Mike Cook said. "I want to give Lisa a quick rundown of what happened this morning."

"Who is Lisa?" Tony Martin asked.

"My boss," Mike replied.

As the two men drove to Mike's office to meet with Lisa, they had no idea what they were looking for with regard to all those records. What they did know, or should have realized, is that they had more leads to follow up on than they could imagine.

A Brief Discussion of Crime Scenes and Collecting Evidence

Many crime scenes are like puzzles. Sometimes, the pieces fit together very nicely, painting a clear picture for investigators. Sometimes, the pieces don't fit as well as investigators would like them to. And sometimes, the pieces investigators need to complete the picture are simply not there. As Dr. Thomas J. O'Conner states, "physical evidence is part of the 'holy trinity' for solving crimes—physical evidence, witnesses, and confessions. Without one of the first two, there is little chance of even finding a suspect. Physical evidence is also the number one provider of extraordinary clearances, where police can link different offenses at different times and places with the same offender."[1]

Analyzing a crime scene is much more than simply searching and processing it. Indeed, managing the crime scene and the preliminary investigation is considered by most investigators, to be the most important aspect of any investigation. And it is much more than documenting it as in making notes, taking photographs, and making sketches. As Connie Fletcher (2006) points out in her book, *Crime Scene, Inside the World of the Real CSIs*, "Before any investigation can start, evidence must be collected. The scene itself, whether inside, outside, or mobile, has to be gone over as if the processors were exploring a site on mars. What's this? Why is *this* here? Why *isn't* this here? What does this all mean? And—how do we get the evidence back to the lab without destroying it?"[2]

If done right, crime scene analysis involves a slow, methodical, systematic, and orderly process. The question here, is, did Detective Tony Martin and Special Agent Mike Cook conduct a well-planned search of the destroyed aircraft and/or D & B Environmental? Their crime scene, as far as we know so far, was in two readily defined areas, and both were of limited size. This is not always the case. Sometimes, crime scenes are large and vast as in the 9/11 attacks on the World Trade Center or as in the bombing of Pan Am Flight 103 over Lockerbie, Scotland on December 21, 1988. A suitcase bomb exploded aboard the New York bound flight out of Frankfurt, Germany killing 259 passengers and crewmembers along with 11 people on the ground in Lockerbie. These types of crime scenes can create a host of problems including having a lack of equipment necessary to conduct the search; the media, who storm the scene to bring breaking news to their viewers, and occasionally, other police officers, especially supervisors, who simply drop by the on the pretext of seeing if they can help. What those responsible for the crime scene must always remember, is to control the crime scene. Without controlling the scene, evidence can easily be destroyed resulting in the investigation being conducted in a very careless manner.

Another example of multiple crime scenes might involve computer-related crimes. In our constantly expanding cyberspace world with computers and smart phones, the crime scene might be less obvious. We find this to be prevalent in virtually all types of crimes these days from narcotic trafficking to child pornography, where the victimized and abused children might be located to the various websites where their pictures might be found, to sexting photos on cell phones, and to one of the fastest growing crimes in the United States, identity theft.

Figure 2.1 Photo Depicting Plane Destroyed over Lockerbie Being Reconstructed.

It's important for investigators to identify the crime scene or scenes as quickly as possible so that evidence can be discovered, documented, and collected for examination.

It's important to understand that there are basically four types of evidence; testimonial, physical, documentary, and demonstrative.

- Testimonial evidence is evidence offered by witnesses speaking under oath or affirmation during a legal proceeding. The witness might be testifying about something they saw (eyewitnesses), something they heard (hearsay witnesses), something they smelled, or something they know (character, habit, or custom witnesses).

EVIDENCE

Submitting Agency_____

Data Collected _____ Time _____

Item # _____ Case # _____

Collected By _____

Description of Evidence _____

_____

Location Where Collected _____

Type of Offence _____

CHAIN OF CUSTODY

Received from: _____ By: _____

Date: _____ Time: _____

Received from: _____ By: _____

Date: _____ Time: _____

Received from: _____ By: _____

Date: _____ Time: _____

Figure 2.2 Example of Evidence and Chain of Custody form.

- Physical evidence, which includes trace evidence and includes tangible objects that are real, direct, and not circumstantial. Some examples of physical evidence might include the knife used to commit the crime, trace particles found at the crime scene, fingerprints, handwriting, and so forth.
- Documentary evidence is usually any kind of writing, sound, or video recording. It may be the transcript of a telephone intercept. This type of evidence usually needs to be authenticated by expert testimony, or, from someone who has custody and control of the documents often referred to as the "custodian of records."
- Demonstrative evidence is to illustrate, demonstrate, or recreate a tangible thing. Think in terms of a model mockup of the crime scene, other constructed-to-scale models, or a time line of the events.

While these are often considered the four main types of evidence, students should be familiar with Associative Evidence, which is bidirectional in nature in that it connects a perpetrator to the scene of the crime and/or the victim.[3]

Trace evidence, which falls under physical evidence, refers to small evidence that is often but not exclusively microscopic in size and is yet another type of evidence that investigators should be aware of. Trace evidence can aid the investigators in many ways. Nicholas Petraco has categorized the most commonly found types of trace evidence as either fibrous substances or particulate matter. Fibrous substances include hair, plant fibers, and synthetic fibers, often found in carpet. Particulate matter includes building material, paint chips, and soil, just to name a few. Petraco notes that human hair and other fiber evidence are frequently encountered at the scenes of violent crimes such as homicide and robbery. Keep in mind that the trace evidence is usually so small and it requires the examination by trained forensic specialists.[4] Blood would also be considered trace evidence.

Investigators should develop a system for carefully documenting a crime scene. And often, this system requires swiftness. It's your author's opinion that the most precious commodity an investigator has is not the new computers the department or agency gives you; not the smart phones you carry; and not the new cars nor the multitude of informational websites that are available to you as you research information related to your investigations. The most precious commodity you have is your TIME. You only have so much of it. With regard to documenting your crime scene, be thorough, but also be swift. Use initials in place of full names. But whatever system you use, remember that you may very well be required to produce your field notes in court. Organize your information and proofread and evaluate your report. You don't want to create an opportunity for a defense attorney to discredit your testimony. Keep strictly to the facts and do not offer opinions. Always use the term "alleged" if you are unable to substantiate a fact.

Questions for Discussion

1. How is a fingerprint classified and identified?
2. What is meant by ridge lines?
3. Fingerprints come in three general types. Research the three types and discuss where an investigator is most likely to find them.
4. Research two cases where the IAFIS system helped law enforcement identify a major felon.
5. Research the following cases. What was/is the impact on law enforcement with regard to searching crime scenes?
   a. Katz v. United States, 389 U.S. 347 (1967)
   b. Mincey v. Arizona, 427 U.S. 385 (1978)

6. Who was Edmond Locard and what is his principle? How did he employ this principle to solve a case?
7. What is an Integrated Automated Fingerprint Identification System (IAFIS) and how does it work?
8. What type of evidence might Tony and Mike be looking for with regard to the remnants of the two explosive devices they recovered?
9. Do some additional research and discuss the concepts of:
   a. Evidence tampering
   b. Evidence contamination
   c. Evidence substitution

10. What is the most important part of an investigation? Why?
11. What are the purposes of a crime scene search?
12. Why does your author suggest an investigator's most precious commodity is his/her time?

Work Sheet

Notes

1. Thomas J. O'Connor, Dr. Criminal Justice Mega Links. Austin Peay College.
2. Fletcher, Connie. (2006). *Crime Scene: Inside the World of the Real CSI's,* 8. New York: St. Martin's Paperbacks.
3. Thomas J. O'Connor, Dr. Criminal Justice Mega Links. Austin Peay College.
4. Petraco, N. (1985). The Occurrence of Trace Evidence in One Examiner's Casework. *Journal of Forensic Sciences* 30.2: 486.

Supplemental Reading

Fletcher, Connie. (2006). *Crime Scene: Inside the World of the Real CSIs.* St. Martin's Press.

Osterburg, James W. and Richard H. Ward. (2014). *Criminal Investigation: A Method for Reconstructing the Past,* 7th Edition. Anderson Publishing.

Swanson, C., N. Chamelin, L. Territo, and R. W. Taylor. (2009). *Criminal Investigation,* 10th Edition. McGraw Hill Publishing.

Thomas J. O'Connor, Dr. Criminal Justice Mega Links. Austin Peay College.

CHAPTER 3
INTERVIEWS AND INTERROGATIONS

Sincerity is the key to success; when you can fake that, you've got it made.

George Burns
Everybody lies

Cops lie. Lawyers lie. Witnesses lie. The victims lie. The trial is a contest of lies. And everybody in the courtroom knows this. The judge knows this. Even the jury knows this. They come into the building knowing they will be lied to. They take their seats in the box and agree to be lied to.

Michael Connelly, Author
The Brass Verdict

Chapter Objectives

1. Understand the basic differences between an interview and an interrogation.
2. Compare and contrast interrogation and interviewing as they pertain to the questioning process.
3. Identify the various methods of acquiring the significant details a complainant or witness may possess.

Recommended Reading

1. *How to Win Friends and Influence People*, by Dale Carnegie.
2. *The Art of Investigative Interviewing*, by Charles L. Yeschke.
3. *Interviewing & Interrogation for Law Enforcement*, by John E. Hess.

Lisa Swanson had been with the Bureau of ATF for about 14 years. During her tenure with the agency, she had demonstrated that she was not only capable, but in many respects, a far better investigator than many of her counterparts. Lisa was always an over achiever. She had to be, she told herself, to make it in this business. She learned quickly, that sometimes, one had to get their hands dirty when dealing with people who had no reservations about their doing so. She also realized that she had turned into a divorced, 40 something workaholic that left little time for any social life. What she learned to live for, instead, was the occasional fast investigative pace of trying to solve a crime that required every bit of her attention. Now, she sat behind a desk shuffling more paper from an inbox to an outbox than she ever dreamed possible. The bureaucracy made sure that there was a never-ending supply of paper to move. But she also supervised a dozen agents, some older, set in their ways and reluctant to embrace change, and some younger ones who thought that they could change the world but who had yet to hone their craft enough to much more than cause her a few headaches. Lisa knew that in time, the young agents realize that they too, couldn't change the world, but in some cases, could certainly make it a better place to live and work for a small group of people. Her biggest regret was giving up the independence she had as a senior investigator for the more mundane task of supervision. Her days now, consisted mostly of moving paper from the inbox to the outbox; preparing budgets, conducting case reviews, reviewing status reports, mediating petty disputes between agents, and briefing senior management on everything from ongoing investigations to satisfying training requirements. Lisa only agreed to go into supervision because she was convinced that she could do it better than some she had witnessed and worked for who held those positions. And, mentoring young agents was one of the things that made the decision to become a boss palatable. But as this day approached mid-afternoon, all Lisa could think about was lacing up her running shoes and heading out to the trail along the river for a long run. When her phone vibrated indicating she was receiving a text message, she somehow knew her run was going to be postponed. Lisa was right. The message was short and direct. "Will be in the office in 20 minutes. Need to speak to you ASAP." The text was from Special Agent Mike.

It was almost 5:00 p.m. when Mike Cook and Detective Tony Martin sat down in Lisa's office to tell her about the events of the day involving the airplane that had been blown up and the attempted bombing of the environmental plant.

"Lisa, this is Detective Tony Martin," Cook said as he made the initial introductions and pointed to Tony to take a seat.

"Nice to meet you Tony," Lisa said as she extended her had. "So, I heard about the plane that was blown up. What else can you tell me?"

Tony Martin and Mike Cook told Lisa everything they knew so far. They told her about the two rudimentary devices found at both crime scenes. They told her about the plane being owned by the same people who owned the D & B Environmental. They told her the office manager was trying to locate the owners and that they would be available for interview in the morning. They also told her about the fact that they suspected the company records had been saturated with gasoline and had been meant to be destroyed. And, they told her that Sara Howard had personally supervised the transfer of the evidence at the lab.

"This all sounds good," Lisa said. "So where do you want to go now with this?" Before directing any agent in an investigative direction, Lisa always sought out their thoughts first. She wanted to see what their thinking was on any given set of circumstances. She knew that if you left one alone, they more than often came up with their own investigative solutions. At least the good ones did. Mike Cook was young but Lisa saw potential in him. She believed he had the tools to be one of the good ones.

"We have to start interviewing a lot of people," Mike Cook said. "I think this is going to take some considerable time."

"You two are going to have to conduct a lot of interviews," Lisa told Mike and Tony. "In cases like these, where you're dealing with company owners, who, might or might not be involved in the crime, you have to tread lightly at first. Remember, you're dealing with people who have probably never been involved in any type of criminal activity in their life, nor, have they probably ever been the victim of a crime before. You're not dealing with your everyday witness, nor, are you necessarily dealing with bad guys who know how to play the system," Lisa continued.

"I've never worked anything like this," Detective Martin said.

"We know we're going to have to examine those records at some point, and soon. But they need to be dried out first. In the meantime, I think we should start gathering information from the major players in this as soon as possible. We're both open to any ideas you might have," Mike Cook added.

"Interviewing is art," Lisa told the two men. "Keep two things in mind: First, people like to talk about themselves not YOU. They don't really care about your dog(s), cat(s), what shoes you recently purchased, where YOU went on vacation, unless they're going there soon and need some personal information about the place. They don't care who you went out with, or that you had a great meal last night and that it was 'delicious.' And they certainly don't want to hear about some crazy dream you had last night. They don't really care. Oh they'll listen, sometimes. But what we all want most is to talk about what WE like and what WE did. How many times have you been in the middle of telling a story when the person you're telling it to interrupts you and says, 'oh, but let me tell you about what happened to my friend . . .,' who you may not even know, because their story is so much more interesting and important?"

"That happens all the time," Detective Martin said. "I can't tell you how often this guy I golf with does that."

"My sister does that every time I talk to her, Mike added. "She starts telling me stories about friends of her neighbors that I've never heard of or care about."

"Well, your friend Tony, and your sister, Mike, don't know to listen," Lisa replied. And this brings me to my second point, and this is very important; good investigators need to learn to listen. It's investigators who solve the majority of crimes, because they got somebody to 'talk.' I want to be painfully clear here: 'Somebody talked.' They didn't text, tweet, email, or send a smoke signal. An investigator, who has developed the art of listening, figured out what questions to ask a person and either obtained the necessary information to proceed and/or make an arrest. This is what solves the majority of crimes."

Lisa paused and took a drink of water from her plastic water bottle. She was hydrating in anticipation of the long run she hoped to have shortly after this meeting. Looking at both men she continued, "It's not lasers, DNA analysis, although it does certainly help, along with other high-tech procedures. And from my perspective, interviewing and interrogation is a dying art. Why? Well, let's see: Maybe because we spend so much time texting these days, we've lost the skill set to actually have a conversation with people. Let's also be clear about something: criminals rarely come forth voluntarily and, witnesses are more often than not, reluctant to get involved in any investigation. In fact, reading people, as far as I'm concerned, is usually far more important than reading clues."

"This all sounds about right," Mike Cook replied.

Lisa Swanson continued, "An interview should resemble your having a conversation with someone but in this case, for a specific purpose. You're going to want to be prepared for each interview, which I know you both will do, but don't let the conversation lose the quality of spontaneity and flexibility."

"What do you mean?" Tony Martin asked.

"It means a number of things," Lisa replied. "A lot of people who work at D & B are feeling a lot of different emotions right now. In some cases, there is a sense of loss. Some are scared of losing their jobs. Others, if involved in some way, are scared of what you two might find out. They're feeling fear, anger and host of other emotions. Keep all that in mind when you start questioning the employees and owners. You're going to want to have some prepared questions for sure, but make sure that you're flexible enough with your questions to get through those emotions.

"Don't rush your interviews either. And be aware of where you conduct your interview. For instance, if it's in the interviewee's office, take a few quick seconds to access the surroundings. Look around. Is the office neat and clean or in disarray? What pictures are on his/her desk and/or hanging on the wall? Where did he/she go to school? Do they have pictures of kids, pets, a boat, ski vacations, etc. Use this information to your advantage and to set the person at ease, if, they appear to be a reluctant witness."

"This is quite a different approach than dealing with a drug informant," Tony Martin said.

"All interviews are different," Lisa replied. "You have to access your subject, witness, surroundings, and so forth. You might interview the CEO of a company in the morning and the dregs of society late at night. Keep in mind, they all want respect, and have information that you want. The way everyone defines ethics is different, including investigators. The problem is, there is no universal definition of what ethics are. It's up to you to maneuver through the ethical values of your witnesses and targets in order to get the information you're looking for."

"What ever happened to the simple, Who, What, Where, When, Why, and How?" Detective Martin asked.

"Nothing," replied Lisa. "Those are still the basics of any interview. You've already started doing that, I presume, with the people you've already spoken to with the fire department and at D & B Environmental."

"We have," Mike Cook replied. "But things were moving fast this morning. I'd like to get back up there in the morning and start interviewing the two owners."

"That's a very good place to start," Lisa replied. You're going to want to develop a plan with regard to conducting the interviews."

"A plan?" Mike asked.

"Yes, a plan. Do some background work. Become as familiar as you can with the people and business operation. I know you already know this, but conduct the interviews in private. Place the people at ease. Start with casual conversation. Don't interrupt like your sister. And avoid hypothetical questions. And don't dispute the subject's answers, not yet. Keep your emotions under control. Don't lose eye contact with your subject. Not even to take notes. One of you do the primary questioning while the other takes notes. And the owner interviews are going to be the most important interviews you do in this case. Keep in mind, you're going to want to ask some specific questions of these people."

"Such as?" Mike Cook asked.

"For instance, you're going to want to ask, 'How and when did you learn of the fire?' When you ask them where they were when they heard about the fire, keep in mind, they're establishing an alibi. Then, you're going to want to know some basic things about them and the business.

Lisa Swanson sensed that she was giving the two men a lot to think about. But she also knew, from her experience, that the interviews of the two owners were the most critical part of the investigation. As such, she didn't want them to leave anything to chance.

"During the course of the interview, look for dry mouth on the owners. It's something I always liked to keep an eye on. It's just a red flag that they might be lying. Watch for simple things like them licking their lips or swallowing to overcome the dry mouth. Watch their hands; if they're covering their mouth, it could indicate an attempt to prevent some sort of disclosure. Foot and toe tapping might also indicate nervousness. Taken alone, it's not proof of anything tangible but I've found that it does help me question whether someone is telling the truth or not. And one of my favorites," Swanson added, "is when they repeat the question I just asked. That tells me they're trying to buy time. And be wary of general verbalizations such as my favorite; 'I swear to God', or, 'as God is my witness' and, 'on my mother's grave.'"

"We'll keep an eye out," Cook replied.

"And make sure that you thoroughly record the details of each interview. Just a note of precaution. I don't like reading reports and finding out that investigator's failed to accurately record the details of an interview because of preconceived notions, time constraints, or just carelessness. It's just one of the major mistakes investigators make when conducting interviews. Don't make assumptions. Let the evidence take you where the case goes. And, I suspect that this case is going to create a lot of obstacles for you. Remember the river that flows to the sea—it takes a natural path going around obstacles instead of always through them. Find ways to go around the obstacles. And don't hesitate to let me help you get around those obstacles."

Both men nodded. And just like that, the meeting with Lisa Swanson was over. Several minutes later, Special Agent Mike Cook and Detective Tony Martin found themselves in a coffee shop going over the conversation they just had with Lisa.

"Does Lisa always remind you of what to do when you work a case? I could sure use a beer instead of this coffee," Tony Martin said.

"Same here," replied Mike Cook. "She's just being a boss I guess. And I could use a beer too. I don't know about your agencies policy, but in the federal service, even thinking about having a drink and driving a government car will get you fired."

"It's no different with us," Martin replied. "It's one of the quickest ways to an internal investigation you can get. We just don't do it."

"The old guys keep reminding me of how different our world is with all the policies and politically correct procedures we have to adhere to these days," Cook said. "I wonder what it might have been like to investigate this kind of stuff before computers, smart phones, DNA, and all the other things we have that a lot of these older guys didn't have back in their day."

"I have no idea," Martin replied. "Our department is even using social media in our investigations."

"Social media?"

"Yeah. Especially Facebook. A lot of these guys are posting stuff on their Facebook accounts. Seems like criminals still like to brag about their exploits. I guess that hasn't changed so much since the old timers' days."

"You had much luck using Facebook to solve anything?"

Martin said, "Some. Once these guys post information on a social media website, it's open to the public. Their friends can share the information with anyone they want. We have one guy dedicated to simply creating fake online identities to befriend suspects in child porn investigations. It's also a great way to gather intelligence."

"Maybe somebody will post something on Facebook that helps us solve this investigation," Cook said with a smirk on his face.

As the two investigators drank their coffee, neither man realized, that in many respects, the investigation they were embarking upon would require them to learn firsthand just how much computers, smart phones, and DNA analysis were NOT going to play an integral part in their query.

A Brief Discussion about Interviewing and Interrogations

Good investigators need to learn how to *listen*. And second, and this is very important, it's investigators who solve the majority of crimes, because they got somebody to "*talk.*" I want to be painfully clear here: "*Somebody talked.*" They didn't text, tweet, email, or send a smoke signal. An investigator, who has developed the art of listening, figured out what questions to ask a person and either obtained the necessary information to proceed and/or make an arrest. This is what solves the majority of crimes.

It's not lasers, DNA analysis (although it does help), along with other high-tech procedures. And from my perspective, interviewing (and interrogation) is a dying art. Why? Well, let's see: Maybe because we spend so much time texting these days, we've lost the skill set to actually have a conversation with people. Or, maybe some police and investigators demonstrate a lack of patience in the art of interviewing like Sergeant Joe Friday of the old TV show, *Dragnet*. Friday's stock and trade comment was, "just the facts." Let's also be clear about something: criminals rarely come forth voluntarily and, witnesses are more often than not, reluctant to get involved in any investigation. Yes, way too many people have no enthusiasm for getting involved in anything that doesn't involve them, especially if it means cooperating with the police.

Let's look at structuring an interview. One must first *prepare* for the interview. What does this mean? We'll think about treating each interview as a "first date." Leave nothing to chance. That means preparing, as if it were a first date. I'm not even sure your generation dates any more, but more about that later. That means gathering simple facts about the case, the person to be interviewed, where you're going to discuss the interview; such as an office, police station, or neutral location. If in the interviewee's office, take a few quick seconds to access the surroundings. Is the office neat and clean or in disarray? What pictures are on his/her desk and/or hanging on the wall? Where did he/she go to school? Do they have pictures of kids, pets, a boat, ski vacations, etc. Use this information to your advantage and to set the person at ease, if, they appear to be a reluctant witness. Also, prepare for the timing of the interview. You don't want to interview someone prematurely.

The next step in the process is the *Introduction*. Let the person know your name, your position, and the purpose of the interview. Do it up front and set the stage. You want to avoid having the person you're interviewing asking you what this is all about. Make a good first impression.

Next, *establish a rapport* with the interviewee. Think about ways you can reduce his/her anxiety. Create a sense of harmony by emphasizing with the person being interviewed. Now come the questions. For this, I want you to think in terms of open- and closed-ended questions. Open-ended questions produce better results. Think back to treating this like a first date. "Tell me about yourself," you might ask. Get the person talking. Remember, people like to talk. Follow up with closed-ended questions as needed. But get the person talking.

Some schools of thought suggest starting with closed-ended questions in order to put the person being interviewed at ease and to encourage affirmative responses.[1] It's true, this limits the number of responses one might receive from the person being interviewed. And, it helps the person conducting the interview maintain control of the interview itself. I leave it up to the investigator to determine which method, open or closed questioning, is best used given a certain situation, person being interviewed and the environment. Remember, open-ended questions start with the basics of what we hope to learn in any interview, who, what, where, when, how, and why. Open-ended questions require the person being interviewed to think clearly. Or in some cases, think about the deception they want to relay to you.

Conducting interviews is an art. Like playing an instrument, one must practice to become proficient at it. Texting does not count as practice. Nor does sending emails. To become proficient at interviewing, one must engage in conversations with people and find ways to keep the conversation going. Think back to times when a conversation you were having came to a standstill. When there is that lull in the discussion, often, one of the parties will find a way to excuse themselves. That's fine if you're at a social gathering. It can prove disastrous if you're conducting an interview.

While there are numerous ways to question people, Charles L. Yeschke (2003), in his excellent book, *The Art of Investigative Interviewing*, points out several techniques that I've found useful over the years. Below are just a few of the types of questions investigators might consider while conducting an interview.

There is the "You" question. Here, the interviewer might begin by telling the person that it's important to get things cleared up, and, that you're asking the question in an effort to determine what happened. For instance: "If you did this, it's important to get this cleared up." Someone with a high level of shame or guilty mind might not be able to deal with the stress of what they did and confess. This is somewhat rare. And will probably never work when dealing with a sociopath.

There is the "Who" question. Here, the interviewer asks if the person knows "for sure" who committed the crime.

There is the "Suspicion" question. If the person doesn't know for sure who committed the crime, ask if they have any suspicions as to who may have done it.

There is the "Approach' question. An example might be something like this: "Did anyone ever ask you to transport drugs for them?" This allows guilty parties to cast blame on others.

Interrogation

The guiding principles of an interrogation differ greatly from those of an interview. Interrogation usually means questioning a suspect, or a suspect's family member or associates. These are the people the investigator or interviewer is likely to find to be withholding information. You'll find them to be deceptive, in large part, because they are either involved in some way with the crime being investigated, or, are simply trying to protect someone close to them. It is here, that the well-trained investigator will use the skills he/she has developed over a period of time in order to extract the information they need. Of course, some investigators have found that having some evidence of the person's involvement in the crime to go a long way in getting that person to talk or cooperate.

According to Dr. Thomas O'Connor, interrogations frequently lead to confessions. Police agencies in America are particularly good at it. The United States has the highest confession rate and we achieved this without torture. Dr. O'Connor points out that "three out of four people waive their Miranda rights" and roughly 50-75% of police interrogations end in confession. Compared to other country's confession rates, such as Germany's 40%, the United States is clearly the leader in the industrialized world when it comes to confessions. Dr. O'Connor states, "A confession is regarded as the "holy grail" of evidence collection. It's prima facie, direct evidence of guilt." This means that it's not a "presumption of guilt" or a piece of evidence that can be used in court. It's what "cinches" a conviction.

The statements that suspects make to the police during an interrogation can be categorized as:

- Full confession (24% of the time)
- Partial confession (18% of the time)
- Incriminating statement (23% of the time)
- No incriminating statement (36% of the time) (Leo, 1996a)

Many of the same principles and techniques used in interviewing are applied to the concept of conducting an interrogation. One of the more significant differences is in the "accusation." Without this accusation, one really isn't starting with an interrogation. The accusation is simple enough, i.e. "you're not being candid with me." I think you assaulted that woman." People usually do not confess to anything unless confronted with their guilt. Think about the time(s) your parents caught you doing something. The power to resist confessing was no doubt, overwhelming. It's human nature to resist unpleasant things. As an interrogator, you must destroy all hope in the mind of the suspect that you believe his/her lies. Let's also be clear, this is an adversarial situation. The nature of the business of "criminal investigation" often puts the inquirer, i.e. you, the investigator, in a confrontational situation. And while some might argue that conflict builds character, it's stressful. If engaging in adversarial situations is not for you, than more probably than not, neither is this profession. There are numerous books about how to read body language; how to interpret responses from people being interviewed and/or interrogated; all best left for another time and place, more appropriately in your case, for advanced courses in interviewing and interrogation. Suffice to say, that you should consider something called the "sales pitch." In other words, minimize the magnitude of the crime. Don't oversell it. At the same time, don't allow the suspect to continue denying his/her participation in the crime.

One technique, developed by the FBI and used by many law enforcement organizations, as well as your author prior to retiring from a career in law enforcement, is creating a setting designed to let the person know that you have a great deal of evidence on him/her. Using props such as photos of the suspect meeting other suspects; pieces of evidence, tagged and left in plain view of the suspect on the table, file folders with his/her name on it as well as enlarged surveillance photos, all suggesting that the person being interrogated, is a target of a large-scale investigation. These props, such as pictures, can be worth their weight in gold. Remember the old saying, "a picture is worth a thousand words."

In our fictional story, Lisa Swanson points out that one of the biggest mistakes investigators make when conducting an interview is not recording the details when conducting an interview. In their book, *Criminal Investigation; a method for reconstructing the past*, the late James Osterburg and Richard Ward point out that another major mistake often made by interviewers is not realizing the important aspect of the facial expressions of the interviewee. While the facial expressions of those being interviewed or interrogated can, and often do, reveal a great detail as to the subject revealing fear, anger, or lying, studying these facial expressions is best left for an advanced course in criminal investigation or interviewing techniques. It is suffice for this course however, that students understand a change of facial expressions can, and do, reveal a lot to the interviewer. For the purposes of this course, focus on a person's eyes. What does their eye contact tell you? Are they genially interested in what you're saying? Do they indicate sadness, hostility, or a lack of interest? Investigators are taught to look for behavioral symptoms or indicators of truth and deception in the form of verbal clues. These clues are something you'll learn as you develop your interviewing and interrogation skills. In the meantime, when talking to people (not texting), start looking for subtle signs of deception such as people having long pauses before responding to your question, or, giving you a rehearsed response. Look to see if they are slouching or anxious when they respond to you. This doesn't mean they're lying, but it should be a cause for doubt that they're telling the truth. Start paying attention to the people you talk to and practice these techniques.

Regardless of the age, mental state, or capacity of the confessor, what most have in common is a decision, at some point in the interrogation process, that confessing will be more beneficial to them than continuing to maintain their innocence. An interrogation, by definition, is, in part, a "guilt presumptive process." The interrogator, in this case, a law enforcement official, holds a strong belief that the target is guilty. Success is measured by his/her ability to extract an admission from the suspect. Think back at a time when you confessed to your parents about some wrong you had committed. They, no doubt, had a strong suspicion that you were guilty of whatever it was they were accusing you of. So, why did you confess? Was it time to cut your losses? Were you looking for absolution as some suspects do when they confess?

There is no way this course or the exercises in this chapter can make anyone a good or seasoned interviewer or interrogator. That will take time, practice, and lots of trial and error. One way to begin this process is to start having actual conversations with people. I've found, over the past 15 years, that students who have worked in any job, that requires them to interact with people, such as being a waiter or waitress, helps them develop communication skills quicker than those who have little to no real personal interaction with people, especially ones they really don't know. And keep in mind, you can't study one's eyes if you're texting with them.

Good investigators know that all investigations start and end with the interview. How you conduct and manage them is up to you.

Key Terms

Interview
Interrogation

Questions for Discussion

1. In our fictional story, Lisa Swanson tells Mike Cook that as far as she's concerned, "reading people is usually more important than reading clues." What does she mean by that? Do you agree or disagree? Support your position.
2. What are two common mistakes investigators make with regard to conducting interviews?
3. How might social media help and hinder an investigation?
4. What is the difference between an interview and an interrogation?
5. Why might witnesses be reluctant to cooperate in an interview?
6. What are some reasons why people confess?
7. What is meant by a "guilt presumptive process?"
8. What does Lisa Swanson mean by "not letting the conversation lose the quality of spontaneity and flexibility?"

Work Sheet

Exercises

1. Develop at least 10 questions that you'd want to ask the two owners about themselves and/or the business. Do not include the obvious such as name, address, phone number, and date of birth. Expand on the questions suggested of the owner interview in Chapter 1. Keep in mind, the principles of who, what, when, where, why, and how.

2. Develop five closed- and open-ended questions for Angela Lyle, the office manager of D & B Environmental.

3. Develop five closed- and open-ended questions for John Thomas, the foreman of D & B Environmental. Do not include the obvious, such as name, address, phone number, and date of birth.

Work Sheet

Notes

1. Yeschke, Charles L. (2003). *The Art of Investigative Interviewing*. 2nd Edition, 162. Butterworth and Heineman.

Supplemental Reading

Gudjonsson, G. (1992). *The Psychology of Interrogations, Confessions and Testimony*. NY: Wiley & Sons.

Harney, M and J. Cross. (1960). *The Informer in Law Enforcement*. Springfield: Charles Thomas.

Hess, John E. *Interviewing & Interrogation for Law Enforcement*. 2nd Edition.

Leo, R. (1992). From Coercion to Deception. *Crime, Law & Social Change* 18:35–59.

Leo, R. (1996a). Inside the Interrogation Room. *Journal of Criminal Law and Criminology* 86:266–303.

Leo, R. (1996b). Miranda's Revenge: Police Interrogation as a Confidence Game. *Law and Society Review* 30:259–88.

Leo, R. (1996c). The Impact of Miranda Revisited. *Journal of Criminal Law and Criminology* 86: 621–92.

Osterburg, James W. and Richard H. Ward. *Criminal Investigation: A Method for Reconstructing the Past*. 7th Edition.

Thomas O'Connor, Dr. Austin Peay State University.

Yeschke, Charles L. (2003). *The Art of Investigative Interviewing*. 2nd Edition, 162. Butterworth and Heineman.

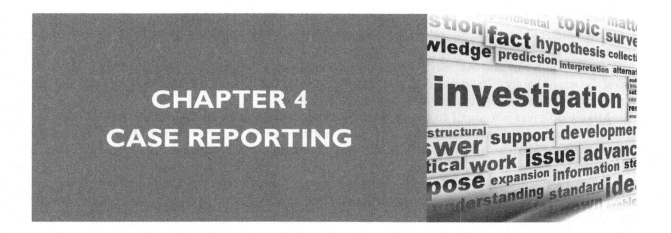

CHAPTER 4
CASE REPORTING

"Atticus told me to delete the adjectives and I'd have the facts."

Harper Lee,
To Kill a Mockingbird

Chapter Objectives

1. Identify and understand the six interrogatory investigative questions.
2. Become familiar with the common elements of an incident report.
3. Become familiar with how to write a narrative report.

It had been a long and filthy day for Special Agent Mike Cook and Detective Tony Martin. Cook had learned long ago, that rummaging through fire debris is not as exciting or glamorous as it's sometimes made out to be on television; especially when you have limited resources and much of the crime scene searching falls directly on the back of the investigator. After saying good-bye to Tony the night before, Cook drove home, stopping first to pick up some Chinese take-out, showered, and ate. And, he thought about the long day ahead of him the next morning. He tried sleeping but that eluded him. All he could think about was how he was going to proceed with his investigation in the morning. Mike Cook was a young agent. While aggressive, he did lack some of the experience more seasoned agents had. But Lisa Swanson was enough of a supervisor to know when to trust her people. She also knew that if you left good people alone to do their jobs, they would often surprise you by achieving things you might never have considered doing yourself. Cook knew that Lisa would be watching to see how he responded to her "suggestions." It hadn't been that long ago when he failed to follow one of her suggestions. The end result was an opportunity lost in an ongoing investigation. The follow-up conversation with Lisa didn't go well.

"I notice you didn't follow up on the lead I suggested," Lisa had told Mike.

"No, I didn't," Mike replied. "I thought it might be better to wait until I was able to recover some more information from the documents."

"Well, as you can see, that was the wrong decision," Lisa said calmly, but sternly enough that Mike knew she wasn't happy. "The next time I make a suggestion on handling a lead, you might be better served, if you simply consider my suggestion to be an order," Lisa said.

Mike Cook was not about to disregard any of Lisa's suggestions anytime soon. At 6:30 a.m., he was up, showered, dressed, and driving an hour north to meet Detective Tony Martin. They were scheduled to meet that morning with both Alan Thompson and Eric Mann, the owners of D & B Environmental.

On that same morning, and just one day following the destruction of the Twin Engine King Air and the attempted bombing of D & B Environmental, Detective Tony Martin, who was more used to investigating burglaries, assaults, robberies, and the very rare and occasional murder, found himself telling Ed Van Pelt, his Lieutenant, about the prior day's events. Martin explained to Van Pelt everything that had transpired the day before. He shared with him the fact that the two explosives devices, based on what the fire department, and from what he and Cook had found, appeared to be almost identical in nature. He also told the Lieutenant about having transported the evidence to the ATF crime lab and having met with Lisa Swanson, Cook's supervisor.

"So, what do you think is going on here?" Van Pelt asked.

"I'm not sure yet Lieutenant. Never handled anything quite like this. The feds are taking lead on this. I suggest we work with them for now, see where this goes," Cook suggested.

"Okay," Van Pelt replied. "But if we let the feds run lead on this, make sure that they keep you and me in the loop. Don't let me find out they're keeping information from us."

"I don't think that's going to be a problem with this guy Cook," Martin told his boss. "It's only been one day, but something about this guy tells me he's not out to hide things from us."

"That's fine," Van Pelt added. "But remember, most feds don't carry as heavy a case load as you do. You have other cases to work. So manage your time accordingly."

Tony Martin didn't expect anything less from Van Pelt. He had known the Lieutenant since he was his patrol sergeant. The two men got along just fine. But Martin also knew that Van Pelt was right; he had a heavy case load and couldn't devote, all, of what some investigators consider their most precious commodity, time, to just one case.

"I'll have a better handle on this later today," Cook told Van Pelt.

"What's happening today?" Van Pelt asked.

"We're interviewing the two owners of D & B Environmental. "Can't wait to hear what these two have to say."

It was unusually cool that morning. Clouds were rolling in, and the threat of rain was in the forecast. Special Agent Mike Cook met Detective Tony Martin in the parking lot of the police station.

"It's a good thing this didn't happen yesterday," Cook said, handing Tony Martin a Styrofoam container of black coffee.

"I know. We'd be soaked for sure. I think this rain is coming in sooner than later. Thanks for the coffee. Any sugar?" Martin asked.

"In the bag. You weren't in the Marines were you?" Cook asked.

"No. Why?"

"We drink it black. Don't usually have time to doctor up our coffee. Besides, you ruin the taste with milk and sugar."

"Well, I don't use milk, but I do need some sugar," Martin replied, smiling at Cook. Martin sensed that Cook was lightening the mood and hoping to develop a partner relationship in this investigation. A bit unlike some of the other feds he had met in the past.

"So, how do you want to handle this?" Martin asked.

"You and I both question Thompson and Mann; separately of course. I'll take Thompson first, you take the notes. Afterwards, we can switch roles. I'll leave that up to you."

"Sounds good. Let's go. We don't want to be late."

The two investigators arrived at D & B Environmental at 8:30 a.m. They were met by Angela Lyle who was trying to put her office in some order after the previous day's events. John Thomas, the foreman, was also there and talking to what appeared to be several yard employees.

"How are you doing Angela?" Mike Cook asked.

"Fine. Still a bit upset over all of this. Can't imagine who'd want to do this to us."

"Well, we're going to do our best to find out," Mike Cook replied.

Moments later, Alan Thompson and Eric Mann walked in the office. Each man extended their arm to Mike Cook and Tony Martin. Thompson was the older of the two men; about 50, Cook thought. Thompson was of medium height, overweight, and balding. But he was impeccably dressed. The suit, Cook thought, had to be tailored made just for him. Mann was about 10 years younger and far more fit. He was dressed more informally than his partner opting for a light blue oxford shirt and khaki slacks. Cook's first impression was that these are two very different people.

After the introductions and pleasantries were dispensed of, Alan Thompson asked the expected questions of the two investigators, namely, who did this to us? Cook told both Thompson and Mann they had no idea and that the investigation was just starting.

"We're hoping you both can help us get started," Special Agent Mike Cook said.

"Of course, we'll do whatever we can." Alan Thompson replied.

"How about if start with you first Mr. Thompson. Do you mind if we call you Alan?" Cook asked.

"Yes, please. But wouldn't it be easier to talk to both of us at the same time?" Thompson asked.

"We'd prefer to talk to everyone privately. We find that's more beneficial to everyone."

Being interviewed separately was not what either Alan Thompson or Eric Mann had expected. But it was clear to both men that the two investigators were not letting them have that option.

Mike Cook and Tony Martin followed Alan Thompson into a small conference room opposite of Angela Lyle's office. Except for several bound notebooks of what appeared to be books dealing with regulations related to the industry, the room was devoid of any personal photos, certificates, or professional licenses. After sitting down, Mike Cook began.

"Alan, can you tell us, where were you when you heard what happened yesterday?"

"Eric Mann and I were at a business meeting at Price Environmental, about an hour north of here. We both had our cell phones on vibrate so we didn't take any calls until after 12 noon. That's when we heard what happened. Our foreman, John Thomas had called several times and left messages. By the time we got here, it was a bit after 1:00 p.m."

"What were you doing at Price Environmental?" Cook asked.

"Just a business meeting. We were going over some potential new contracts to transport and dispose of some of their waste."

"I'm curious, how is this business structured?" Cook asked.

"It's an LLC."

"A limited liability corporation?"

"That's right. Me and Eric Mann are the two owners."

"And when did you two start this business?"

"About four years ago."

"Is there anyone else who has a financial interest in the company?"

"No, just me and Eric Mann."

"Exactly what is it you do here at D & B Environmental?" Cook asked.

"We mostly transport hazardous waste from companies that produce it to facilities that are licensed to dispose of it. We really don't do any disposal ourselves. We're not equipped to do that."

"And just how many employees do you have?"

"About eighteen."

"I'd like to get a list of the employees and their address if you don't mind. Do you have any other business locations for D & B other than here?"

"No. This is our only facility."

"I noticed a number of trucks in the yard. Are they used to transport the hazardous waste?"

"Most are; yes."

"And do you own or lease the trucks?"

"We lease most of them. But, we do own a couple of them."

"Are there any judgments or liens against D & B?"

"None," Thompson said, shifting in his chair. "I'm not sure what any of these questions have to do with finding out who did this to us?"

"It's important background information. We're going to need to know as much about your company as possible if we're going to have any chance of finding out who did this," Cook said calmly. "Any ideas as to who may have done this?"

"I have no idea," Thompson replied.

"Had any trouble with former employees, people you do business with; that sort of thing?"

"None that would cause anyone to do something like this."

"Do you own the airplane?"

"No. It's in the company name; yes, but Eric Mann is really the sole owner of the plane. When we took over the company, he bought the plane and put it in the company's name. I have virtually nothing to do with it other than fly in it from time to time."

The initial interview with Alan Thompson ended with Thompson agreeing to cooperate with the investigation in any way possible. Mike Cook and Tony Martin predicted that this first interview would not reveal much in the way of helping them identify who may have been involved in trying to destroy D & B Environmental. And, they did not want to press Thompson during the initial interview especially, if he were in any way involved in the crime. There would be time for that later. For now, it was simply a meet and greet with the intent of learning as much about the company as they could, and exactly what the company did. Before the interview was over, Alan Thompson told the two investigators that the company and the airplane were both insured by Practical Insurance.

It was now time to interview Eric Mann. Mann told the Cook and Martin virtually the same thing Alan Thompson had said. He and Thompson were meeting with Price Environmental and did not hear about the destruction of the aircraft, or, the attempt to destroy their company until about noon the day prior.

"And exactly how did you hear this news?" Detective Martin asked.

"Had a couple of voice mail messages along with text messages from our foreman, John Thomas," Mann said.

Mann also confirmed what Thompson had told the two investigators about how the company was set up, what the company did, the number of employees it had, and that he had no idea as to who would have done this to them.

"How's the company doing financially?" Martin asked.

"We're doing okay," Mann replied. "Not getting rich, but doing okay."

"Tell me about the airplane."

"What do you want to know?"

"Who owns it? What's it used for? How often do you use it?"

"It's a Twin Engine King Air. I've had it about 10 years. Put in the company's name as we often use it for business."

"Who flies it for you?"

"I fly it myself."

"You're a pilot?"

"I am. Been flying for over 15 years."

"So you're the only one who flies the plane?"

"No. Occasionally, I lease it out. But not often."

"Do you have records of who you lease it out to and how often?" Martin asked.

"I'm sure I can find them somewhere," Mann replied.

"Who has keys to the business?"

"All the drivers have keys to the gate. As far as the office goes, me, Thompson, John Thomas, and Angela Lyle have keys."

"That's it; just the four of you?"

"That's right."

"I noticed a gas pump out back. What's that used for?"

"It's where we gas up our trucks."

"Is that pump operational all the time?"

"It's supposed to be. The drivers sometimes leave early and come back late. We want the trucks topped off whenever they're in the lot."

Cook and Martin thanked Eric Mann for his time. They told them they'd be in touch soon and would no doubt, have some additional questions for him. They had one more interview to conduct that morning. It was now time to talk to the foreman, John Thomas.

John Thomas told the two investigators what he had said the day prior, that he had arrived at D & B Environmental around 7:00 a.m., opened the bay doors, and saw what he thought was a ticking time bomb.

"What else did you see?" Mike Cook asked.

"What do you mean?"

"I mean, what else did you see? Did you notice anyone around? Did you see any signs of a break-in?"

"No, nothing."

"So you saw just the device with the wind-up clock?"

"And?"

"That's it."

"What about the papers that the device was on top of?"

"Oh yeah, the papers. The bomb was on top of all those papers."

"We know that. Anything else?"

"The place smelled like gasoline."

"And?"

"The smell was strong. Like someone had poured gasoline everywhere."

"And what did you do when you saw the bomb?" Cook asked.

"I called the police."

"Then what did you do?"

"I waited for the police to arrive."

"That's it?"

"Yes."

"Did you try to contact Mr. Thompson and Mann?"

"Yes. But not until after the police and fire department arrived."

"And when did you do that?"

"Sometime later in the morning?"

"Do you know when?"

"Not exactly. Sometime later."

"And what did Mr. Thompson and Mann say when you told them what you found?"

"First, I left them a message. They didn't call me back until later."

"And what did they say when you finally told them?"

"They said that they were on their way."

"How long have you worked here?" Cook asked.

"Since the company opened. About four years."

"And what did you do before that?"

"Worked in shipping and on the loading dock for a few local companies. But mostly worked on my family's farm about 20 miles from here."

"How big is your farm?"

"About 200 acres. We grow some corn, raise some cattle. Not much. Lots of work for little money."

"Who was the last person on the premises the night before this happened?"

"What do you mean by premises?" Thomas asked.

"The company . . . Who normally locks up? Who locked up that night?"

"Oh . . . Most of the drivers have a key to the gate. If they're late coming back, they unlock the gate, park the trucks, and then lock up when they leave."

"So how many people have keys to the gate?" Cook asked.

"Just about everybody who works here."

"And security cameras?"

"We don't have any. Never thought we needed them. Nothing to really steal here."

Cook and Martin ended their interview of Thomas telling the foreman that they were certain to talk to him again as they continued to learn more about what had happened at D & B Environmental. Thomas extended his hand and told the two investigators that he'd help in any way that he could.

An hour later Mike Cook and Tony Martin were sitting in a coffee shop going over the three interviews they had conducted that morning.

"Does this make much sense to you?" Cook asked Martin.

"What exactly are you talking about?" Martin asked.

"The two owners have their cell phones either off or on vibrate most of the morning. The foreman, not the most articulate guy you'll ever meet, doesn't get in touch with them until hours after he discovers the device on a pile of company gasoline saturated records, and none of them seem to have any idea as to who might have done this."

"No, it doesn't make a lot of sense to me at all," Martin replied. "But right now, it's plausible. I'm suspicious, but I'm always suspicious. But again, it could have happened that way."

"Could have, yes. But I'm not so sure," Cook said.

A Brief Discussion about These Three Interviews

Did Mike Cook and Tony Martin ask enough questions in these "initial" interviews to answer the basic Who?, What?, When?, Where?, Why?, and How? related to this investigation?

With regard to the Who, think in terms of who was the victim? Who discovered the crime? Who reported the crime.? With regard to the What, think about what crime was committed.? What did the suspects do or not do? What did they take or not take?

The Where includes where the crime was committed? Where was the victim when the crime was committed? Where are the witnesses or potential witnesses?

When refers to things such as when was the crime discovered? When was the crime committed?

How includes how the crime was committed? How did the suspect get to and from the scene? How did the suspect gain entry to the premises? How much damage was done?

The Why might take a bit more investigation to determine why the crime was committed?

If not, what else might they have asked? From the information provided in this chapter, it's clear that the two investigators were conducting an interview and not an interrogation. And, they were conducting it in an informal manner.

Virtually every police department in the United States uses some form of incident complaint form to report crimes. Indeed, some departments have forms specifically for certain types of crimes adding to what many officers feel is an overabundance of forms and paperwork that they must complete when answering a call or investigating an offense. And while the forms vary from one department to another, they all have similarities that include blocks or spaces for basic information such as the type of crime committed, who reported the crime, when the crime was reported, and so forth. Below, in Figure 4.1, is an example of one such form.

Federal law enforcement agencies are less apt to use incident reporting forms. Instead, they rely more on a report that is focused on narrative format. In such a report, federal investigators are more inclined to report what they did and who they interviewed in narrative style. And, while not employing incident reporting forms, federal agencies, such as the FBI, DEA, and BATF, use a standard "narrative" reporting format. This allows an office in New York, Detroit, Miami, and Los Angeles to see and use a report that fits the agency guidelines. One thing that federal law enforcement does not promote in its reporting is individual style.

The investigative "narrative" of any report is critical. Writers of such reports should keep in mind that their reports will be made available to suspects and defense attorneys. More about this in a later chapter. And those reports should be written in the most concise and direct manner as possible. One of the *pitfalls* of narrative report writing is that if something can be *misinterpreted*, it will be misinterpreted, perhaps not by all, but certainly by some. That's why it is critical for all narrative reports to reflect information as to what people actually said, and whether it was something they heard, simply believed, or something they actually knew to be true. There is no substitution for being clear and precise in one's narrative writing.

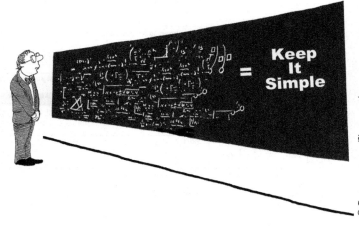
© Cartoonresource/Shutterstock.com

County Sheriff's Office
Offense/Incident Report

Case Number:

Date of Report:

Report Status: (Check one) ☐ OFFENSE or ☐ INCIDENT   If this is an OFFENSE: (Check one) ☐ Felony or ☐ Misdemeanor or ☐ Petty Offense

Reporting Officer: (Your name goes here)

Date & TIme of Offense/Incident:

Name of Person who Reported the Offense/Incident:

For all people on report, use the following codes:

V = Victim
W = Witness   Ex:
S = Suspect   Sam Smith (V) reported that...

Address and/or Location of Offense/Incident:

Reporting Officer's Summary of Offense/Incident:

_____

_____

_____

_____

_____

_____

_____

_____

_____

_____

_____

_____

_____

_____

_____

I hereby attest that the following report is an accurate representation of witness accounts reported to me and my own personal observations of the offense/incident scene.

_____
Signature of Reporting Officer

Suspect Information

Name, if known:	Gender:	Age:	Height:	Weight:	Hair:	Eyes:

Was an arrest made? (Check one)   If no, the suspect's last known location:
☐ YES or ☐ NO

On the reverse side of this paper, Reporting Office must draw a sketch of the crime scene/incident layout. Be sure to label any important details.

Figure 4.1 County Sheriff's Office Report.

Such narratives are not the place for the writer to add opinions, nor make assumptions. When completing either an incident report and/or a narrative report, investigators should always include the name of the individual being interviewed, or, who reported the incident; their age, physical and E-mail address(s), and all telephone numbers associated with that person. And by all means, check your spelling. People form opinions of you based on a variety of factors including your appearance, voice, tone, ability to listen, and so forth. And, in this profession, your ability to write. How you express yourself in writing can make or break a career. Misspelled words can change the meaning of a sentence. And by all means, edit what you write.

On one occasion, while I was a very young officer, I came across a vehicle with three white males in it. The vehicle and the occupants matched the description of car and occupants that had beaten and robbed a young man, and, stripped him virtually naked and left him on the ground by the side of the road.

When I stopped the vehicle, it was clear to me that the three people inside where the suspects in this offense. Actually, I immediately knew they had done it when I saw what appeared be bloodied clothes in the back seat of the car. But that was just me. More evidence would be needed to convict them, but for now, I had the guys. Back up help arrived and, when I wrote up the report, I stated that when I approached the vehicle, I saw clothes covered in blood. It seemed fair, and accurate, at the time. In court, my first ever such appearance on the witness stand in a felony trial, I was asked by the defense attorney how I knew that the cloths were covered in blood.

"It looked like blood," I said.

"Did you analyze the blood?" the defense attorney asked.

"No."

"Can you tell if something is blood simply by looking at it officer?"

"Usually, yes."

"Can you explain to the court how you've come to have this extraordinary capability?"

Well, you can see where this line of questioning went. I was put through the ringer and embarrassed myself. I did not make a good impression on the prosecutor either. In my defense, a good prosecutor would have caught this earlier. But this was not only my first case; it was the prosecutor's as well. We didn't prepare for my testimony properly. And, the narrative of my report did not reflect exactly what I knew to be true. It contained information as to what I thought was believed to be true but was interpreted as my claiming it to be "true."

Keep the narrative short, direct, and to the point. These reports are no place to try and impress people with YOU trying to display your mastery of the English language.

What makes a report effcient?

It . . .

- includes only necessary words and facts
- organizes the facts in a clear and logical sequence
- can easily be understood by anyone doing a follow-up investigation

Questions for Discussion

1. In the narrative, Detective Tony Martin suggests that some investigators consider "time" to be their most precious commodity. Argue for and against this statement.
2. What are the six basic interrogatory investigative questions?
3. What did the two investigators learn from their interview with Alan Thompson? Eric Mann? and John Thomas?
4. Alan Thompson asks why he and Eric Mann can't be interviewed together. Why is it important to separate witnesses when questioning them?
5. What should the next step(s) taken by Mike Cook and Tony Martin be in this investigation?

Work Sheet

Research the Following:

1. Research the National Incident-Based Reporting System (NIBRS) program. Describe its purpose and the format used in this program. Be prepared to discuss in class.
2. Research the interviewing mistakes made by the police in the JonBenet Ramsey murder case in Colorado. Be prepared to discuss, in class, the case and how the mistakes made by the police impacted on the case.

Work Sheet

Exercise

1. Write up a narrative interview for Alan Thompson, Eric Mann, and John Thomas. In the narrative, use whatever local address, phone number, and email you like to identify each of the three people interviewed. Make sure that you address all of the pertinent facts outlined in the interview conducted in this chapter. Use your name as the writer, not Mike Cook or Tony Martin's.

Work Sheet

References

Osterburg, James W. and Richard H. Ward. *Criminal Investigation.* 7th Edition.

Swanson, C., N. Chamelin, L. Territo, and R. W. Taylor. *Criminal Investigation.* 10th Edition.

CHAPTER 5
SOURCES OF
INFORMATION

"One may smile, and smile, and be a villain."

Hamlet, William Shakespeare

Chapter Objectives

1. Identify the various methods of acquiring the significant details a complainant or witness may possess.
2. Identify various methods of obtaining information from people.
3. Understand the various motivations of informants.
4. Describe the types of people used as informants.
5. Understand the concept of entrapment.

© GlebStock/Shutterstock.com

It had been two days since BATF special agent Mike Cook and Detective Tony Martin had interviewed the two owners of D & B Environmental. Martin, of course, had other cases that demanded his attention while Mike Cook worked for the second largest bureaucracy in world; that being the U.S. Government. And, they were second only to the bureaucracy found in Russia. And like all bureaucracies, the United States demanded paperwork for everything, including buying more paper. Literally everything Mike Cook would do in connection with this investigation would be have to be documented. In some instances, the amount of time completing the paperwork would rival the amount of time spent actually investigating the crime. And, for the past two nights, Mike Cook had not slept well. The case involving D & B had preoccupied his mind to the point that he could think of almost nothing else. There was something about this case that he simply could not put his finger on; not just yet. Normally, had the business been totally destroyed, the BATF Arson and Explosives response team would have descended on the scene like vultures over dead prey with a team of investigators and crime scene technicians. And that meant that while he might still be the case agent, he'd have a lot of assistance. In this case, since the bomb malfunctioned, there was no need for the Arson and Response team to get involved. The Twin Engine King Air that blew up created a small and well-contained crime scene worked by the local fire and police department. The cause was quickly established, so again, the response team was not necessary. So, Mike didn't sleep well. And, he spent the next two days completing a variety of paperwork associated with his new case. There was the case opening report describing what the case was about along with the written statements of Alan Thompson, Eric Mann, and Angela Lyle.

No sooner was Mike Cook getting ready to draft yet another report on his computer when the door to his small office opened. It was his supervisor Lisa Swanson. Lisa had no qualms about offering her guidance to young agents. She had done it before and would do it for Mike Cook.

"How's it going?" Lisa asked.

Mike said, "Fine. Just getting all this paperwork done."

"It's never ending. If you think you have a lot of paperwork to do, think about my having to read yours and everyone else's. Plus all the admin paperwork I have to do."

Mike said, "That's why they pay you the big bucks."

Lisa had heard that response many times before. Mike's comment was certainly not original. If he only knew how just how much "little" more bucks she was making than senior agents, his response would have been different.

"I want to talk about what you have so far," Lisa said.

"Is there something wrong with the paper work?" Mike asked showing a concerned look on his face.

"Not at all. The paper is fine. What I'm concerned about is where you plan to go with this. According to Alan Thompson and Eric Mann, they have no idea who may have done this or why. And the foreman, this guy Thomas, doesn't sound like the brightest guy around. So right now, you have no suspects and no motive. Is that about right?"

"So far, yes. But we just started this."

"I understand. And, I didn't expect much more than what you have this quickly. But I can't imagine why neither of the owners have any idea as to why this was done. Don't you find that odd?"

"I do. And so does Tony Martin. I think one of them, especially the foreman, John Thomas, might know more than they are telling us right now. But we have a considerable amount of work to do before we can prove or disprove what they're telling us."

"I agree. That is part of what I want to talk about. You're going to want to think about flipping somebody somewhere down the road. And, you're going to want to explore a variety of sources for information to help you determine who is telling the truth, who is lying, and, ultimately, what happened."

"Well, I have one informant, but he lives about 50 miles away and is only good for limited information concerning illegal gun sales. I'm not sure if he can help."

"I wouldn't expect him to. However, let's think about where you're going to go to get information on Thompson and Mann along with D & B Environmental," Lisa Swanson offered. "For instance, you haven't had much experience looking into businesses yet, so you're going to want to start with getting a Dunn and Bradstreet report on D & B."

"What's that?" Cook asked.

"A Dunn and Bradstreet report will provide you with information about the company such as verifying that the business exists; its size and purpose; it will review the background of the owners and key employees, and, identify the company's financial trends. Of course, we have a form for you to fill out to request the report," Lisa said as she handed Mike the form from a folder she was holding.

"And, you're going to want to get your hands on the company's financial records."

"Financial records?"

"Of course. You're going to want to know how the business was doing financially. If they were making lots of money, I doubt they'd want to destroy it. That would make the financial motive hard to prove. However, if the business was losing money, they might have been better off destroying it for the insurance money. So you're going to want to see the financials."

"You're talking about the company's bank records?"

"Yes. But there is more to it than that. You're going to want both the business and personal financial records of the owners. And, you're going to want to look for things such as decreasing revenue, increased production costs, lease and rental agreements, and were there any personal expenses paid with corporate funds. Look too for bounced checks. Find out if they're able to pay their bills. That sort of thing."

"Sounds like the work of account, not an agent," Mike said.

"You're right. And you're not an accountant, as far as I know. You did take some basic accounting in college didn't you?" Lisa asked.

"I did, thanks to a professor who was relentless with me. It wasn't easy, but I got through it. But I wouldn't tell anyone I could work as an accountant."

"Well, you may not need an accountant but you're certainly going to need an auditor on this case. I hope that you remember enough of your basic accounting to at least have an intelligent conversation about the subject once we get an auditor assigned to the case," Lisa said. "I'd hate to see you making a fool of yourself as the auditor tries to explain things to you, or, asks you for direction."

"How do I get an auditor assigned to the case?"

"I'm glad you asked. You have to put in a request of course. Here's the form," Lisa said as she handed Mike yet another form from the folder she was holding.

"How many more forms do you have in that folder for me to fill out?" Mike asked.

Lisa smiled but didn't answer Mike's question. However, she was nowhere near being finished providing guidance to her young agent. She knew that this case had the potential for being a bit more complex than what an agent with Mike's experience might have to deal with. Still, she was convinced Mike Cook was aggressive and thorough in his work. As long as she oversaw his actions, she was confident he would weave his way through this case. Her experience reminded her again, that left to their own accords, good people would often surprise you with what they could accomplish.

"Remember when I said you're going to need sources? Well don't always think in terms of criminals trying to bargain their way out of a something they'd gotten themselves into. Sources come from a variety of places. For instance, I know you have a call into the insurance company that had the policy for both the plane and D & B. When the agent calls back, you're going to want to meet with him or her as soon as possible. More importantly, find out who the arson investigator is for the company that's getting the ticket on this case. That person is going to run a parallel investigation into this. Make that person one of your new best friends. They can get their hands on records that you're going to need a subpoena for. Speaking of subpoenas, I've taken the liberty of requesting an Assistant U.S. Attorney (AUSA) be assigned to this case for you. You'll be getting a call from AUSA Carlos Sanchez soon. Set up a meeting. I know you've testified before the grand jury before but I don't think you've ever used a grand jury as an investigative tool. Carlos is a good man, a little absent minded sometimes, but he'll walk you through the process. And smile, you don't need to fill out a form for that.

"Getting back to sources, think about the insurance investigator as a major source. Find out who the company's book keeper and/or accountant is. That can be another good source. And, find out who their customers and competitors are. Those too, are very good sources. Also, the employees. You're going to want to interview each and every one of them. I'll try to get you some help but we're really swamped here. Are you comfortable with Detective Martin doing some of the interviews himself?"

Mike Cook said, "Absolutely. He knows what he's doing. This is new to him too but he's a good investigator. He'll know what to do."

"Okay then. You two divide and conquer the best you can. See what the employees have to say. My bet is that somebody knows more than what they're saying."

"Will do."

"Also, make sure you have a talk with him about the rules relating to entrapment. Make sure, as the two of you make attempts to develop sources, and, especially if you think you may wire them up somewhere along the way, that Tony understands the guidelines regarding entrapment."

Again, Cook said, "Will do."

When the meeting was over, Mike Cook walked back to his office, sat down at his desk, and logged on to his computer. While the computer fired up, he sat there staring at the screen and thought, "*Lisa is right. Someone at D & B knows more than they're telling us.*"

A Brief Discussion of Sources of Information and the Concept of Entrapment

Some argue that good investigators have a variety of "good sources." And in the business of criminal investigation, good investigators are always looking to increase the number of "sources" they have at their disposal. Simply put, investigators deal in information. So who has information? The answer is short and simple: Just about everyone. And that makes just about "everyone" a potential source. Try talking to any bartender about what he/she hears during the course of their night shift in a well-trafficked watering hole. I've had students who tended bar and were able to tell me who was cheating on who; who was dealing drugs; who was trafficking in stolen property; and who might one see for getting their hands on false identification.

Ever try asking a cab driver in Las Vegas where "the action" off the strip might be? Well, depending on the "action" you're looking for, more than just a few cabbies will be able to tell you where you might look for whatever it is you're looking for. How about waitresses; especially the ones working the midnight shift at 24 hour diners? Imagine what they "see and hear." Some of the best sources available are other members of the law enforcement community. And, private investigators with financial institutions, including credit card companies, along with cable and utility providers can be a wealth of information. These are not criminals but simply people who work with people and "hear" things; things that might be of benefit to you, the investigator. Everyone, no matter what they do for a living is a "potential" source of information. And as soon as you run afoul of one of these people, you lose a potential source. And good investigators need all the sources they can get. Some argue that investigators are only as good as the number of sources they have. And sources, or informants as they are often referred to, are often needed to help the investigator establish probable cause.

The courts, however, have weighed in on informant reliability. Needless to say, the courts have shown a distinct lack of reliability on the use of informants. One such case in point is Draper v. United State; 1959.

The facts of this case are as follows:

A federal narcotics agent was given information from a reliable informant that the Petitioner (suspect/Draper) was dealing drugs from his apartment. The informant stated that the Draper had gone to Chicago to purchase heroin. The informant told the agent the date the Draper would return to Denver from Chicago, the clothes he would be wearing, and the color of the bag he would be carrying. Based on this information, the agent waited for Draper at Denver's Union Station on Draper's expected date of return. When Draper disembarked the Chicago train, he was wearing clothes and carrying a bag fitting the informant's description. Based on this information, the agent arrested Draper without a warrant. Heroin and syringe were found on Draper and seized pursuant to this arrest. Draper was subsequently convicted of transporting heroin.

The court dealt with two issues related to this case: First, did the surrounding facts and circumstances give the federal agent probable cause to believe that the Petitioner (Draper) had committed, or was committing a crime. And second, Can probable cause be based on hearsay?

The court ruled yes to both questions. According to the Supreme Court, "The informant's past reliability, accurate description of the Petitioner's clothing, bag, and date of arrival gave the agent probable cause to arrest the Petitioner without a warrant." With regard to the issue of hearsay, the court also ruled yes, stating, "Hearsay is an evidentiary rule dealing with guilt beyond a reasonable doubt. Excluding facts that are hearsay from probable cause confuses the common sense standard of probable cause from the technical, legal standards of proving guilt beyond a reasonable doubt."

However, the Supreme Court did not end its argument over the use of sources/informants with the Draper decision. The court followed up with two additional cases important for investigators to understand. They are Aguilar v. Texas and Spinelli v. United States. Those cases will be part of this chapter's assignment.

Cultivation and Management of Informants

According to Dr. Thomas O'Connor, a cultivated source is someone who has connections with the criminal underworld and is able to give advance warning of things that are going to happen. O'Connor states that "cultivated sources make the best informants". Criminals who want to have their charges dropped or reduced and turn into police informants (or "flip) in order to do so are not considered cultivated sources. Under evidence law they appear to be working out of self-interest and therefore their claims don't have as much value. Truth is assumed in the words of someone acting outside of their own self-interest. It is better to have active informants coming forward with information about future crimes as opposed to past ones.

A cultivated source is someone who does business in the same vicinity as criminals. Examples of cultivated sources are taxi drivers, hotel employees, airline employees, automobile salespeople, doormen, gun dealers, bartenders, private investigators, apartment managers, package delivery employees, and proprietors or employees of restaurants. O'Conner states, "The idea is that such people can get as close to criminal suspects as possible (for example, their regular barber or prostitute) without getting so close you're treading on privileged relationships (for example, their wife or psychotherapist). These types of informants work as eyes and ears for the police that are watching for signs of a crime in the making.

Managing informants is a matter of keeping them motivated and ensuring that the motivation continues to have some type of value. There are many different motivation based typologies of informants. Osterburg and Ward (2000) present one that distinguishes the following:

- Volunteer informant—usually an eyewitness to a crime or jealous spouse with specific information about vice activity or income tax evasion motivated by civic duty or vanity and kept motivated by gratitude
- Paid informant—usually someone involved in a crime with particulars about a person they feel the police should know about and motivated by revenge or money and kept motivated by money
- Anonymous informant—usually someone with precise or imprecise information about suspicious activities or a crime that is being planned or they believe is not yet discovered by police and motivated by repentance and kept motivated by reward or gratitude

Finally, there is the oldest typology of motives which has been around for some 40 years simply because they never change (Harney & Cross, 1960):

- Fear—people who feel threatened by the law or by other criminals (*most police believe this is the best motivation*)
- Revenge—people such as ex-wives, ex-girlfriends, ex-employers, ex-associates, or ex-customers who want to get even
- Perversity—people who are cop wannabes or think they're James Bond and/or hope to one day expose corruption
- Ego—people who need to feel they are smart "big shots" and/or outwitting those they see as inferiors
- Money—people who, like mercenaries, will do whatever it takes if the money is right
- Repentance—people who want to leave the world of crime behind them and/or citizens fed up with crime

The concept of entrapment is an issue often raised by the defense whenever sources/informants are used when they've acted in or on behalf of law enforcement. In essence, an informant, when acting on behalf of a law enforcement officer, is, in fact, an arm of the officer. He/she (the informant) is acting on behalf of law enforcement and is, therefore, prohibited from engaging in any conduct that would constitute a criminal offense. What investigators and other law enforcement officers can do is provide individuals with the opportunity to commit a crime. What they cannot do is entice someone to commit a crime that they might not otherwise be predisposed to commit.

"Entrapment defenses in the United States have evolved mainly through case law. Two competing tests exist for determining whether entrapment has taken place, known as the "subjective" and "objective" tests. The "subjective" test looks at the defendant's state of mind; entrapment can be claimed if the defendant had no "predisposition" to commit the crime. The "objective" test looks instead at the government's conduct; entrapment occurs when the actions of government officers would usually have caused a normally law-abiding person to commit a crime."[1]

Exercises

1. Do some independent research and discuss four major problem areas that arise in the management of informants.
3. Discuss briefly, in 200 words or less, how you might develop sources who have not been arrested. What type of people and in what professions would you target as sources if you were a detective in your community. Explain how and why you think the sources you identify would be of significant value to you.
4. In Draper v. United States, the court held, "A tip from a reliable informant, which is corroborated by predicting facts unknowable to a stranger, gives rise to probable cause. In determining what facts and circumstances will give rise to probable cause, one must view the facts and circumstances as a reasonable person would view them, and not how they would be viewed in a courtroom." Explain what is meant by this.
5. Provide a summary of the facts, the courts findings, and decision on the following cases:
   A. Aguilar v. Texas, 378 U.S. 108 (1964)
   B. Spinelli v. United States, 393 U.S. 410 (1969)

Work Sheet

Notes

1. http://law.jrank.org/pages/1091/Entrapment-two-approaches-entrapment.html.

Supplemental Reading

Gudjonsson, G. (1992). *The Psychology of Interrogations, Confessions and Testimony.* NY: Wiley & Sons.

Harney, M. and J. Cross. (1960). *The Informer in Law Enforcement.* Springfield: Charles Thomas.

Hess, John E. *Interviewing & Interrogation for Law Enforcement.* 2nd Edition.

Osterburg, James W. and Richard H. Ward. (2000). Criminal Investigation: A Method for Reconstructing the Past. 7th Edition.

Leo, R. (1992). From Coercion to Deception. *Crime, Law & Social Change* 18:35–59.

Leo, R. (1996a). Inside the Interrogation Room. *Journal of Criminal Law and Criminology* 86:266–303.

Leo, R. (1996b). Miranda's Revenge: Police Interrogation as a Confidence Game. *Law and Society Review* 30:259–88.

Leo, R. (1996c). The Impact of Miranda Revisited. *Journal of Criminal Law and Criminology* 86:621–92.

Thomas O'Connor, Dr. Austin Peay State University.

Key Legal Cases

Draper v. United States, 358 U.S. 307 (1959)

Aguilar v. Texas, 378 U.S. 108 (1964)

Spinelli v. United States, 393 U.S. 410 (1969)

CHAPTER 6
INVESTIGATIVE SOURCES

Sometimes if I tell people, 'I'm afraid that I'm really a fraud,' or 'I have a lot of self-doubt,' they go, 'Oh, no, you're kidding.' I go, 'No, I'm really honest.'

Al Franken

© Dale A Stork/Shutterstock.com

Chapter Objectives

1. Become familiar with the role of the insurance investigator in certain types of investigations.
2. Become familiar with the basic types of questions to ask of insurance representatives in a variety of investigations.
3. Become familiar with the role of investigative units within private insurance and financial institutions.
4. Become familiar with the provisions of the Arson Immunity Reporting Act.

After three fruitless days of interviewing the yard workers and truck drivers at D & B Environmental, Mike Cook and Tony Martin failed to come up with any clue that might have helped them identify who might have been involved in the attempted destruction of D & B Environmental and/or the blowing up of the airplane. Even though the investigation was still new, the two investigators were frustrated. Each driver and yard worker had basically told them the same thing. They had worked there for anywhere from as long as three years or for as little as six months. Each person claimed to have no idea as to who would want to destroy the company; no idea if either of the owners had any enemies; could not recall anything unusual or out of the ordinary, and, each of the workers and driver's had an alibi for where they were the night prior to the destruction of the aircraft and the attempted bombing/arson of the company. It was almost as if each had been programmed to say the same thing.

"Maybe we're not asking the right questions," Tony Martin said as he sat with his feet on his desk late in the afternoon.

"Perhaps," Mike Cook replied, sitting across from Detective Martin. "I still think someone knows more than they're telling us."

"Probably so. But unless we can squeeze one of these people, they're not going to tell us a thing."

"Maybe when we get a chance to look at the records that were piled in the office, we'll come up with something," Cook offered.

Their conversation was cut short when one of the secretaries in the detective bureau walked in and said, "There is a John Sherry here to talk to you. Says he's an investigator with Practical Insurance. He standing over there."

"That old guy?" Tony Martin said. "It's about time he got here. Send him in."

John Sherry was a few years younger than he looked, although he was and did look old. That's because he was old. And, he didn't try to pretend otherwise. He'd long ago given up working out opting instead, to concentrate on his golf game. And when he wasn't golfing, he was reading; mostly history books dealing with World War II or watching the History Channel about WW II. The insurance investigator gig was his second career. He'd had a very successful career years ago as a state police office and federal investigator doing background investigations for people needing top secret security clearances. Sherry knew how to dig into both crimes and people's backgrounds. He didn't believe in spending one minute longer in the office than necessary. He knew people did not usually surrender and to catch criminals, one had to be out there among them. He was gone so much from the office when he was back on the job that his nickname was the "ghost." Sometimes quick-tempered, and irascible, Sherry knew that he should have more patience with all things in life but that wasn't his make-up. As he grew older, he had less patience with just about everything, especially slow golfers and incompetent young investigators. When he had not one but two voice mail messages from Special Agent Mike Cook asking to meet, he was certain he'd be dealing with yet another overly aggressive young agent who thought he had all the answers. As was often his custom, John Sherry went into his initial meeting with the two young investigators predisposed in his thoughts, thinking that he was about to have to deal with yet another young federal agent who thought he could catch criminals by use of the Internet and not having to get out among them as was his philosophy. Sherry was soon to learn that his fears were unfounded.

"Nice to meet you," Mike Cook said as he and Tony Martin both stood to shake the "old man's hand."

"My pleasure," Sherry said almost as if he didn't really mean it.

"We've been waiting to talk to you," Mike Cook said. "We're investigating the bombing of the plane your company insured for Eric Mann as well as the attempted bombing of D & B Environmental."

"I know that," Sherry replied. "What can I do to help you two?"

"What can you tell us about the insurance policies on both the plane and the company?" Cook asked.

"Well, the plane was insured for $1,800,000. Looks like we might be on the hook for the full amount. Depending of course, what we find out as to who did this. As for the company, they had a three million dollar policy on the property and the contents. Not much actually, but the funny thing is, they increased the amount from two to three million about six months ago."

"But you're not on the hook for any payout on the business since the business didn't burn, are you?"

"Not sure just yet," Sherry replied. "They haven't submitted any claim just yet for damages or loss of business due to the records being destroyed or, seized by you guys. And, depending on what we find, we might not have to pay anything on the plane. A bit too early to say."

"We've never worked with an insurance investigator before. Can you tell us exactly what it is you do or plan to do regarding the bombing of the airplane and the attempted bombing of the plant?" Mike Cook asked.

"First, just so you know, before I came here, I met with Lt. Gonzalez. I went over his report and his findings as to what he found at the airport the morning the plane blew up. He was kind enough to give me a copy of his report. I also went with him to the airport and took some pictures of the burnt plane. In this case, the plane was destroyed by fire caused by an explosive device placed on top of a gasoline container. So, we know that it was intentionally set. That is not going to be in dispute. Normally, I would concentrate on determining if the fire was intentionally set or not. In this case, we know that it was indeed intentionally set.

"I'm also going to do many of the exact same things you are including, checking Thompson and Mann's prior criminal records; checking to see if they had or have any prior lawsuits; and see if they've had any former insurance claims. I'm going to also look for any judgments they may have against them, and I'm going to look for any liens against the property as well as any tax liens they might have. I'm going to interview them both, just as you did. That is what I'm going to do. Now maybe you can tell me, what have you two discovered that might be of help?"

Mike Cook and Tony Martin exchanged startled glances at each other. Here was this "old guy" telling them what he was going to do regarding their investigation. And now, this "old guy" was asking what they've discovered.

"I'm not sure we can discuss much with you right now," Cook said. "This is a federal investigation."

"You can discuss anything you want as long as it's not part of a federal grand jury investigation," Sherry said, coolly. If we're going to work this together, and you're going to want to do that, we need to share information. I am not required by law, to voluntarily turn over any evidence I might discover during my investigation. I only have to turn over evidence upon receipt of an official letter from your agency. In fact, just so you know, that's the only way I can turn the information over to you that I have. So, we either work together on this, or, I'll take my leave."

Detective Tony Martin asked, "How can you get things easier than us?"

"Because I represent a private party. In this case, it's the insurance company. And I'm investigating this from a civil perspective. Not a criminal case. That's what you two are doing, or so I presume," Sherry said half sarcastically. "My authority falls under contract law and the provisions of the insurance contract," Sherry said as he reached into his canvas bag and handed Cook a copy of the insurance policies on both the airplane and D & B Environmental. "As you'll read, they are required to cooperate with me on a variety of matters and providing information in order to have the claim for the airplane honored. If they fail to do so, we can deny the claim for the aircraft.

Special Agent Mike Cook wasn't quite sure how to respond to Sherry. It was clear that this old guy knew what he was talking about. But working with him to the extent he was proposing was not something he had anticipated. After all, he thought, this guy wasn't a cop.

"Let me make a quick call," Mike said to Sherry. "I'll be right back."

Mike Cook excused himself and went into the hallway to make a phone call leaving Tony Martin alone with John Sherry. Mike took out his cell phone and called Lisa Swanson. After explaining to her the meeting he and Tony had just had with John Sherry, the insurance investigator, and, what he was suggesting, or more demanding, with regard to working together on this case, Lisa's advice was short and to the point: "Do what you want, but I would strongly advise you to work with this guy. Make him your new best friend. But it's your call."

Once again, Mike Cook decided to take Lisa's advice and treat it like an order. Walking back into Tony Martin's small office, Mike Cook smiled and said, "Okay. What do you need from us right now?"

John Sherry grinned. He didn't usually smile, but he grinned, almost like the look on a cat after it had just eaten a canary. "So, how is Lisa Swanson?" he asked.

"She's fine. She said to say hello," Mike Cook replied. Lisa had said no such thing, but he wasn't going to give Sherry the last word on this subject.

"I'm going to need a letter from your agency to mine making a formal request for information related to this insurance file. I have to follow strict legal guidelines here because I'm not part of a public safety investigation. But once you send the official letter asking for information in our file, the insurance company is protected under the *Arson Immunity Reporting Act*. So, have you two spoken to EPA yet?" Sherry asked.

"EPA?" Tony Martin interjected.

"Yeah; the Environmental Protection Agency. EPA. Have you contacted them about this?"

"No. Why would we want to do that?" Cook asked.

"Because this is an environmental transportation company, that's why. The company deals in hazardous waste. It's clear that someone blew up the plane. We know that. And, they tried to blow up the plant. So, we can operate on several theories. One, the plane was deliberately blown up for the insurance money, or, it was blown up by someone very angry with the owner. Two, the real objective was to destroy the business and the records, either by the owners or by someone very upset with them, such as a competitor or former employee. Third, the plane was the only objective and the company was made to only look like it was the target. From my perspective, the insurance money on the plane only comes to a small amount and will not readily replace it. The real money to be made here, if, it was an inside job, was destroying D & B's building and whatever property the fire may have also destroyed. And since the plane was most often used for business, and the companies business was environmental transportation, makes sense to me that we learn as much as we can from our local EPA investigators as possible. Actually, I'm surprised you haven't spoken to them already. They should be sitting here with us right now."

"I didn't realize EPA had investigators near here," Cook replied.

"They're feds, just like you. They cover the whole country. Who do you think is going to help you understand all those gas downed documents your recovered?"

Mike Cook said, "We were going to do that."

"Really. Do you understand EPA shipping manifests, and so forth? Because I don't. It might help to have some experts on EPA rules and regulations," Sherry said.

"What do you propose?" Cook asked.

"Let's get EPA in on this now. No matter what direction this goes, it's going probably involve issues, people, and or competitors who are in the environmental business. In most arson cases, we always tell people, 'follow the money.' To do that in this case, we need to follow the money and what went on with regard to the transportation of the waste D & B was hauling. For that, we need EPA."

The meeting ended with Cook, Martin, and John Sherry agreeing to set up a meeting with the Environmental Protection Agency. Cook called Lisa Swanson back and told her what he was planning to do.

"Sounds like a very good idea," Swanson said. "Sounds like you're getting your team in place. And, I have an auditor assigned to this for you. His name is Alan Pinette. Quite the numbers guy. Lives for numbers and not much else. Nobody can trace money and count better than this guy. If he tells you five and seven equal 11, believe him because more often than not, he believes it. I played golf with him once in a tournament. If says he got a five or will take a five when he got a six, go with the five. This guy knows numbers."

Mike Cook was happy that Lisa couldn't see him roll his eyes as they spoke on the phone. If she could, she would have certainly noted his displeasure with the fact that she was behind adding a cast of participants to his investigation.

The investigation was only a week old and the list of people who were in the need-to-know as participants was growing. And, with a meeting the following day with an agent from the EPA, the list was going to get even bigger.

"So much for you and I working this little airplane explosion ourselves," Detective Tony Martin said. Mike Cook replied, "Yeah, seems like this is going to be a cast of thousands before it's over."

Before the day was out, Lisa Swanson had one more meeting to make before she could even think of getting in another run. John Sherry was the first to arrive at the coffee shop near Lisa's condo. It had been several weeks since they last met; longer than either had wanted it to be. Drinking a cup of coffee, which he could do almost any hour of the day, Sherry stood when Lisa entered the shop. Lisa ordered a bottled water before sitting down to talk to Sherry.

"So, what do you think of Mike Cook and his detective friend Tony Martin?" Lisa asked.

"Both young, that's for sure. But everyone is young to me. They don't seem to mind getting out from behind a desk, that's a good thing."

"I'd appreciate it if you'd help guide them along as you work with them. This is not going to be the usual type of case Mike might be involved in, especially at this point in his career. Seems like a good 'who-done-it' to me, if, it's not a clear arson for profit case."

"I'll help guide them to the extent they'll let me," Sherry replied. "But I think you're right; this is going to involve some old time investigating to solve this one. I doubt the lab is going to be much help. They're going to have to ask the right questions of the right people, and soon. But don't expect me to back channel all my concerns and what I find to you. If that gets back to them, they won't trust me. And, I'm not going to put the company at risk by acting in bad faith. Your young agent is going to have to work his way through this."

"I wouldn't expect otherwise dad," Lisa said as she kissed her father on the cheek. "I'm off to get in run before dark. Talk to you later."

A Brief Discussion about Private Insurance Investigators

"Typically, an insurance company, a private organization, is not a government agent for purposes of Fourth Amendment Search and Seizure Law. However, if the insurer appears to be acting on behalf of the State (or federal government), then the insurer can open itself up to potential liability. To prevent that liability, the immunity statutes create a safe haven for insurers to cooperate with law enforcement authorities in the investigation of arson and fraud. Likewise public authorities (in the case of our ongoing investigation, the BATF and the local police) may provide information to insurance company representatives, i.e. John Sherry. But this cooperation should never take the form of coordination of investigative activities in which one investigator seeks to direct or guide the investigative activities of another investigator. The insurer's investigator must avoid the appearance of being a "state actor." In other words, neither Mike Cook nor Tony Martin can direct John Sherry to do something on their behalf in order to avoid the rules of criminal procedure.[1] The two investigators in our story must not instruct John Sherry, the insurance investigator, as to what it is they want him to do as that would make him (Sherry) arm of law enforcement. More discussion on this will follow later in the text.

"The investigation of a criminal arson case is subject to a set of rules that differ greatly from the rules governing a civil arson investigation. The two investigations proceed along parallel lines. While the lines may be closely parallel, they do not intersect. The fundamental objectives are different: a criminal investigation seeks to solve a crime and bring the responsible party to justice, whoever it may be; a civil investigation seeks to determine whether a specific individual—the claimant—was responsible for the fire and to refuse payment if he was."[2]

As Guy E. Burnette, Jr. writes in his article, *Coordinating Civil and Criminal Arson Investigations*, "A criminal investigation of arson is subject to a set of rules determined by the criminal code and constitutional law. A civil investigation of arson is controlled by the insurance code and contract law. A criminal investigator can do things which a civil investigator cannot do, and vice versa. A criminal investigator can gain access to information which a civil investigator cannot obtain, and vice versa. A criminal investigator has resources available to his or her investigation which are not available to the civil investigator, and vice versa. Between the two investigations, virtually all of the resources and information an investigator could ever want are available."[3]

Good investigators will make every effort to coordinate their criminal investigation with their private civil counterpart. Promoting this type of cooperation between the two investigations will enable all parties to not only carry out their investigative function, but maximize the information available from all available resources and sources of information that might be available.

When dealing with an arson for profit case, there are three people in the insurance chain that an investigator might consider interviewing. They are the Agent or Broker, the Claims Adjuster, and the Insurance Investigator. Very often, the insurance investigator can and should be able to answer all the applicable questions the criminal investigator might have. Some of the more obvious questions include:

a. Is there more than one person insured?
b. Who is the beneficiary?
c. What is the amount of the policy?
d. When does the policy expire?
e. Have there been any increases in the amount of the policy? If so, when did the increase take effect?
f. Are the payments up to date?
g. Does the insured have any other policies?
h. Have you investigated past fires or claims involving the insured?

For investigators who find themselves working with insurance investigators or adjusters, or members of a Special Investigative Unit of an insurance company, they should keep in mind that while they cannot instruct or direct the representative of the insurance company to do things on their behalf, they can, and should, make a formal request asking for any and all information in the insurance file related to the insured. This includes getting copies of the policy. The file would also, normally, contain a copy of the initial claim made by the insured. This is referred to as the *"Notice of Loss."* This is often done by telephone, and is often recorded. Most companies have the person taking the initial claim call follow a standard company script, which varies from company to company. This is the first statement the insured makes. Additional statements are often taken by cause and origin specialists working for the insurance company as well as to adjusters. It would be wise for investigators to examine all such statements to look for consistency and contradictions in those statements.

Insurance companies, and investigators, have a wealth of information available that can be readily made available to investigators. A simple formal letter requesting the information is virtually all that is legally required to obtain that information. However, investigators should not stop there. A good school of thought is to always follow up with a phone call and request or discuss how the information will be delivered. Make sure that you establish a contact with someone at the company. Once that is done, investigators get everything in the file. And that file will often contain financial records, including tax records, contact information related to company employees and vendors, just to name a few. But tread lightly. Insurance companies, agents, and investigators cannot work for you. They cannot act as your agent or on your behalf. You must avoid the appearance of collusion. Failure on the part of the insured to totally cooperate with the insurance company can result in the denial of their claim. Collusion on the part of the government and the insurance company can result in triple damages being awarded to the insured.

Exercises

1. Most states requirements have statutes that create an obligation for insurance companies to participate in third-party governmental investigations of arson and fraud claims. Many such statutes authorizes or, in some cases, requires insurers to release information to state or local fire investigators/departments when facts gathered by the insurer raises the possibility of arson. Similarly, most states also have a Fraud Reporting Statute, which insulates insurers from civil liability when insurers in good faith report fraudulent insurance claims to state investigative agencies. Research the statutes in your state and provide a detailed list of what exact information the statutes require an insurance company to release and the degree of cooperation they must provide to authorized officials with regard to that official's investigation of suspected arson or fraud.

2. Explain the provisions of Arson Immunity Reporting Act.

3. Research the facts of, and discuss the following cases:
   a. Michigan v. Tyler, 436 U.S. 499 (1978)
   b. U.S. v. Jacobsen, 466 U.S. 109 (1984)

4. Do an Internet search of five insurance and/or financial institutions and discuss three types of criminal offenses those organizations might investigate. Include in your discussion the name of financial institution and/or insurance company, the name of the unit that conducts such investigations, and types of crimes/offenses that unit specializes in.

Work Sheet

Notes

1. Mark T. Dietrichs and Sara M. Andrzejewski. Cooperation Between Insurance Investigators and Law Enforcement in Arson and Fraud Cases. Swift, Currie, McGhee & Hiers, LLP.
2. http://www.interfire.org/res_file/coordcc.asp; Coordinating Civil and Criminal Arson Investigations; Guy E. Burnette, Jr., Esquire.
3. ibid.

Notes

CHAPTER 7
ENVIRONMENTAL CRIME

"Raising awareness on the most pressing environmental issues of our time is more important than ever."

Leonardo DiCaprio

Chapter Objectives

1. What constitutes an environmental crime?
2. What laws are applicable to environmental crimes?
3. The history behind the legislation regarding environmental crimes.
4. Become familiar with several key investigative steps associated with investigating these types of offenses.

© guentermanaus/Shutterstock.com

Mike Cook was complaining about the morning traffic on his way to meet with an agent of the Environmental Protection Agency (EPA).

"I don't want to hear it," Tony Martin said with a look of frustration on his face. "I had to leave over an hour ago to meet you before you even got behind the wheel. So quit complaining," he added as he sipped his coffee.

Both men engaged in light conversation, mostly related to their concerns as to what exactly it was that EPA could do to help them with their investigation in the issues related to D & B Environmental.

Tony Martin asked, "You know anything about this guy or EPA?"

"About as much as you do," Mike Cook replied. "Which is nothing."

It was almost 9:00 a.m. when Mike Cook and Tony Martin pulled into the parking garage of the private high rise building that housed the office of the regional EPA office. Minutes later, after riding the elevator to the 12th floor, the two men were identifying themselves to the middle-aged woman who stood behind a secured glass window. After examining the badges and credentials of the two men, the woman buzzed them into the office.

"Special Agent Jackson will be right with you," the woman said.

Latrelle Jackson grew up in the inner city. His one and only love was sports. Any sport. Anything that involved a ball was fine with him. And, if the game called for some physical contact, that was okay too. His love for sports eventually landed him a full scholarship to play football. He wasn't big enough to play for a Division I team, but his speed made him a Division II standout. There was even some faint hope of being drafted by the NFL. But that dream was shattered during his senior year when a knee injury ended any hope of playing professional ball. Like so many student athletes who think they might actually have a shot at the big money a major sports contract might bring, Latrelle Jackson didn't spend much more time studying that which was absolutely necessary to maintain a grade point average high enough to satisfy the requirements of the NCAA in order to maintain his eligibility to play football at Morehouse College in Atlanta, GA. Once his hopes of playing pro ball ended with a knee injury brought on by an illegal hit from a defensive back, Latrelle quickly realized that he was going to have to do something to earn a living after college or face the unbearable fate of moving back home to live with his parents. With an interest in science, Latrelle was able to get himself admitted to graduate school. Two years later, he had a Master Degree in Environmental Management. Latrelle was, in spite of his knee injury, able to pass the physical of Officer's Candidate School in the U.S. Coast Guard. After four years of serving his country, Latrelle Jackson found himself as a Special Agent with the EPA.

"Nice to meet you," Latrelle Jackson said, extending his hand to Mike Cook and Tony Martin.

After a few minutes of pleasantries, the three men sat down in the EPA conference room to discuss the bombing of the King Air plane and the attempted destruction of D & B Environmental. It took ATF Agent Mike Cook close to an hour to brief Latrelle Jackson as to what he and Tony Martin had learned and done so far in their investigation. When Mike Cook finally finished his briefing, Latrelle said, "Sounds like we might need to look into this with you."

Mike Cook said, "We really don't know much about EPA or what you folks do. And neither Tony nor I really know anything much about what EPA does or its laws. What can you tell us about what you do and how you think you might fit into this investigation."

Latrelle Jackson paused for a moment, nodded and smiled at the two men sitting across from him. "Well, the short answer is that EPA investigates cases that threaten people's health and the environment. We investigate violations of the environmental laws. There are of course, a number of laws that when violated, constitute an environmental crime For instance, Congress passed what is known as the Comprehensive Environmental Response, Compensation, and Liability Act (CERCLA) better known as the Superfund in 1980. This was a political response, as so many laws are, in response to an environmentally related incident. In this case, it was in response to the public outcry over the Love Canal scandal where Hooker Chemical dumped a lot of toxic waste into a canal. This caused a lot of people a heck of a lot of medical problems. Basically CERCLA requires companies to clean up sites they've created, usually from illegal dumping or discharge of waste products, or pay for the federal government for the cost of the cleanup.

"Unfortunately, this legislation has little teeth. This can only happen in the government. I share this with you just so you know that some of these laws can be confusing. What isn't confusing is the illegal dumping of hazardous waste. Simply put, an environmental crime is a negligent, knowing, or willful violation of a federal law. For instance, one of the more common violations involves the illegal disposal of hazardous waste. Another is the illegal discharge of pollutants to a waterway. We also investigate money laundering related to environmental crimes.

"And now, especially since 9/11, EPA is part of the National Infrastructure Protection Center (NIPC). In fact, we're the lead federal agency on critical infrastructure protection issues for the water supply. We are part of a joint effort that coordinates research to develop a vulnerability assessment methodology with private industry representatives, along with technical support from water associations and federal agencies such as the FBI and the Department of Energy. That's an official way of saying we're part of a task force that looks into ways to prevent a terrorist attack on our water supply," Jackson added.

Mike Cook looked at Tony Martin then back to Latrelle and said, "Well, so far, we don't have any evidence of any of these types of crimes."

"No it doesn't sound like you do, not just yet anyway," Latrelle replied. "But it's still early in your investigation. Give me a couple of minutes. Let me see if we have anything on D & B Environmental."

Latrelle Jackson excused himself leaving both Mike Cook and Tony Martin alone in the conference room.

"So, what do you think?" Martin asked.

"I'm not sure why we're here actually. This could prove to be a waste of time."

"I agree. We certainly haven't come across anything that suggests any environmental crimes here."

Minutes later, Latrelle Jackson returned to the conference room with a small folder. Inside was a computer printout that reflected the fact that two years prior, D & B Environmental and its owners, Alan Thompson and Eric Man had been cited for not having the proper manifest on hand during a shipment of hazardous waste.

"What do you mean by cited?" Cook asked. "I ran them through all the data bases and found nothing on them."

"It's not criminal," Latrelle said. "It's a civil action. EPA has authority to take non judicial enforcement action. As such, they don't involve the judicial process as you may know it. Some violations simply result in a letter or notice directing someone to come into compliance. That's what happened here. D & B got a letter demanding they come into compliance. It's almost like receiving a traffic ticket."

"Come into compliance with what?" Cook asked.

"Their manifests. It wasn't on the truck when they were stopped by local police."

"What's a manifest?"

"A *manifest* is a document that accompanies hazardous waste from the time it is generated until it's ultimately treated or disposed of. It's actually a system designed to track hazardous waste. Almost like a chain of custody form for evidence."

"So this guy doesn't have a shipping document one day. So what does that mean?" Cook asked.

Latrelle Jackson paused momentarily and looked at both men and said, "Maybe nothing. It might also be something they deliberately did to mask where the waste was really going when they were transporting it."

Mike Cook asked, "How can we find out if the waste was actually disposed of properly?"

"We have to examine the documents you found piled up in the building. And then we start checking with the companies they were supposed to deliver it to. We're going to need to find out who they had contracts with. What we do know, according to your insurance man, is that they had recently increased their insurance policy on the company and they've been cited for at least one EPA violation. Not sure about you, but it makes me just a little curious," Latrelle said.

Detective Martin asked, "Does that document have the name of the driver on it?"

"It would," replied Latrelle. "But we don't have the document."

Please print or type. (Form designed for use on elite (12-pitch) typewriter.)   Form Approved. OMB No. 2050-0039

UNIFORM HAZARDOUS WASTE MANIFEST	1. Generator ID Number	2. Page 1 of	3. Emergency Response Phone	4. Manifest Tracking Number

5. Generator's Name and Mailing Address   Generator's Site Address (if different than mailing address)

Generator's Phone:

6. Transporter 1 Company Name   U.S. EPA ID Number

7. Transporter 2 Company Name   U.S. EPA ID Number

8. Designated Facility Name and Site Address   U.S. EPA ID Number

Facility's Phone:

9a. HM	9b. U.S. DOT Description (including Proper Shipping Name, Hazard Class, ID Number, and Packing Group (if any))	10. Containers No.	Type	11. Total Quantity	12. Unit Wt./Vol.	13. Waste Codes
	1.					
	2.					
	3.					
	4.					

14. Special Handling Instructions and Additional Information

15.   **GENERATOR'S/OFFEROR'S CERTIFICATION:** I hereby declare that the contents of this consignment are fully and accurately described above by the proper shipping name, and are classified, packaged, marked and labeled/placarded, and are in all respects in proper condition for transport according to applicable international and national governmental regulations. If export shipment and I am the Primary Exporter, I certify that the contents of this consignment conform to the terms of the attached EPA Acknowledgment of Consent.
I certify that the waste minimization statement identified in 40 CFR 262.27(a) (if I am a large quantity generator) or (b) (if I am a small quantity generator) is true.

Generator's/Offeror's Printed/Typed Name	Signature	Month	Day	Year

16. International Shipments   ☐ Import to U.S.   ☐ Export from U.S.   Port of entry/exit: _____
Transporter signature (for exports only):   Date leaving U.S.:

17. Transporter Acknowledgment of Receipt of Materials

Transporter 1 Printed/Typed Name	Signature	Month	Day	Year
Transporter 2 Printed/Typed Name	Signature	Month	Day	Year

18. Discrepancy

18a. Discrepancy Indication Space   ☐ Quantity   ☐ Type   ☐ Residue   ☐ Partial Rejection   ☐ Full Rejection

Manifest Reference Number:

18b. Alternate Facility (or Generator)   U.S. EPA ID Number

Facility's Phone:

18c. Signature of Alternate Facility (or Generator)	Month	Day	Year

19. Hazardous Waste Report Management Method Codes (i.e., codes for hazardous waste treatment, disposal, and recycling systems)

1.	2.	3.	4.

20. Designated Facility Owner or Operator: Certification of receipt of hazardous materials covered by the manifest except as noted in Item 18a

Printed/Typed Name	Signature	Month	Day	Year

EPA Form 8700-22 (Rev. 3-05) Previous editions are obsolete.   DESIGNATED FACILITY TO DESTINATION STATE (IF REQUIRED)

Figure 7.1

"So that doesn't help us," said Martin.

"That's not necessarily true. We can track this event back and get the name of the driver."

"That would be good," Mike Cook said. "We interviewed all of the drivers and of course, they knew nothing."

Latrelle asked, "When can I look at the documents you recovered?"

"How soon can you get started?" Cook asked.

"How about tomorrow? I have an intern from the university working here. I've been looking for something of substance for her to do."

"That sounds good," Cook replied. The three men shook hands and agreed to talk again the following day. Cook thanked Jackson for his time and headed out of the office.

A few minutes later, riding down the elevator, Mike Cook looked at Tony Martin and said, "Why do I think EPA is about to join in our case?"

"Because they just did," replied Tony Martin. "Because they just did."

A Brief Discussion about Environmental Crime

The Environmental Protection Agency (EPA) has urged courts to "view environmental crime for what it really is—a crime of violence and an egregious departure from responsible citizenship."[1,2] According to one EPA study, they estimate that of the [over] 100 billion tons of hazardous waste produced each year in the United States, 90 percent is disposed of in an environmentally unsafe manner.[3,4]

EPA's criminal enforcement program was established in 1982 and was granted full law enforcement authority by Congress in 1988. It enforces the nation's laws by investigating cases, collecting evidence, conducting forensic analyses and providing legal guidance to assist in the prosecution of criminal conduct that threatens people's health and the environment.[5]

"Is it possible that toxic dumping could create a vile organism? Nah."

© Cartoonresource/Shutterstock.com

What students should be aware of, although not necessarily be an expert in, nor try to memorize, is that there are about 18 federal environmental laws that form the basis for the EPA. Of course, these laws include a variety of issues that pertain to the environment including, but not limited to, issues dealing with chemical safety, clean air and water, oil pollution, toxic-substance control, and environmental cleanup. And, both businesses and people are subject to both criminal and civil penalties and in some cases, administrative sanctions for violating the environmental laws. What the environmental laws seek to do is to protect our health and safety with regard to things like making sure we have clean air to breathe and that our drinking water is not contaminated; things we often take for granted. When hazardous waste is illegally dumped or disposed it can and does often result in our water supply being contaminated. People need air and water to survive. Without it, they die. And, contaminated water has been directly linked to disease and death. According to the World Health Organization, more than three-quarters of all human disease is waterborne.[6] Toxic water has also been linked to a variety of ailments including kidney disorder, digestive problems, chronic headaches, blurred vision, and peeling skin.[7]

One of the most famous cases of contaminated waste finding its way into the water system is the case of LOVE CANAL in upstate New York near Niagara Falls.

Case Study

Love Canal—A Brief History

Love Canal branches off the Niagara River, about four miles south of Niagara Falls in upstate New York. It was one of two initial excavations in what was to be a canal to provide inexpensive hydroelectric power for industrial development around the turn of the 20th century. The abandoned excavation, partially filled with water, was used largely for recreational purposes. The canal was about 9,750 feet long and ranged in depth from 10 to 25 feet. Hooker Chemicals & Plastics Corporation (now Occidental Chemical Corporation, or OXY) disposed of over 21,000 tons of hazardous chemicals into the abandoned Love Canal between 1942 and 1953, contaminating soil and groundwater. In 1953, the landfill was covered and leased to the Niagara Falls Board of Education (NFBE). Afterwards, the area near the covered landfill was extensively developed, including construction of an elementary school, as well as many residential properties.

The fenced 70-acre Site includes the original 16-acre hazardous waste landfill and a 40-acre cap, as well as a drainage system and leachate collection and treatment system that are in place and operating.

Beginning in the 1970s, local residents noticed foul odors and chemical residues and experienced increased rates of cancer and other health problems. In 1978 and 1980, President Carter declared two federal environmental emergencies for the Site, and about 950 families were evacuated from their homes within a 10-square-block area surrounding the landfill. This area was eventually referred to as the Emergency Declaration Area (EDA) and was subsequently divided into seven areas as related to habitability concerns.

The severity of the Site's contamination ultimately led to the creation of federal legislation to manage the disposal of hazardous waste. This legislation was named the Comprehensive Environmental Response, Compensation and Liability Act (CERCLA) (Superfund Law) of 1980.

In September 1983, the Environmental Protection Agency (EPA) listed the Site on the Superfund program's National Priorities List (NPL) and began to work with New York State (NYS) to clean up the Site. In 1999, the EPA and the New York State Department of Environmental Conservation (NYSDEC) completed remedy construction in 1999. The EPA deleted the Site from the NPL in 2004.

As a result of the extent of the contamination at the Site, the response action was addressed in several stages focused on landfill containment with leachate collection; treatment and disposal; excavation and treatment of the sewer and creek sediment and other wastes; cleanup of the 93rd Street School soils; the purchase, maintenance and rehabilitation of properties; and, other short-term cleanup actions.

Lawmakers used the national publicity from the disaster at Love Canal to ultimately pass legislation that mandated that those responsible for causing polluted sites be held financially liable for cleaning up the toxic waste sites they generated. The end result is what has become to be known as Superfund, or, the Comprehensive Environmental Response, Compensation, and Liability Act.

"Some of the most reckless tales of toxic dumping involve the waste-hauling practices of illicit truck-ing operations."[9] Legally hauling and disposing of hazardous waste can be very expensive. Illegally dump-ing hazardous waste simply cuts the cost of overhead and results in bigger profits for the trucking business. What it also results in is disease which often leads to death. One can see, why EPA looks upon such crimes as a crime of violence and not simply a white-collar crime committed by corporations.

Environmental violations take many forms. There are laws in place to protect us from air pollution, E waste, which is a direct result of the dumping of old computers, televisions, and other appliances; all of which contain toxic chemicals such as lead and cadmium; all of which can be hazardous to one's health. And, while it might necessarily be information of significant value to investigators, students should know that environmental racism exists in this country. In short, toxic waste dumps are not found just anywhere in this country. Instead, you'll find many of these waste dumps in communities inhabited with large per-centages of minority residents.

Another major concern of law enforcement is the possibility of a terror attack on the United States involving our water supply. This is not a new idea. It was first brought to light by J. Edgar Hoover, the first director of the FBI in 1941 shortly before the Japanese invasion of Pearl Harbor. Hoover wrote:

> "It has long been recognized that among public utilities, water supply facilities offer a par-ticularly vulnerable point of attack to the foreign agent, due to the strategic position they occupy in keeping the wheels of industry turning and in preserving the health and morale of the American populace . . ." (Hoover, 1941).[10]

There are a number of case studies, many in recent years, available to students to review and be familiar with related to environmental violations or mishaps. One of the more recent and well known is the disas-ter involving The Deepwater Horizon Oil Spill in 2010. On April 20, 2010, at approximately 9:50 p.m., a massive explosion blew through a drilling rig known as the Deepwater Horizon. This rig was operating in the Gulf of Mexico, 49 miles off the Louisiana coast. Eleven crew members died that night. The rig was owned by British Petroleum (BP). After the rig collapsed, for almost three months, oil continued to flow from the uncapped well. Over this period of time, billions of oil spilled into the Gulf of Mexico. Government estimates suggest that almost five billion barrels of oil spilled into the Gulf. A presidential commission investigating the cause of the explosion and spill found that BP implemented polices that focused more on cost savings over safety. For instance, on the day of the explosion, BP had arranged for a team to test the cement barrier which had recently been poured and which would have normally kept the pressure even, helping to prevent the well from blowing out. But on the morning of the 20th, BP made the decision to send the team home without conducting the test, saving the company at least $128,000.[11]

It is clear that EPA's efforts to have many of these crimes considered *crimes of violence* are not without merit. In the case of BP, people died, in part, it could be argued, from failed actions designed to save the company money. While it is not the intent of this chapter to make one an expert on the various environ-mental laws, or understand the many confusing aspects of these rules and regulations, it is the intent to familiarize the student with the fact that such laws exist and how they might find their way into an array of investigations.

Questions for Discussion

1. What is the "real" potential threat posed by terrorists with regard to delivering a bio-chemical assault on a city in the United States?
2. What is the history behind the passing of the Superfund Act?
3. What are the major criticisms of the Superfund Act? How would you refine it?
4. What is meant by cradle to grave handling of hazardous waste? More specifically, how is this of value to you as an investigator?
5. What role, if any, does traditional organized crime play in the transportation and disposal industry related to hazardous waste? Do some research. Give specific examples.
6. With regard to the BP case mentioned in this chapter, do some additional research and discuss what impact it had on the economy of the various states effected by the oil spill. What was the ultimate outcome of this case? Did BP receive any penalties?
7. What does the term, "sludgerunner" mean?

Work Sheet

Exercise

1. Imagine you have an allegation of company XYZ dumping waste illegally at a landfill. Give me a list of your first 10 investigative steps and identify three critical documents you'd want to get your hands on.

Work Sheet

Notes

1. Quoted in Parker, Patricia. (1992). Crime and Punishment. *Buzzworm: The Environmental Journal*, March/April, 35.
2. Rosoff, Stephen M., Henry N. Pontell, and Robert Tillman. *Profit Without Honor, White-Collar Crime and The Looting of America*. 6th Edition, 130.
3. Humphreys, Steven L. (1990). An Enemy of the People: Prosecuting the Corporate Polluter as a Common Law Criminal. *American University Law Review*, Winter, 39:311–354.
4. U.S. Environmental Protection Agency. (1982). Everybody's Problem: Hazardous Waste 15.
5. EPA Website.
6. Guest, Ian. (1979). The Water Decade 1981–1990. *World Health*, January, 2–5.
7. Suro, Robert. (1990). Refinery's Neighbors Count Sorrows as Well as Riches. *New York Times*, April 4, A 14.
8. https://www.geneseo.edu/history/love_canal_history.
9. Profit Without Honor, pg. 133.
10. DeNileon, Gay Porter. (2001). Critical Infrastructure Protection: The Who, What, Why, and How of Counterterrorism Issues, January 24.
11. Profit Without Honor, pg. 165.

CHAPTER 8
MANAGING INVESTIGATIONS

"If you don't know where you are going, you'll end up someplace else."

Baseball Great: The Late Yogi Berra

© dizain/Shutterstock.com

Chapter Objectives

1. Gain a basic understanding of the concept of Managing Criminal Investigations (MCI).
2. Identify the five elements of MCI.
3. Gain an understanding of how to develop an investigative plan.
4. Gain an understanding of what solvability factors are.

Recommended Reading

1. *Under and Alone*, by William Queen.
2. *Donnie Brasco: My Undercover Life in the Mafia*, by Joseph D. Pistone.
3. *Serpico*, by Peter Maas.

THE PLAN

The morning after Special Agent Mike Cook met with Environmental Protection Agency (EPA) agent Latrelle Jackson, Cook found himself sitting across from Lisa Swanson in her office. The topic for discussion was the investigation of D & B Environmental.

Lisa Swanson began, "So, bring me up to speed. Where are we right now?"

Mike Cook began with a rundown of what he and Detective Tony Martin had done so far, and with what they discovered.

"As you know, we met with EPA yesterday. Originally, I had thought that was going to be a waste of time. And it still might be. I didn't even know EPA had criminal investigators. However, this guy Latrelle Jackson seems to know what he's doing. And, he's offered to help review the documents that were saturated in gasoline at D & B.

"We also learned yesterday, that D & B had been cited a year ago for transporting hazardous waste without the proper manifest."

"What do you mean by manifest?" Lisa asked.

Mike Cook smiled. It wasn't often that he was able to enlighten Lisa about something regarding their chosen profession. "It's a document that accompanies hazardous waste from the time it's originated until it's properly disposed of. It's an EPA requirement. It may not mean much, but Latrelle thinks it's worth following up on. He's interested in seeing if there were shipments of waste that didn't end up where D & B said they did."

Mike Cook continued stating, "The insurance investigator, John Sherry, is a bit of a curmudgeon."

"Trust me," Lisa said, "You don't know the half of it."

"What do you mean?"

"I'll tell you later," she replied. "Tell me what Sherry said."

"He seems to know what he's talking about. We learned from him that D & B increased the insurance on their business from two to three million dollars in the past year. Again, this isn't evidence of a crime, but it certainly causes me to be a bit more suspicious than I was.

"The lab is of course, behind. The records are dried and ready to be reviewed. We still haven't had time to follow-up much on the plane. As you know, we interviewed the owners of D & B, Alan Thompson and Eric Mann. Neither man could think of anyone who would want to destroy their company. Neither did John Thomas, the foreman. Angela Lyle, the office manager was of little help. She claims to know nothing. And, the drivers we interviewed claim to know nothing as well. That's about where we're at right now."

"So, where do you go from here?" Lisa asked.

"Well I've got some ideas," Mike Cook said.

"Good. I look forward to hearing them and reading your investigative plan. But before you write up your plan for my review, I want to make sure you consider some critical thinking strategies."

"Such as?"

"For instance, take a thorough look at what you already know and determine what still needs to be known. You've told me what you know so far, and that's good. What you haven't told me is what you still need to know. Think about what is missing in this case. What leads do you have other than the fact that D & B increased their insurance and were cited for not having the proper paperwork in place during one of their shipments?"

"Right now, not much."

"That's right, it isn't much," Lisa said. "I'm just playing devil's advocate here. I realize it's early and you still have some work to do on this. However, I want you to consider these things as you prepare your investigative plan. I have bosses to brief too you know. So ask yourself, who had a motive to commit the crime? Who had the opportunity to commit this crime? And who might have been the benefits of the crime?"

"Benefits? What do you mean?" Mike Cook asked looking puzzled.

"Think in terms of money, power, and/or control," Lisa said. "If the owners are involved, follow the money trail. If they're not, someone is seeking vengeance or hoping to control what they do. You have to ask yourself, how are you going to determine that? For instance, who had an opportunity to commit the crime? Why was this crime committed? Was it for money? Power? Control? And most importantly, who stood to benefit from this crime, financially and otherwise?"

Mike Cook was not prepared to answer most of Lisa's questions, especially as quickly as she was asking them. He paused for a moment and just stared at her and said, "Okay."

"When I look at managing a criminal investigation, Mike, I'm looking to see what the solvability factors might be."

"What do you mean by solvability factors?"

"It's how I, and you, should determine where best to employ our resources. For instance, I want to know if there were any eyewitnesses to the crime."

"No," Mike replied.

"None that you've found yet you mean."

"No."

"Can you identify a suspect yet?"

"Of course not."

"Was there any real significant evidence left at the crime scene?"

"Just the remnants of the bomb and gas can from the plane and the actual device found inside D & B."

"Are you aware of any vehicles involved in this crime?"

"No."

"Did yours and Tony Martin's search of the two crime scenes disclose anything that might help you identify who committed this crime?"

Again, Mike Cook just stared and answered, "No."

"These are the questions I'm looking to have answered in order to determine the solvability factor in this case. And at some point soon, you too, should be asking the same questions."

This time, Mike Cook just sat in his chair and said nothing.

"I know you said none of the truck drivers claimed to know anything. Maybe you need to consider looking into some of their backgrounds a bit. Have you run them through the various criminal data bases?"

"I ran Thompson and Mann through TECS and NCIC, but nothing came back on either one."

"When is your meeting with Assistant U.S. Attorney (AUSA) Sanchez?"

"Tomorrow at 4:00 p.m. Getting on this guy's calendar wasn't easy. Seems like this guy has a lot on his plate."

"Most of the prosecutors do. But that gives you the rest of the day and part of tomorrow to get ready for your meeting with him. He's going to ask you the same questions I'm asking, and then some. What about the auditor, Alan Pinette; when are you meeting with him?"

"The day after tomorrow. Right now, all I seem to be doing, is attending meetings?"

"These meetings are important. You have a lot of things to deal with in this case and it's going to require a team of people. You're going to want to think about what it is, specifically, you're going to want Pinette to do."

The meeting ended with Mike Cook feeling downtrodden. He knew Lisa was not berating him. Still, he felt as if he hadn't been prepared for her questions. He thought he had, but Lisa threw questions at him that he certainly had not fully considered.

Mike Cook walked quietly back to his small office, sat down at his desk and picked up the telephone to check his messages. There was a message from John Sherry that was short and direct: "Call me. I just learned that Alan Thompson had taken a photo from his office the day before someone tried to blow the place up. This picture was allegedly one of his grand possessions." And with that short message, the line went dead.

The phone rang four times before the voice on the other end, which was exactly the same voice millions of other cell phone recorded messages had on them, in part because people did not want to take the time to leave a personal message, that informed the caller that someone wasn't available and to leave a message. Mike listened as the pleasant recorded voice that accompanied most all cell phones began the message when suddenly, a very gruff voice that sounded as if the person being called didn't want to be bothered, infiltrated the standard recording with just two words, "John Sherry," the voice said, as the pleasant voice continued instructing the caller to leave a message.

"John; it's Mike Cook. Please give me a call when you get a moment," Mike said as he thanked Sherry in advance for calling him back later.

A Brief Discussion on Managing Criminal Investigations (MCI) and Preparing an Investigative Plan

"Managing Criminal Investigations (MCI) is designed to determine which crimes are most solvable and to use limited investigative resources to solve them."[1] Its a good idea that all investigations, well, at least those investigations that involve more than just a few hours to investigate, have a plan. Think of the plan as your road map. If you're going to get in your car and drive to the west coast or east coast, depending on where you live, you're probably going to have a "plan" as to how to get there. And while many of us might be going to the same place, it would not be unusual for several of us to take a different route to get to our ultimate destination. What many investigators, especially state and local police often fail to consider, is asking, "What is my investigative plan?" Federal law enforcement, in many cases, whether the investigators like it or not, requires that they develop an investigative strategy. Sort of like taking our fictitious road trip without a mapped out course of travel or strategy as to how to get there.

Investigators should ask themselves:

A. What is being investigated?
B. What is not being investigated?
C. Do I have a hypothesis based on what I already know?
D. What evidence do I have?

E. What special personnel do I need to conduct the investigation? For instance, what are the amount of anticipated face-to-face interviews? Does the case require any specialists to provide assistance?

F. Are there any special considerations that need addressing in this investigation?

G. What is my strategy for getting there?

Investigators should also set the framework for their investigation. There should also be goals that should be set as the investigation progresses. For example, an investigator might want to consider setting out an anticipated chronology for the investigation. If documents are recovered at the crime scene, or during the crime scene search, or, documents are being subpoenaed, when will the documents be received and when will they be reviewed? Who will actually review the documents? When will the witnesses be interviewed? When will the interviews be conducted?

Marilyn B. Peterson, Intelligence Management Specialist, New Jersey Department of Law and Public Safety, Trenton, New Jersey writes in her article, *An Analytic Approach to Investigations* "Investigative plans help investigators identify and organize what is needed to complete an investigation. The plans can be simple or lengthy, depending upon the complexity of the work being undertaken. In the simplest form, the plan should include the following elements:

- Objective of the investigation
- Potential sources of information
- Investigative resources needed
- Estimated timeline for completing the work
- Estimated likelihood of success

Peterson also states, "In addition, the investigative plan will reflect the depth of the investigation and the resources to be assigned. Is a search warrant or electronic intercept anticipated? Should an undercover operation be used? What analytic products need to be produced (link charts, indicator listings, flow charts, threat assessments)? The more complex the investigation is, the greater will be the need for a plan to obtain the necessary investigative resources.

"Investigative plans are developed by analysts, investigators, and prosecutors. Investigative plans are particularly critical when working on a multiagency investigation where assignments cross jurisdiction lines. Having a plan that is known and agreed to by all can eliminate costly duplication of efforts and predicate the likelihood of a successful conclusion."[2]

One particular step that Marilyn Peterson touches on is the possibility of using an undercover approach to an investigation. Law enforcement has used this approach, with great success, for decades. A much more intensive operational plan is required when implementing an undercover operation in connection with any investigation. An undercover approach should almost always, be considered, if the opportunity presents itself. Of course, an agent or officer working undercover usually means that he/she is working in secrecy and, under an assumed identity. Many state and local agencies don't have the resources, i.e. time and money, to provide the necessary training for those asked to work in an undercover capacity. At the federal level, undercover officers or UCO's, often undergo a screening process that involves a psychological evaluation and personal interviews with family members. If selected to be a UCO, they are often provided with extensive training which teaches them how to operate in a variety of covert capacities.

But all the training and screening in the world doesn't always prepare the UCO for what he/she will be faced with. William Queen, a former BATF agent who infiltrated the Monguls motorcycle gang, says in his excellent book, *Under and Alone*, (and in this writer's opinion, the best book ever written on what one might experience while working in a covert role), "there was one thing I didn't realize when I accepted this undercover assignment: [i.e.] how much it was going to change me. I'd been all fired up to infiltrate the Mongols and do the grueling investigative work; I'd been mentally prepared for the danger, the violence, the guns and drugs, the challenges to my undercover identity. What I hadn't fully anticipated was the emotional turmoil. I really had to abandon all semblance of my personal life for the duration of the undercover role."[3]

If using a UCO to further an investigation is a technique being considered, the investigative plan should include additional items such as not only identifying the right person for the assignment, but who is going to handle or back-up the UCO (this should be someone other than the case agent or lead investigator). This person has to be aware of the emotional toll and stress the UCO is under and know when to pull him/her from the assignment. Other considerations include funding (these operations don't work without money), what type of backstopping, in the way of protecting the UCO's assumed identity, is required, and what, if any, special needs such as vehicles and other surveillance might be needed. And those are just a few of the things to be considered depending on the type and duration of the undercover approach.

In their book, *Criminal Investigation, a Method for Reconstructing the Past*, the late James Osterburg and the late Richard Ward, write that there are, "five elements viewed as significant in the management of criminal investigations:

1. The initial investigation
2. Case screening
3. Management of the ongoing investigation
4. Police–prosecutor relations
5. Continuous monitoring of the investigative process[4]

While there has been a trend to give greater responsibility for many initial investigations to the first responding officer, the real responsibility still lies with the investigator who is leading the case.

"Case screening is used to determine whether a case should be followed-up on because it appears to be unsolvable."[5]

When engaging in the case screening process, a number of questions that should be asked and answered, are:

1. Is there a witness to the crime?
2. Is a suspect named?
3. Is physical evidence present?

There are certainly other questions to ask in this phase, but these are just a few.

The management of the continuing investigation is usually a function of supervision. By conducting case reviews and reporting, as was witnessed by Lisa Swanson's questioning of Mike Cook, management can help eliminate shortcomings that one or more of the investigative team may be exhibiting as well as helping to take advantage of having specialists assigned to the instant investigation.

Police–Prosecutor Relations have always been a professional challenge to say the least. Indeed, many police officers, detectives, and federal agents often feel that the relationship with the prosecutor is adversarial. And while heated arguments sometimes do occur, the relationship is not an adversarial one. Investigators and prosecutors have different roles and responsibilities. It is not the investigator that argues on behalf of the state or federal government when the court, i.e. a judge, asks, "Is the government ready?" All prosecutors are trained in the law. Very few investigators are. Prosecutors are responsible for meeting the standards of the law to gain a successful prosecution.

Investigative monitoring of a case gives supervisors continuous feedback on an investigation. "If sufficiently detailed, the system will identify problems and facilitate the development of remedies."[6]

Young investigators should realize early on, that if there is a state, local, or federal agency, whereby supervisors DO NOT want to be kept in the "loop" as to significant ongoing investigations, your author has yet to recognize such a place. Supervisors hate surprises. The more thorough one is in planning and documenting their investigation, the better all concerned will be. A very wise supervisor once told this author, "small cases, small problems, and big cases, big problems." Big, complex investigations usually involve numerous investigators and multiple agencies, crossing multiple jurisdictions, along with an array of specialists, i.e. forensic accountants, prosecutors, auditors, computer specialists and so forth. That's why, many agencies employ a case monitoring system. This allows supervisors an opportunity to receive continuous feedback on an investigation. It's during this feedback or review, supervisors can identify problems and hopefully, if their good supervisors, find ways to help facilitate remedies to solve those problems. On one occasion, many years ago, your author was running a very large undercover operation. The operation involved the use of two different civilian sources working in a meat processing plant. An agent, posing as a meat inspector, was working in yet a third meat packing facility. The targets of the investigation were bribing inspectors to allow inferior or tainted meat (carcasses) to pass inspection for shipment when in fact, they should have been rejected. On several occasions, bribes were made and all the money paid to the civilian inspectors was tagged and placed into evidence. One day, a young meat inspector, working for me in the investigation, received a bribe totaling about $500. He put the money into a white overcoat or smock, worn by inspectors and subsequently hung the coat on a hook in a common area as he went and used the restroom. When he returned, the money was gone. Needless to say, this young man panicked, fearing he would not be believed that the money was stolen, and, that he too, might be the subject of an investigation. I was only about five years older than this young man and as much as I tried, I simply could not get him to believe that it was going to be okay and that we looked forward to his continued support in the ongoing investigation. He wanted to quit. But that was really not an option for me. So, I took the problem to the boss. At the time, the boss, our Special Agent in Charge, (SAC) was what we called, "a very old man, with totally white hair." Your author now fits this same description, but more about this later. Simply put, our SAC looked like a father figure. He could be stern one day, and quite sensitive the next. When I explained the problem, he said, "Ernie, let's get in the car and go see this kid."

We met the cooperating source for lunch and when the meeting was over, the SAC was the consoling father figure assuring "the son" that everything was going to be okay. The inspector, of course, continued helping in the investigation, which later, resulted in over a dozen indictments and convictions. The SAC simply found a way to facilitate a remedy to what could have been a real problem for those of us running this major operation. And in this case, it didn't take additional manpower, money, cars, computers, cell phones, etc. All it took was reaffirming someone's value to continuing their participation in a case. When other resources are needed that do require assets and/or money, good supervisors will help find a way to get the investigator the things they need, provided, in most cases, that the investigator ensures there are no surprises, and, the solvability factors continue to be answered in the affirmative.

Remember, big cases require a team effort. If you're not helping the team, you probably shouldn't be on it.

Questions for Discussion

1. What is TECS?
2. What is NCIC?
3. What are solvability factors?
4. What is a case monitoring system and why is it important?
5. What evidence, to date, in our fictional story, have you recovered?
6. What value do you expect this evidence to have on this investigation?
7. What investigative techniques do you propose using in the short term in order to identify some of the solvability factors discussed in this chapter?
8. What investigative resources, if any, do you anticipate needing, in the short term, to address the needs of the case?
9. Who, if anyone, is a potential source of information in this investigation? How do you plan to solicit information from this source or other sources?

Work Sheet

Exercise

1. Prepare an investigative plan of action for supervisory review. This plan should include, but not be limited to:

   A. A brief statement as to the offense being investigated. Remember to include as much as possible of the Who, What, When, Where, How, and Why elements of statement. Include in the opening paragraph, the objective of your investigation.

   B. A list of those participating in the investigation, to date, and what each person's role is.

   C. What immediate short-term steps you plant to take to address the issues related to the investigation.

   Note: Do not include an undercover approach at this time as part of your investigative plan. Write the investigate plan as if you were in Special Agent Mike Cook's shoes and had to submit it to your supervisor, Lisa Swanson.

Work Sheet

Notes

1. Becker, Ronald F. and Aric W. Dutelle. *Criminal Investigation.* 4th Edition, 152.
2. Peterson, Marilyn B. (2005). An Analytic Approach to Investigations, *Police Chief Magazine,* July.
3. Queen, William. *Under and Alone.* 172.
4. Osterburg, James W. and Richard H. Ward. *Criminal Investigation: A Method for Reconstructing the Past.* 7th Edition, 306.
5. Ibid. pg. 307
6. Ibid. pg. 308

CHAPTER 9
LEGAL ASPECTS OF AN INVESTIGATION

"The Police Must Obey the Law While Enforcing the Law"

Former Chief Justice Earl Warren

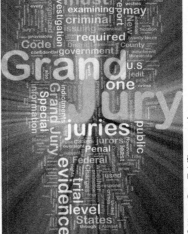

© Kheng Guan Toh/Shutterstock.com

Chapter Objectives

1. Define probable cause.
2. Understand the concept of "Fruits of the Poisonous Tree" doctrine.
3. Understand the role of the Federal Grand Jury.
4. Understand the concept "reasonable expectation of privacy."
5. Understand the meaning of "due process under the Fourteenth Amendment."
6. Understand the concept of preparing a search warrant affidavit.
7. Understand the concept of prosecutorial discretion.

Mike Cook and Tony Martin waited patiently in the lobby of the U.S. Attorney's Office. The meeting scheduled with Assistant U.S. Attorney (AUSA) Carlos Sanchez was already 30 minutes behind schedule. And, it was getting even later in the afternoon. Mike Cook took it all in stride. Detective Tony Martin, on the other hand, was getting impatient. He had over an hour's ride back to his office once the meeting ended. Martin sat quietly, his legs crossed and clearly irate. He knew that if he left later than 5:30, traffic would choke the city streets preventing him from getting home anytime soon that evening. And still the meeting hadn't yet started. The two men kept looking at their watches as if doing so would magically make AUSA Sanchez appear quickly.

"I'm sorry about this," Mike Cook said. "I thought it important that you be here for this initial meeting. I had no idea this guy would be making us wait."

"It's the same way with our local DA," Tony Martin quipped. "These guys have no idea as to how to keep an appointment. I'll bet they never keep a judge waiting," Martin replied, his frustration clearly starting to show.

"No, they don't," Cook replied. "But it's not like we can do anything about it," Cook added as he nervously tightened his tie.

Cook said, "I've been meaning to tell you, I received a message from John Sherry telling me to call him. Said he learned that Alan Thompson had taken some important photo from his office the day prior to someone trying to blow the place up."

"When did you talk to him?"

"I didn't. He left me a message yesterday. I called him back but haven't heard from him."

"Did he say how he found this out?"

"Nope. Just said he found out about it."

"What kind of picture?"

"I have no idea."

Cook looked at his watch again. It was almost 5:00 p.m.; a time when most people were getting ready to go home. For Carlos Sanchez and most of the prosecutors in the U.S. Attorney's Office, it was still early in the day.

Both men knew that in the criminal justice system it's the prosecutor who often wields the greatest power. What the two young investigators could not fully appreciate was the fact that it is the prosecutor who, more often than not, endures the greatest stress and deals with most of the dilemmas associated with cases facing criminal prosecution.

Just as the two men were about to look at their watches yet once again, AUSA Carlos Sanchez appeared.

"Sorry to keep you waiting," Sanchez said in perfect English with only a hint of his Cuban dialect present as he extended his hand in greeting the two men. "Sometimes our days get away from us. Follow me and let's go to my office and see what it is you two have going on. Lisa Swanson tells me you have an interesting case you're looking into."

Mike Cook and Tony Martin got up, shook Sanchez' hand, and followed the prosecutor who was impeccably dressed in what looked like a blue pinstripe suit that was tailor made for a man more than just a little bit overweight. The three men walked down a carpeted hallway past several offices that seemed to be busy with people talking and/or engaged in a telephone call.

Carlos Sanchez had graduated from George Washington University Law School in Washington D.C. where he concentrated mostly on criminal law. But his rise to the prosecutor's office was a long and challenging one. Having immigrated to the United States at the age of nine, along with his mother, Carlos Sanchez arrived in Miami speaking not a word of English. A difficult obstacle for a young man trying to learn the accepted practices of his new country. Aided by family living in south Florida, Sanchez eventually learned English from watching endless American television shows and from attending a Jesuit high school where he excelled in golf. In his senior year of high school, he almost led his team to the golf state championship by sinking a 60-foot putt; a feat he's never been able to repeat. But while the putt would have won his team the championship, Carlos failed to record one of his strokes on the 16th hole par four. When he signed his card, it was wrong. And the strict rules of golf show no mercy for such an infraction during tournament play. As a result, Carlos was disqualified and his team settled for a distant third place. When asked later by his coach, known simply as "T" by all his players what had happened, Carlos' response was short and direct, "I forgot," was all he said.

That infraction didn't keep Carlos Sanchez from getting a golf scholarship to a small division II school where he continued to perform well. But now, he was playing against some of the very best young players in the country. And winning didn't come as easy as it did in high school. When he graduated from college with a degree in business administration, he knew two things: First, he didn't have the skill set to take golf to the next level of competition, and two: he didn't really want to start working in an office. So, he applied for some student loans and went to law school. After graduation from the University of Miami School of Law, he clerked for a federal judge. It was through the clerkship, that Carlos Sanchez caught the eye of the sitting U.S. Attorney, who at the time, was looking for a Hispanic-speaking prosecutor to join the office.

The three men sat across from each other at a very small conference table in Sanchez' office.

"Okay, tell me what you've got," Sanchez said.

Mike Cook and Tony Martin wasted no time detailing the events surrounding the attempted bombing and arson of D & B Environmental and the destruction of the Twin Engine King Air. Cook did most of the talking while Tony Martin, who had never been to the U.S. Attorney's Office prior to this meeting, remained mostly silent, offering little to what Cook was telling Sanchez.

Mike Cook also told the federal prosecutor about him and Martin having met with Latrelle Jackson of the Environmental Protection Agency (EPA) and how they had spoken to John Sherry, the insurance representative for Practical Insurance.

"So far, the two owners of D & B Environmental, Alan Thompson and Eric Mann, claim to have no idea who might have done this," Cook said. "What we do know is that D & B was cited over a year ago for not having a shipping manifest properly filled out during the shipment of some hazardous waste."

"I'm not that familiar with EPA regulations," Sanchez said. "What does that mean?"

"From what I understand, according to Latrelle Jackson, this manifest is an important document. It tracks the waste from the time it is generated until it's disposed of."

"Okay," was all Sanchez said, as he took notes on a yellow legal pad. "What else have you got?"

"I heard yesterday from John Sherry. He's an insurance investigator for Practical Insurance that holds the policy on both D & B and the airplane. He left a message saying he heard that Alan Thompson had taken some sort of prized photograph from his office the day prior to the attempted bombing of the business. I haven't been able to reach him today to follow up on this."

Cook and Martin spent the next 30 minutes briefing Sanchez about what the drivers at D & B had told them, which actually wasn't much, and, what the secretary, Angela Lyle, had told them. Cook also told Sanchez that in the morning, he was going to deliver mostly all of the documents he and Tony Martin recovered from D & B to Latrelle Jackson.

"Jackson has agreed to have his intern pour over the documents to see what, if anything we might learn from these company records. We're hoping that it will provide us some leads," Cook added. "What we'd like to know is what your thoughts on this are? Lisa Swanson wanted us to make sure that we coordinated with your office and were up to speed on the legal issues associated with this investigation."

When they were done, it was time for Sanchez to talk. "First, Lisa was right sending you here. Normally, on most cases, we don't see the investigating agent until the investigation is almost complete and it's time for an indictment. So while it's early and you really don't have much, I'm intrigued by what you've told me. Second, while I'm not sure what you've got here, it's clear someone blew up the airplane and someone, no doubt the same people, tried to blow up the company. So let's take a look at a few things to see how best to explore these events.

"I don't want to overwhelm the two of you with legalese; I'm sure you've had enough of that in your career. However, I think it's good that we review some things for you to keep in mind as you pursue this.

First, I want to consider using an investigative grand jury to help you along. I find that people who are reluctant to help or be more forthcoming with investigators are more apt to be helpful when faced with appearing before a federal grand jury."

"This is new for me," Detective Martin said. "I've never worked with a federal grand jury before."

Carlos said, "Think of federal grand juries as an investigative tool. It's not like a jury in a criminal trial. Federal grand juries have a maximum of 23 members. Sixteen must be present to form a quorum. As a rule, they sit for a term of 18 months, meeting at regular intervals, usually for three or four days in a row each month. In order to indict someone, we need 12 or more members to vote in the affirmative."

"But we're nowhere near getting ready to indict someone," Martin replied.

"That's true. But grand juries can do so much more. We can subpoena someone to provide testimony who otherwise might be reluctant to talk to you."

"Won't they just lawyer up? If they ask for a lawyer, how does that help us?"

"They still have to appear before the grand jury unless they are the target of the investigation. Well, actually, I can subpoena a target, although it's the Department of Justice's (DOJ's) policy that we don't. So even if I did, he/she would have to come in and invoke their 5th Amendment privilege. But I'm getting ahead of myself. Basically, everyone I subpoena has to appear. In other words, they have to come and testify. If a witness then feels they might incriminate themselves, they can always take the 5th. And, they can't have their lawyer in the room with them when they do. They can confer with their lawyer outside the grand jury room but not for such a period that they are disrupting the grand jury process. I'm not sure what the state law is regarding a witness lying to a detective, although I probably knew but forgot. But lying to a federal agent during an interview and/or lying to the federal grand jury is a federal crime."

"So if these guys lie to Mike Cook or in the grand jury, that's a crime?"

"It is indeed. But keep this in mind; what is discussed in the grand jury is a *secret*. This is a strict rule known as Rule 6(e). That means when we put you two on the 6(e) list, you can't discuss the grand jury testimony of witnesses with anyone. Nor, can you share any information from records or documents that we might subpoena. I hope that's not going to be a problem for you Tony. Sometimes bosses in local departments don't like being out of the loop."

"I'll explain it to my bosses. If it's a problem, I'll let you know."

Sanchez continued, "So, we can subpoena testimony, records, or both from people. As you identify what records you might want to subpoena, think about who it is who might potentially have to testify to the authenticity of those records. In many cases, you're going to need to find the custodian of records."

"I also want to touch upon your maintaining good notes throughout the case. As you know, the notes you take, especially in connection with interviews you conduct and that you use to prepare your written reports, are discoverable under Brady."

"What do you mean by discoverable under Brady?" Tony Martin asked.

"Brady is a famous case from 1963 that originated in Maryland. What happened was that the prosecution withheld evidence from the criminal defendant violating his due process. And by discoverable, I mean any information and/or evidence that is material to the guilt or innocence of the defendant. In Brady's case, his conviction was overturned. Now, anything that violates due process, where the evidence is material to either guilt or punishment, is discoverable. And that has been broadened to include an investigator's notes. So make sure that all your notes are maintained. If this case, or any case for that matter, were to ever go to trial, those notes could be subpoenaed by the defense."

Martin asked, "What was Brady charged with?"

"Murder," Sanchez replied.

"It's our policy to keep our notes," Mike Cook said. "I hadn't even considered mentioning it to Tony."

Martin said, "We keep them too."

"Good," replied Sanchez.

"Now let's talk a few minutes about *probable cause*. At some point, you might consider getting a search warrant. To do so, you're going to need probable cause. This is where many investigators seem to have difficulty with prosecutors. We tend to ask questions that you folks don't ask. It's not to be difficult, but we have to get a judge to sign off on these warrant requests. And the last thing anyone wants, is to have their warrant challenged and overturned. The 4th Amendment generally requires the police to obtain a search warrant unless it falls within the exception to the warrant requirement. So keep in mind, when thinking of probable cause, think about the simplistic definition of the requirement. Simply put, it refers to *information upon which a reasonable person would need to believe that an item is where it is supposed to be, and, that the item is part of a crime, or otherwise illegal to possess*. And remember, probable cause can be supported by *hearsay information*. If you're able to get information from a reliable source, that you can corroborate, you can use that hearsay to support your probable cause in your search warrant affidavit. If and when it comes time to get a warrant for anything, we'll work through it together. But right now, I'm not sure what you have justifies getting a warrant. But then again, it's early."

Mike Cook acknowledged that it was indeed, early in the investigation.

"As you think about your investigative approach to this case, please keep a few things in mind. People have an *expectation of privacy*. For some reason, over the many years, law enforcement has encroached on this Fourth Amendment Constitutional guarantee. This has resulted in an array of Supreme Court decisions impacting on how law enforcement is able to conduct business. For instance, we all have an expectation of privacy in our homes and even in hotel rooms. The expectation of privacy is crucial to distinguishing a legitimate, reasonable police search and seizure from an unreasonable one. But not all places guarantee privacy. For instance, a person cannot have a reasonable expectation of privacy in things held out to the public, such as leaving their garbage out for collection."

"I think we have a good idea about this," Cook said.

"That's good. Because under the Doctrine of the '*Fruits of the Poisonous Tree*,' any violation of the Fourth Amendment that results in your obtaining evidence will taint any further evidence you discover. In other words, we won't be able to use that evidence. It will be excluded."

"Fruits of the Poisonous Tree?" Detective Martin asked.

"It started back in 1920 with a case known as *Silverstone Lumber v. U.S.* However, in 1961, another case, known as *Mapp v. Ohio*, applied this concept to state and local police departments. It was the first time the Supreme Court suppressed evidence because the police violated the 4th Amendment regarding search and seizure. It's one of the biggest cases ever to impact law enforcement regarding search and seizure that applies to this very day."

Cook said, "We studied that in the Academy."

"Good. Then you know that the Court followed up on the Mapp decision a few years later in 1963 with the Wong Sun case where we actually learn about the fruits of the poisonous tree for the first time. You probably also know that Dollree Mapp's conviction was overturned because the officers who searched her home did not have a valid warrant. In fact, they didn't have a warrant at all. So when the search produced what, at the time was considered obscene materials, Mapp was arrested and subsequently convicted. Basically, the high court held that any evidence that was obtained illegally would be excluded from evidence. More important, while the feds were actually operating under this provision, this case applied the Fourth

Amendment protection from unreasonable searches and seizures to all the states under the Due Process Clause of the Fourteenth Amendment."

"So, she got away with it," Cook said.

"She did on that case. But that isn't the end of her story. After her conviction was overturned, or *vacated*, Mapp moved to Queens, New York. In the early 1970s, the police searched her home—this time with a valid warrant—and found about $250,000 worth of heroin; that was a lot of money at the time, and some stolen property."

"So what happened to her?" Cook asked.

"She was convicted of possession of drugs and sentenced to 20 years to life."

"Don't you just love it when a story has a happy ending," Cook added, with a degree of sarcasm.

"In this case, yes, she did finally go to jail. But it took years for that to happen. We don't want that to happen in this case," Sanchez said.

Cook said, "We get it. We'll be careful not to violate anyone's right to privacy during this case."

"I know you will," Sanchez said. "But sometimes, investigators do things thinking they're doing the right thing. Then later, because of some new interpretation of the law, we find that with all their good intentions, the court decides that they still violated someone's right to privacy."

"What are you talking about?" Martin asked.

"As I'm sure you're aware, police officers can usually search a person without a warrant incident to their arrest simply for the officer's safety, and to prevent the destruction of evidence. And up until just recently, law enforcement officers believed they were permitted to search a suspect's cell phone incident to arrest; they believed they could examine the call history, review the internet searches, and scroll through the text messages. This was, at least in part, a reasonable belief. Then, came the case of *Riley v. California*. Riley was arrested on weapons charges. When he was arrested, the police seized his cell phone—a smart phone—from his pant pocket. The police found information on the cell phone that implicated him in some street gang activity. A short time later, a forensic specialist examined the contents of the cell phone and found evidence connecting Riley to a shooting that had occurred several weeks earlier. That evidence was later used to enhance his sentence."

"Are you saying we can't check someone's cell phone now?" Tony Martin asked.

"That's right. According to the Supreme Court, you have to get a warrant unless you have some *exigent* circumstances. In other words, you better be able to articulate to a judge that some emergency existed preventing you from getting a warrant. Short of that, get a warrant. So you see what I'm saying?" Sanchez said looking directly at the two men sitting across from him. "We're learning new stuff all the time. The Supreme Court is interpreting the Constitution on a continuing basis. There were no smart phones when Dollree Mapp was arrested. And who knows what new technology is on the horizon that people who break the law will use, or that police will employ to obtain evidence of a crime. I'm sure you've both been following the legal battle between Apple and the FBI over the Bureau wanting them to help develop technology that will enable them to decrypt cell phone passwords."

"I have," replied Mike Cook. "I just don't understand why Apple doesn't do the right thing and help the FBI in the fight against terrorism."

"Because it's not that simple," Sanchez said. The issues involve not only national security, but privacy and individual rights. And, the two sides don't necessarily agree on a number of basic technology issues. I don't want to get distracted from our case here, just to let you know that things are not always as simple as they seem. The point is, no matter how this plays out down the line, advances in technology are going to present law enforcement and the courts with an array of new issues to deal with. So let's keep that in mind."

Carlos Sanchez stood up signaling that the meeting was over. He shook both men's hands and told them to keep in close contact with him.

"Our office will help you in any way we can," Sanchez said. "And let me know about this so-called painting or picture this guy Thompson allegedly removed the day before the attempted bombing of his business. I'm very curious about that."

And just like that, the meeting was over. Mike Cook was feeling a bit frustrated but anxious at the same time. He wanted to get in touch with John Sherry and find out about this picture Alan Thompson supposedly removed from his office.

"I'll write this meeting up and get you a copy," Cook told Martin. "Good luck getting through this traffic." Mike Cook would prepare a memorandum for the file detailing the time, place, and participants of the meeting that just ended. The memorandum would also detail the issues discussed. This memorandum would become part of the investigative file and would serve to aid another investigator in the event he/she had to assume responsibility for the investigation.

As soon as the two men got off the elevator and walked into the lobby, they said good-bye. Mike Cook then called John Sherry again. This time, John Sherry answered the phone.

A Brief Discussion about the Law and Prosecutors

It is not the intent of the chapter to delve deep into the subject matter dealing with legal and constitutional issues that students will no doubt be better taught during courses dealing with criminal law and criminal procedure. For the purposes of this chapter, however, it's important to understand the more significant legal issues and the processes dealing with criminal investigations.

As James B. Stewart (1987) writes in his book, *The Prosecutors*, "Much of what prosecutors do is shrouded in secrecy."[1] Prosecutors have a profound influence over the justice system. It is prosecutors who decide whether to prosecute or not. The term *"prosecutorial discretion"* refers to the fact that under American law, government prosecuting attorneys have nearly absolute and unreviewable power to choose whether or not to bring criminal charges, and what charges to bring, in cases where the evidence would justify charges. This authority provides the essential underpinning to the prevailing practice of plea bargaining, and guarantees that American prosecutors are among the most powerful of public officials.[2] Indeed, they play a vital role in both the American political system and the criminal justice system.

And to be clear, while their decisions are expected to be apolitical, such is not always the case. The sad reality is that while politics is often subtle, it does occasionally influence a prosecutor's decision whether or not to prosecute. Investigators, especially those tasked with investigating large white-collar crimes, would be well served to keep this in mind. Large corporations yield a tremendous amount of influence in many areas, especially when they impact on the economy. As such, it is not always easy to disregard the political impact it might have when considering to indict a company.

Earlier in this chapter, AUSA Sanchez was explaining to Mike Cook and Tony Martin, how the federal grand jury could possibly help them during their investigation. Grand juries basically serve to listen to evidence in order to determine if criminal charges should be brought. *Grand juries do not determine guilt or innocence.* That is for a trial jury; something students will learn more about in their criminal procedure course. "Grand juries are a crucial interface between government authority and the private citizen, and provide a recognition that even bringing of criminal charges is a momentous step that can have dire consequences for the accused. Grand juries themselves do not investigate, but subpoenas are issued in their name, thus providing a powerful tool for investigators."[3] It's important to note that not all states employ an investigative grand jury similar to federal grand juries.

Investigators investigate crimes. And crime is simply defined as, "an act committed or omitted in violation of law forbidding or commanding it, and for which punishment is imposed upon conviction."[4] And, what is or is not a crime is defined by our elected officials who serve in our legislatures. Punishable behavior is either (a) inherently bad (*malum in* se, e.g. murder, or killing another human being) or (b) against public policy (*malum prohibitum*, e.g., committing arson in order to defraud, or, stealing a car).

Dr. Thomas O'Connor says that "everything about criminal law in America today (defining, classifying, grading, prohibiting, and punishing) is in the hands of the legislature or law-making body for each jurisdiction. Crimes are 'owned' by the state, prosecuted by the state, and the only thing separating a civil wrong from a criminal wrong is that fine line that exists because some legislature says it exists."[5]

Once an investigator understands the type of crime he/she is dealing with, especially those passed by our legislatures, he/she can proceed accordingly. It has been your author's position, for many years, that a good investigator should be able to investigate virtually any type of crime as long as they know the elements of the crime being investigated. For instance, the basic elements of arson are generally accepted as being (a) burning by fire or explosion, (b) the intent to start a fire, and (c) the burning of a building. The elements of murder are (a) the voluntary act of killing another person, (b) purposely, or knowingly, or extremely recklessly, and (c) aggravating circumstances prescribed in first-degree murder statute. Again, there are variations of these, from state to state, especially as it relates to the last element. Armed with the elements of a these two different crimes, a good investigator should be able to conduct either investigation.

As the late James Osterburg and the late Richard Ward write in *Criminal Investigation, a method for reconstructing the past,* "the phrase elements of the crime describe the specific acts that, taken together, compose the crime. For example, loosely stated, the elements of burglary are (a) breaking, (b) entering, and (c) with intent to commit a crime; the elements of robbery are (a) the taking of property, (b) from another person, and (c) by force or the fear of force. If each and every element of a crime is not proved, a defendant cannot be convicted for that crime."[6] Understanding and knowing the elements to any crime you are investigating is paramount. A good rule to consider following is making the elements to the crime(s) you're investigating part of your overall investigative plan as was discussed in the previous chapter.

The use of a *search warrant* is a vital investigative tool. What many young first-time investigators fail to realize is that obtaining a search warrant is a two prong process. First, the officer, or investigator, must complete a *warrant affidavit*. In this affidavit, the officer, or investigator, completes a narrative outlining the information he/she has obtained that provides sufficient probable cause to execute a search warrant. This affidavit should contain as much information as possible to support the request for obtaining the warrant. Under no circumstances, should this warrant affidavit contain abbreviations, especially "lol" or ####'s. You are not creating a text message. What you are doing is creating a document that might come under legal scrutiny. The affidavit must also contain information as to what is being sought in the warrant, i.e. stolen televisions. And, it must contain the identification of the places to be searched. In other words, the house number, street, color of home, etc. There should be no doubt as to where the search is to occur.

The second document that is prepared is the actual warrant itself. Warrants, at a minimum, must contain the authorization by a magistrate or judge of the state issuing the warrant, the authorization to seize specifically described items, a specific location to be searched, and a return that includes information relating to the date of the search, the items seized, name of the officer serving the warrant, and the officer's signature. A copy of the warrant is left with the person whose property is being searched.

IN THE CIRCUIT COURT OF _____

Judge or Division: _____	Case Number:	
	do not fill in	
Name and Title of Person Making Application:		(Date File Stamp)

Search Warrant

State of _____ to any Peace Officer in _____:

Based on information provided in a verified application/affidavit, the Court finds probable cause to warrant a search for and/or seizure of the following:

☒ Property, article, material or substance that constitutes evidence of the commission of a crime;
☐ Property that has been stolen or acquired in any manner declared an offense;
☐ Property for which possession is an offense under the laws of this state;
☐ Any person for whom a valid felony arrest warrant is outstanding;
☐ Deceased human fetus or corpse, or part thereof;
☐ Other

You are commanded to search, size, and photograph or copy, as applicable, the person, place, or thing described below. Photographs or copies of the seized property, article, materials, substance, or person shall be field with the Court within 10 days.

The person, place or thing to be searched is described as follows:

Currently stored at _____

The property, article, material, substance or person to be searched for and seized is described as follows:

What you want seized and for what criminal offense

_____ at _____	☐ AM ☐ PM	_____
Date and Time		Judge

This warrant is issued by: ☒ hard-copy   ☐ facsimile   ☐ other electronic means: _____

Directions to Officer: Make a complete and accurate written inventory of any property seized pursuant to this warrant. When possible, complete the inventory in the presence of the person from whose possession this property is taken, and give a receipt for the property, as well as copy of this warrant to that person. If no person is found in possession of the property, leave the receipt and warrant copy in the premises searched. Immediately deliver photographs or copies of the seized property, article, materials, substance, or person, the written inventory, and the warrant return to this Court.

Officer's Return

I certify that I am a peace officer within the State of _____ and executed the above search warrant as follows:

Date and manner of execution: _____

Name of possessor (and owner if known and if not the same) of property _____

A property receipt and a warrant copy were left   ☐ with possessor   ☐ in the premises.

The inventory receipt is attached to this return ☐ Yes ☐ No

Property seized (general description): _____

Attached to this return are: ☐ Photograph(s)   ☐ Copy/copies of items seized   ☐ Inventory.

_____	_____
Date	Signature of Officer Making Return

In the story, AUSA Carlos Sanchez talks about a person's expectation of privacy. Students should keep in mind that the U.S. Supreme Court is constantly dealing with new issues involving this topic as it relates to search and seizure, due in part, to the rapid advances in technology. For instance, in "Florida v. Jardines," the Supreme Court ruled on March 26, 2013, that police violated the Fourth Amendment rights of a homeowner when they led a drug-sniffing dog to the front door of a house suspected of being used to grow marijuana.

In a 5-to-4 decision, the court ruled that the police conducted a "search" when they entered the property and took the dog onto to the front porch of the house. Since the officers had not first obtained a warrant beforehand, their search was unconstitutional. In essence, the court said that the police officers violated Jardine's Fourth Amendment rights against unreasonable search and seizure when they physically intruded into the surrounding area of his private home for the purpose of conducting an investigation.

"When it comes to the Fourth Amendment, the home is first among equals," the late Justice [Antonin] Scalia wrote. "At the amendment's very core stands the right of a man to retreat into his own home and there be free from unreasonable government intrusion."[7]

While the above example deals with the police using a drug-sniffing dog to detect the possibility of a grow house being operated, "this case may provide some argument or protection in the area of reasonable expectation of privacy in one's home and *curtilage* (the *curtilage* of a house or dwelling is the land immediately surrounding it, including any closely associated buildings and structures, but excluding any associated 'open fields beyond,' and also excluding any closely associated buildings, structures, or divisions that contain the separate intimate activities) given the rapid advancement of *drone technology*, particularly given law enforcements' stated intent to deploy these technologies." Think about your expectation of privacy; would you feel it is being violated if a drone, operated by law enforcement, was flying over your home? What is a person's right in using this technology if it interferes with commerce?

The Dollree Mapp Story

It was 1957 and Dollree Mapp, also known as Dolly, was a 30 something, African American woman residing in Cleveland, Ohio. Though Dolly did not have an official police record, she did have some dealings and associations with some known criminals of the area. Dolly had ties to the boxing world as well, she was married, and divorced, to boxer Jimmy Bivins. At one time she was also engaged to Archie Moore, though the two never tied the knot.

In the late 1950's Don King, famous for his big hair and success in promoting the sport of boxing, also had suspected ties to gambling and running numbers used in illegal wagering. It was late spring of 1957 during the month of May and King's house was bombed. Could it be from his suspected criminal activities or something related to boxing? While police were investigating the crime, they received an anonymous tip that the person responsible for the bombing was laying low at the home of Dollree "Dolly" Mapp.

The police went to Mapp's house intent on searching for their bombing suspect. Mapp did what most people, I suspect, especially those trying to hide something from the police would do, she refused to let the police search her home. With the police on her doorstep, Mapp contacted her lawyer and he told her not to allow the police in to search unless they produced a warrant. He further advised her to carefully read the warrant, if they produced one.

During the officers' initial visit to Mapp's home, they did not have a warrant. The officers soon returned to her residence that day with what they called a warrant. One of the police lieutenants lied to Mapp and informed her of the newly obtained warrant. Remember earlier in the text when I said, "everyone lies."? Following directions from her attorney, Mapp demanded to see the warrant that the Lieutenant claimed to have but he refused to give the document to her. True to her bold character, Mapp quickly snatched the paper from the Lieutenant's grasp and shoved it down her shirt. As you can probably imagine, the Lieutenant knew that the paper was false and it was imperative to get it back from Map. He fought her for it and he was able to retrieve the so called, warrant. As one might expect, Mapp was arrested and handcuffed. Below is some of the testimony by Mapp of what happened after she seized the paper,

"What are you going to do?" one of the officers asked.

"I'm going down after it," a sergeant said.

"No, you are not," Mapp told the sergeant.[8]

Though police did find the suspect they were looking for in connection to the King bombing, the officers continued to search Mapp's home. The canvased about every inch of the house and in every piece of furniture. When the police searched the basement of Mapp's home they found a trunk. Inside the trunk they found what was considered obscene material for the time. There was a nude sketch and four books. Two of those books were, "Memoirs of a Hotel Man" and "Affairs of a Troubadour." According to Ohio law, during that time, it was illegal for person to have obscene material and this act was considered a felony.

When questioned about why Mapp had these obscene materials, she claimed they were not hers and was simply holding them for a previous tenant. At trial, Mapp would testify she tried to tell the officer "not to look at them, they might embarrass him."

After discovering the materials in the trunk, police continued their search of Mapp's home. During this time, Mapp's attorney arrived and the police refused him access to Mapp. Simply put, the police refused to let him see his client. This refusal only compounded the problem of the illegal search of Mapp's home.

Later that day, Mapp would be arrested. Police say that she was belligerent, refused to cooperate and was in possession of obscene material. In spite of the fact that during her trial, no search warrant was produced, or any testimony offered explaining why there was no warrant, the jury deliberated for only 20 minutes. Dollree Mapp was found guilty and she was sentenced to up to seven years in prison.

Mapp left prison on bond and decided to try and appeal her conviction. She was unsuccessful with her appeal to the Ohio Supreme Court and lost her case. However, Mapp would later appeal to the United States Supreme Court. Unlike the Ohio Supreme Court, the U.S. Supreme Court found the Ohio obscenity law laughable. The justices continually poked fun at the government's attorney and would ask him why the clerk of court, administrators, university librarians and even psychologists in the state of Ohio had not all been indicted since simply possessing obscene material was a felony?

The nine justices were in agreement that Ohio's obscenity law violated the First Amendment. Focus soon shifted towards the Fourth Amendment when Associate Justice, Tom C. Clark, drafted the majority opinion. The Fourth Amendment prohibits unreasonable search and seizure and this applied directly to Mapp's case. Lewis Katz, a law professor at Case Western Reserve University in Cleveland, would later write: "The illegal entry of Mapp's house by the police was nothing extraordinary; it was an everyday fact of life for blacks and other racial minorities. Police throughout

(Continued)

America were part of the machinery of keeping blacks 'in their place,' ignoring constitutional guarantees against unreasonable arrests and searches . . ."[9]

During the time of Mapp's case, states would allow evidence to be admitted to trial even if it had been obtained illegally. In a 6-3 decision, the Supreme Court justices decided to change that by overturning Mapp's conviction. This ruling is significant because it applied the exclusionary rule to both federal and state prosecutions. From that point forward, this rule is legal doctrine that excludes from a trial any evidence seized illegally by police, now applies in all the states.

Mapp however, couldn't stand prosperity. Several years later, after the Supreme Court overturned her conviction in this landmark case, Mapp moved to New York. Continuing her relationship with seedy characters, sometimes violating the law, the police raided her home in Queens. This time, they had a valid warrant. The police seized approximately $250,000 in heroin and stolen property. Mapp was charged with possession of narcotics and convicted in 1971. Again, she appealed her conviction. This time however, the appeals were all in vain. She served about eight years in prison until December, 1980 when the Governor of New Yew York commuted her sentence. After her release, Mapp worked in variety of jobs including the insurance business. Mapp died in 2014 at the age of 91.

In the story, AUSA Carlos Sanchez is careful to explain to Mike Cook and Tony Martin the idea that even while "acting in good faith," investigators sometime do things that are later interpreted by the courts as being in violation of an individual's rights. As a young federal investigator, your author found himself working on what, at the time, appeared to be a large weapons smuggling operation. The suspect was flying in and out of a major city in the United States and while in town, would almost always stay at the same upscale hotel on the private floor reserved for guests who pay a premium for privacy. This floor, often referred to as the "concierge" floor, required a special pass key to access it. Once the guests exited the elevator, they were often met by a host or hostess that made sure you had fresh drinks, of any almost any kind, and hot and cold hors d'oeuvres to satisfy almost every taste.

The investigation was only weeks old when we set up a surveillance in the hotel. With the full cooperation of the hotel's general manager and the head of hotel security, your author took a room directly across from the subject of this investigation. Throughout various times of the day, the plan was to engage the suspect in the general lounge area on the concierge floor. On one particular morning, about three days into the surveillance, I received a telephone call for the director of security informing me that the suspect had complained about some issues in his room that needed repairing, including an electrical issue that was causing him problems. The director of security was sending two repairmen to the room to deal with the necessary repairs. She asked if I wanted to meet her in the room. Of course, I said yes.

When I walked across the hall, the door to the suspects' room was wide open. Inside were two repairmen making the repairs the suspect/guest had requested. Also inside the room was the hotel's director of security. As I stepped into the room, I looked around but did not disturb any items. I did not open drawers, closets, nor, did I go through any luggage. I simply stood inside the room, talking to the director of security after being invited in and not after any prompting on my part. I saw nothing in plain view, immediately that is, that suggested anything out of the ordinary. Then, on the nightstand next to the bed, I noticed a plain white envelope, the type one would mail a letter in. Some of you may have heard about letters from your history class. It was a way of communicating in a time not so long ago. On this envelope was a series of letters and numbers. I immediately recognized that these letters and numbers related to a "Federal Firearms License." So I wrote the numbers down in my notebook.

I was in the room for less than five minutes. But I had noticed, in plain view, letters and numbers on an envelope that was, in fact, a Federal Firearms License (FFL) issued by the U.S. Treasury Department at the time, to individuals and companies that sold firearms. That number provided a valuable lead in our investigation. Needless to say, I was excited. It was the first big break in the case. But my excitement was short lived. When I shared this information with the federal prosecutor, she flew into orbit.

"How could you do such a thing?" she screamed.

"What are you talking about?" I yelled back.

"You had no right to go in there. He has an expectation of privacy. You violated that right."

By now, my language was a bit more colorful than one might record in a textbook such as this. Needless to say, voices were raised and the shouting continued for several minutes.

"But I was invited in. And he (the suspect) left that paper on his nightstand knowing that people were going to be in his room making repairs," I shouted back.

"It doesn't matter. His expectation of privacy relates to privacy against government intrusion."

"Let's let a judge or a jury decide," I insisted.

Well, my argument was to no avail. Not only did this federal prosecutor refuse my request to test my actions in the courts, the information we developed from the FFL was excluded under the *"fruits of the poisonous-tree-doctrine."*

I share this story because police officers and investigators, local, state, and federal, thinking they are operating with the confines of the law, make mistakes. At the time, I thought nothing of going into that room at the request of hotel security. They had a right to be there; the hotel maintenance staff had a right to be there, so I figured I did too. But not according to the federal prosecutor. Less than two years later, in 1984, the U.S. Supreme Court decided, in the case of *Nix V. Williams* (a case you will research at the end of this chapter), that evidence that would generally be excluded or inadmissible under the fruits-of-the-poisonous-tree doctrine would be admitted, if, the government could show that the evidence would have been discovered anyway in the normal course of the investigation I know that during the course of the investigation I shared above, we would have found this FFL number in due course. But at the time, the prosecutor I was working with would simply not take a chance and allow us to use the evidence I found on that nightstand. Maybe she was right.

Colleges and universities teach a variety of courses dealing with the law, rules of evidence, legal issues, and criminal procedure. In this text, and as it relates to the case study in this book, I've tried to touch upon a *few* of the more significant issues criminal investigators should take into consideration when conducting an investigation.

Question for Discussion

1. After researching Nix v. Williams, argue both for and against, allowing the evidence related to the FFL your author found on the nightstand. Would this be admitted or excluded today under Nix v. Williams? Explain your reasoning.

Work Sheet

Exercises

1. Define probable cause.
2. Define the exclusionary rule.
3. Identify three things a federal grand jury can do for an investigator in furtherance of conducting an investigation.
4. What is meant by "due process?"
5. Prepare a one-page, type-written, double-spaced memorandum detailing the meeting with AUSA Carlos Sanchez. Write up the memorandum as if you were SA Mike Cook.
6. Research the following court cases and provide a capsule summary of the case. This should include a brief statement as to:
   A. The *Facts* of the case.
   B. *The Issue* (the Court dealt with).
   C. *The Supreme Court Decision*.
      i. Rochin v. California, 342 U.S. 165 (1952)
      ii. Nix v. Williams, 467 U.S. 431 (1984)
      iii. Stoner v. California, 376 U.S. 483 (1964)
      iv. Draper v. United States, 358 U.S. 307 (1959)
      v. Aguilar v. Texas, 378 U.S. 108 (1964)
      vi. Riley v. California, 573 U.S. (2014)
      vii. Wong Sun v. United States, 371 U.S. 471 (1963)
7. Prepare a one-page, type-written, double spaced memorandum detailing the meeting with AUSA Carlos Sanchez. Prepare the memorandum as if you were SA Mike Cook.
8. Explain the concept of prosecutorial discretion.
9. Do some research and argue both for and against Apple and the FBI regarding the dispute over Apple assisting the government with developing decryption software to aid law enforcement. Also provide your own opinion on this topic.

Work Sheet

Notes

1. Stewart, James B. (1987). *The Prosecutors*. 10. Simon & Schuster.
2. Gerard E. Lynch. *Prosecution: Prosecutorial Discretion—Varieties of Discretion, Subjects of Prosecutorial Discretion, Standards of Prosecutorial Judgment, Controlling Prosecutorial Discretion*. http://law.jrank.org/pages/1870/Prosecution-Prosecutorial-Discretion.html.
3. Stewart, James B. (1987). *The Prosecutors*. 24. Simon & Schuster.
4. The American Heritage Dictionary of the English Language, 2nd College Edition, s.v. "crime."
5. Dr. Thomas O'Connor. The Mega Study of Law.
6. Osterburg, James W. and Richard H. Ward. (2014). *Criminal Investigation: A Method for Reconstructing the Past*. 7th Edition, 338. Anderson Publishing.
7. https://en.wikipedia.org/wiki/Expectation_of_privacy.
8. Armstrong, Ken. (2014). Dollree Mapp, 1923–2014: 'The Rosa Parks of the Fourth Amendment'. *The Marshall Project*, December 12.
9. Katz, Lewis R. (1997). *Mapp after Forty Years: Its Impact on Race in America*. Faculty Publications. Paper 246. http://scholarlycommons.law.case.edu/faculty_publications/246.

Additional Readings

Armstrong, Ken. (2014). Dollree Mapp, 1923–2014: 'The Rosa Parks of the Fourth Amendment'. *The Marshall Project*, December 12.

del Carmen, Rolando V. and Jeffery T. Walker. *Briefs of Leading Cases in Law Enforcement*. 6th Edition.

Florida v. Jardines, 569 U.S. 1 (2013).

Osterburg, James W. and Richard H. Ward. *Criminal Investigation: A Method for Reconstructing the Past*, 7th Edition.

Robinson, David J. (2014). The U.S. Supreme Court Says 'No' to Cell-Phone Searches Incident to Arrest. *Illinois Bar Journal*, September, 102(9):438.

Ronald F. Becker and Aric W. Dutelle. *Criminal Investigation*. 4th Edition.

Samaha, Joel. *Criminal Law*. 11th Edition.

Stewart, James B. (1987). *The Prosecutors*. Simon & Schuster.

CHAPTER 10
MONEY LAUNDERING

© Kheng Guan Toh/Shutterstock.com

"Follow the Money."

W. Mark Felt, the informant known as "Deep Throat," to reporter Bob Woodward, in All the
Presidents Men

"He's a businessman. I'll make him an offer he can't refuse."

Mario Puzo, The Godfather

Chapter Objectives

1. Gain an understanding of what constitutes money laundering.
2. Obtain a good idea as to what investigative steps are necessary in conducting a money laundering investigation.

3. Be able to identify the steps associated with money laundering.
4. Understand the role of the auditor in criminal and financial investigations.
5. Understand the difference between an Asset and a Liability.
6. Understand the concept of Net Worth.

The meeting the following morning took about an hour. The coffee shop the two men decided to use for their meeting offered a variety of hot and cold caffeine drinks to satisfy most every taste. What irritated the two men most was standing in line for so long just to get a black cup of coffee. It seemed everyone in front of them ordered every type of Frappuccino imaginable; each drink taking an inordinate amount of time to prepare. All the two men wanted was a simple cup of coffee; the type that could be poured into a cup in a matter of seconds. And, the old man was not one who exhibited much patience for anything these days, especially when he wanted his morning coffee. And when the young woman in front of him couldn't make up her mind if she wanted a Java Chip or a Red Velvet Cake Crème Frappuccino, he simply grunted a colorful phrase that he didn't realize was heard by the people in back of him. But it was. And the stares he received didn't seem to bother him. It was the waiting that did.

Once they got to the counter, the young man who took their order looked saddened by the fact that all they wanted was a plain cup coffee.

"Would you like our Blond Roast or maybe our Pike Place Roast?" the young man asked. "Our Caffe Misto is especially nice too."

"I just want two black cups of coffee," the old man said in a voice that left the listener no doubt he was not amused. "I don't care about the kind. Just make it black and hot."

"Would you like one of our homemade muffins today?" "We have."

But before the young man could explain the variety of muffins available, the old man looked him straight in the eye, and said, "No. I don't want any muffins."

Seconds later, while people who ordered before them still stood waiting for their morning beverage, the two men sat down at a table that provided them some privacy. What Mike Cook did that morning was mostly listen. He listened while John Sherry, the old insurance investigator, told him about his having spoken to Angela Lyle, the office manager for D & B Environmental.

"We had a nice talk the other day," Sherry said. "She told you about the same thing she told me. Claimed to have no idea who would want to blow the business up. Nor, was she aware of any hostility between the owners, employees, or from competitors. When I was about to finish the interview with her, she said, 'it's a good thing Mr. Thompson removed that picture of him and his sailing buddies out of the office the day prior to someone trying to blow the place up. He loved that picture.' So, when I asked her how long the picture had been in the building, she said for almost two years. Claimed the picture was taken after he and his friends had won some local sailing event."

"How fortuitous," Cook said.

"Indeed. But that's *circumstantial evidence*. But it's evidence nonetheless."

"Not sure how that helps us."

"Circumstantial evidence can really help, as long as we have enough of it. Remember from your academy training, circumstantial evidence, or presumptive evidence, allows for certain facts to be presumed, or inferred, to have taken place. We use this type of evidence to help us establish the facts by proving another set of facts from which a presumption can be drawn. Simply put, Thompson's taking this picture out of his office the day prior to the attempted bombing is circumstantial. So is the fact that he and his partner increased the insurance on their business only weeks before someone tried to blow the place up. Again, circumstantial. The relevancy here is based on logic."

"What do you mean by logic?"

"It's based on what is considered to be reasonable. Good common sense. If the evidence helps in proving the truth, it is considered relevant. It's largely based on our human experience. For instance, given a set of circumstances, the result of those circumstances is usually the same each time they happen. So, keep that in mind. Right now, we have two pieces of circumstantial evidence that suggest that either Alan Thompson and/or Eric Mann might have had something to do with the bombing and arson of the airplane, and the attempted bombing and arson of the D & B Environmental. But that's all we have right now, two pieces of circumstantial evidence. Not much more."

The two men sat there for a several moments simply staring at each other, neither man saying a word as they drank their coffee. Then John Sherry asked, "What's your next move?"

Mike Cook sat there for a moment pondering the old man's question. He shook his head and said, "What I need is some direct evidence of something."

"Any idea as to how you're going to get that?"

"A few. First, I need to meet with Latrelle Jackson over at EPA. I want to see what, if anything, he found in those records we recovered."

"That's a good move."

"Then I want to run detailed checks on all of the drivers for D & B."

"Good. While you're doing that, I'm going to follow up some things related to the airplane."

"Like what?"

"I want to review the *flight log*. That will tell us a few things about the aircraft. Let's see where it's been to lately. Find out who's been flying it. And if the maintenance has been kept up."

"How's that going to help?"

"Could shed some light on a number of things. Let's see what we find out. Can you get me access to the flight log?"

"Sure. Come by the office and you can take a look at it there."

"Tomorrow. I'll stop by in the morning. First thing. Does that work for you?"

Mike Cook told Sherry that he'd meet him in the morning so that he could examine the flight log that belonged to the Twin Engine King Air that blew up on the tarmac. But he didn't want the flight log to leave the office. It might, at some point, be offered into evidence. Signing it out to an insurance investigator could prove to be problematic. But sharing the information inside the flight log wouldn't be a problem.

That afternoon, Mike Cook found himself seated across from Latrelle Jackson in the same conference room the two men occupied just a few days prior when Cook briefed him on the case involving D & B Environmental. After some initial pleasantries, Cook asked Jackson if they'd found anything of value.

"Certainly some interesting things to look at," Jackson replied. "My intern is doing a good job organizing the records. What we have noticed is that there appears to be a great deal of hazardous waste being transported by this company. Some of the manifests look like they were taking a very large amount of waste to the same two companies for disposal. In some cases, they would have had to make more than one trip to dispose of so much waste in just one day. And, D & B has contracts with a number of private companies and with the Department of Defense."

"Are you telling me that they have government contracts?"

"Yes, several of them."

"You have any suggestions based on what you've found so far?" Cook asked.

"I do. I think you and I, along with Tony Martin, need to visit these two hazardous waste disposal facilities and see if the manifests that were recovered inside D & B match up to what those facilities have on file."

"Sounds good. And if they don't match up?"

"Then there is a lot of hazardous waste out there somewhere."

Mike Cook went back to his office and sat down at his desk. Before he had time to pick up the phone and call Tony Martin, Lisa Swanson walked in and, without waiting for an invitation, sat down.

"How's it going?"

Cook smiled and said, "not bad. I just learned that D & B was moving a lot of hazardous waste. In fact, maybe too much. More than what their drivers and trucks might be able to move in a day. And, they had contracts with the Department of Defense. Jackson, over at EPA, and his college intern are doing a great job pouring through the records we found saturated in gasoline."

"Interesting," Swanson replied. "What's your next move?"

"Jackson and I, and maybe Tony Martin, are going to visit two of the hazardous waste-processing plants to see if they actually received the amount of waste D & B claims to have transported to them. And John Sherry, this insurance guy, is going to follow up on the plane and see what leads we might develop from the flight log we recovered inside the cockpit."

"What's the deal on this picture Alan Thompson supposedly removed from his office the day before someone tried to blow the place up?"

"According to Sherry, he was doing a follow-up interview with Angela Lyle, the office manager, when she just offered up the information as he was about to leave. Sherry claims it was a picture of Thompson and some of his sailing buddies. Apparently, this picture meant a lot to this guy."

"What about looking at the company's financials?" Lisa asked.

"I'm meeting with the auditor, Alan Pinette later this afternoon. I'll go over with him what records we might want to subpoena. I'll have a better feel for this after I talk to Pinette."

Lisa Swanson stood up and smiled. "Good. Now put all of that in your investigative plan and have it on my desk in the morning."

Mike Cook spent the next two hours outlining his investigative plan. In essence, he was creating a road map that would be used to proceed with his investigation. This plan, or road map, could of course be changed or adjusted as the investigation continued. But for now, he had a plan. And, he was developing a team of supporting players to help him uncover the facts surrounding the bombing of the airplane and the attempted destruction of D & B Environmental. He knew not to underestimate or overestimate anything. The facts of the case would direct him where to go next; not the other way around.

Later that afternoon, Mike Cook met with Alan Pinette, the auditor assigned to assist him in his investigation. The meeting was in Cook's office. It was the first time Mike Cook ever had an occasion to work with an auditor. In fact, Cook was now working with an insurance investigator and an auditor, two people who were not in law enforcement; the first time he'd ever had a case whereby he was actually involved in a criminal investigation with non-sworn officers or agents. This was new territory for Mike Cook, and not without its awkward moments.

Alan Pinette was a numbers man. Quiet and reserved, not prone to drama or rumor as were some of his friends, he seldom caused controversy. He preferred working alone usually with a good cigar and a drink as his quiet companion. So working with numbers was a perfect fit for him.

"Nice to meet you," Cook said extending his hand to greet Pinette. "Thanks for coming over."

"My pleasure," replied Pinette. "So what are we doing?" he added, wasting no time on unnecessary pleasantries.

Mike Cook spent the next 30 minutes giving Pinette an overview of the investigation. He explained how the crude explosive device had failed to detonate at D & B, and, that most of the company's records were saturated in gasoline and expected to have been destroyed had the device worked and the building burned down. He also told Pinette about EPA having found some evidence of what appeared to be fraudulent manifests related to the transportation of hazardous waste. And, he told Pinette about Alan Thompson having removed a picture from his office the day prior to the attempted bombing of D & B.

"So, what do you think?" Cook asked.

"I think we need to look at the company's financial records," Pinette said.

"In the spirit of full disclosure," Cook said, "I've never worked with an auditor before. Tell me how this works and what you need from me."

Pinette was prepared for the question. He reached into his briefcase and pulled out a sheet of paper that he handed to Cook.

"Take a look at that," Pinette said. "It contains a list of things I'm going to need to run an audit on the company."

Cook took a few moments to read the list of items Pinette was asking him to obtain for him. The list included bank records for D & B Environmental, personal bank records for both Eric Mann and Alan Thompson, profit-and-loss statements for D & B, along with other financial statements including D & B's balance sheet, their statement of income, statement of cash flows, statement of revenue and expenses, and, if possible, the tax returns for the past three years for D & B and the two owners, Mann and Thompson.

"That's a lot of financial records," Cook said.

"It is. If these people torched the plane and tried to burn the business for profit and, or, are engaged in a money laundering scheme, we're going to have to look at a lot of financial data. And, I'm guessing you're going to have to subpoena them unless the insurance company demands them, which I think they can do."

"Money laundering?" Cook asked.

"Yes, money laundering. It's very possible they tried to destroy their business to cover up or some other crimes they were committing. I'm not sure if an environmental crime would serve as the underlying crime to support a money laundering offense, but who knows what else they may have been involved in. I'll certainly take a look at it through that lens."

"I'm still not sure I understand."

"It's pretty simple really," Pinette said. "Money laundering is basically defined as using money derived from some illegal activity and making it appear as if it came from some legal source. In this case, theoretically speaking, let's suppose they did in fact commit some type of crime associated with the environmental laws, and in the process, took the dirty money from those crimes, and put it back into the system as if it was clean money, or, shown to be money made legitimately."

"I'm listening," Cook said. "Tell me more," as he sat back on his chair and placed his feet on his desk.

"Basically, money laundering involves three stages. First, the illegal money, say from narcotics trafficking, prostitution, or possibly in this case, environmental violations, has to be placed. We call this *placement*. In this stage, the person committing the act takes the money, usually cash, and converts it into cashier's checks or deposits it into or through multiple transactions into bank accounts."

"That's why you want their bank records?"

"Yes. But that's not all of it. The second stage is called *layering*. It's here people attempt to hide their actions. For instance, they might try to layer their money in other businesses or in offshore accounts."

"Sounds like their trying to camouflage the source of the money."

"You're a quick study. That's exactly what they're trying to do in this stage."

"What's the third stage?"

"The third stage is called *integration*. In essence, the launderer is looking for a way to make the illegal money look legitimate and re-introduce it into the economy."

"Isn't that difficult? How might they do that?"

"In any number of ways. One of them is to inflate the sales of a business. That would integrate the money back in the system and make it look legitimate. This is sometimes referred to as the money circle, meaning that checks are written and deposited, but the money ends up back where it all began. Not saying they did this here. I'll have to look at those records to get a better idea as to what is going on. They might also be overstating their revenues. And, they might be overstating expenses. I won't know until I look at the financial records."

"So once I get these records, assuming I can, what do you then do?"

"I'll do a financial investigation. I'll take a look at their assets and liabilities, and try and come up with their net worth."

"Sounds simple enough."

"It is and it isn't. I'll need to look at more than just their financials. Remember, an asset is not only money. It can be anything that can be turned into money such as a house."

"What about liabilities?"

Pinette nodded. "Think of it as an obligation or claim against an asset. For instance, if you own a home worth $500,000, that's an asset. If you owe $400,000 to the bank on that same house, you basically have a liability of that amount. Subtract what you owe on the house from the value of house and you have net worth of $100,000. Assuming, that is, that you have no other assets. That's a simple explanation, I know. But think about all the assets Mann and Thompson might have. We'll have to look at all their assets and then, try to determine their liabilities to come up with a net worth. Once we do that, we can see if the money they're generating from D & B allows them to make the purchases they've made and/ or live the life style their living. I'm basically going to see where they get their money and what they're doing with it."

"But I thought money laundering was basically something drug dealers did. I hear about this from my contacts at DEA all the time."

"Drug dealers are certainly some of the biggest money launderers. But we're finding it now among simple embezzlers, corrupt politicians, and more recently terrorists."

"So exactly what might they do to make this money look clean?"

"They want to avoid having the government knows about the money. That, of course, is why they don't deposit it in U.S. banks. Instead, they deposit the money in foreign banks, or banks outside the United States. Most of these banks, for a fee of course, agree to keep the transaction secret. These guys then create fictitious companies back here in the states and begin transferring small amounts of money into phony business accounts."

Mike Cook was starting to get a headache. Then he said, "I'll try to get a grand jury subpoena for them but it will no doubt take a month or so before we can get all the records."

"That's no problem. Just call me when you get them. And while you're at it, see if you can get me any records associated with leasing out that plane that was blown up."

"Why's that?"

"Plane sales and leasing are big ticket items. They have to be well documented. The FAA should be your first stop. They may have the information you need. And don't forget to check with the maintenance facility that took care of the plane. They might have some interesting information for you."

"That's my next stop actually. We recovered the flight log from inside the plane. I plan to take a close look at that in the next couple of days."

"If you have trouble getting a grand jury subpoena for the records, don't rule out getting some of the records from third parties."

"What do you mean by getting them from third parties?"

"See if either Mann or Thompson has been married before. If so, check with their ex-wives. Do they own or rent? If they rent, check with the landlords, both current and former."

"I hadn't thought of that."

"Most people don't if they haven't been involved in a money laundering case. And I'm not even sure we have one here. But we'll still need to look at Mann and Thompson's financials as well as the company's."

"I'll call the U.S. Attorney's office this afternoon and see about the subpoenas."

"Good. And we're going to want to ask the company accountant some questions."

"Such as?"

"I'd want to know if the company was operating at a profit and loss; what was the net worth of the business? What are their assets and liabilities?

"We'll go together on that interview."

"Good. And let me know when you get those records."

And just like that, Alan Pinette stood up, extended his hand to Cook and said good-bye.

Mike Cook was starting to get a headache. *How could what looked like a simple bombing of a small private airplane and the attempted arson/bombing of a small company now involve the Environmental Protection Agency, an old insurance investigator, and now an auditor who thinks there might also be some money laundering involved,* he thought to himself. Cook's headache and reverie were interrupted when his land line buzzed. It was Lisa's secretary telling him she was transferring a call to him.

"Can you take a message," Cook said. "I'm busy right now."

"It's an agent from the Defense Department. Said it was important."

Mike Cook didn't realize it, but his headache was about to get bigger.

A Brief Discussion about Money Laundering

In order to have any discussion of money laundering, we must have a clear understanding of the nature of money itself. Cleary, money is a concept. It's an idea that some object, for instance, a house, a car, an iPod, and clothes, has an assigned value to it and money is used to trade for it. As John Madinger states in his book, *Money Laundering*, "You simply can't understand the concept of money laundering without a clear understanding of what money is and how it works."[1]

© LZ Image/Shutterstock.com

For most people, money comes in the form of "cash." Money comes in many forms and people are constantly working and fighting for it. Some are even stealing it. While I don't want to bore you with a history lesson on the evolution of money, you should know that money has evolved through the ages. Today, money comes in the form of paper currency, checks, coins, credit cards, etc. As many of you know, we are moving toward a cashless society. Many years ago, in an age long before ATM's, one had to stand in line at banks or grocery stores, to cash a small check in order to have cash. But this was a long time ago . . . . I for one, welcome the forthcoming changes toward a cashless society. Especially being able to use our cell phones to pay for items.

The phrase money laundering was first coined in the 1930s by U. S. Treasury Agents trying to lock up Al Capone. The mob owned hundreds of Laundromats in and around Chicago. It was here that they disguised the earnings from their illegal liquor business as money honestly earned from the laundries.

In the 1970s, one particular pizza business in New Jersey a mom and pop operation, was told, by criminal elements, that "based on the size of their restaurant, it was estimated that they would need 100 pounds of pepperoni and 200 pounds of mozzarella every week." Mom and pop usually needed about a quarter of that for their business. What was happening? They were being extorted. What did they do? They bought the meat and cheese of course; they were too scared to do otherwise.

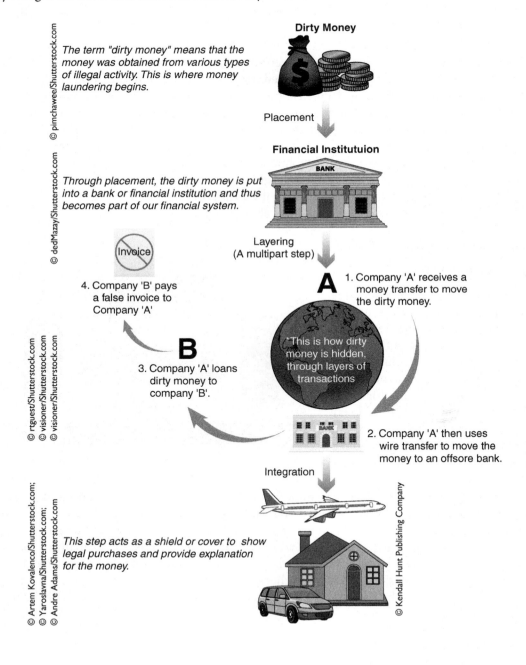

Dirty Money

The term "dirty money" means that the money was obtained from various types of illegal activity. This is where money laundering begins.

Placement

Financial Institutuion

BANK

Through placement, the dirty money is put into a bank or financial institution and thus becomes part of our financial system.

Layering
(A multipart step)

A

1. Company 'A' receives a money transfer to move the dirty money.

*This is how dirty money is hidden, through layers of transactions

Invoice

4. Company 'B' pays a false invoice to Company 'A'

B

3. Company 'A' loans dirty money to company 'B'.

2. Company 'A' then uses wire transfer to move the money to an offsore bank.

Integration

This step acts as a shield or cover to show legal purchases and provide explanation for the money.

© pimchawee/Shutterstock.com
© dedMazay/Shutterstock.com
© rguest/Shutterstock.com
© visioner/Shutterstock.com
© visioner/Shutterstock.com
© Artem Kovalenco/Shutterstock.com;
© Yaroslavna/Shutterstock.com;
© Andre Adams/Shutterstock.com
© Kendall Hunt Publishing Company

The process of money laundering has three stages:

1. Placement
2. Layering
3. Integration

Remember, for the crime of money laundering to occur, i.e., to charge a violation of the Money laundering Control Act, title 18 U.S.C. 1956 (A) (1), there has to be an underlying crime. In other words, the first question you must ask, and prove, is "did the money in fact, come from some specified unlawful activity?" It's important to understand that. Without a crime, there is no money laundering. "Money laundering has to start off by determining the crime behind the money. This is known in legal circles as the 'substantive offense.'"[2]

You must also prove that the defendant, in conducting the illegal transaction, did so with intent. So, how might we prove intent? Intent can be proven in a number of ways. For instance, "paying for drugs with the proceeds from other drug sales or reinvesting the proceeds from an illegal gambling business back into that business."[3]

An Overview of Money Laundering

Illegal sources of income arrive from a variety of criminal activities including but not limited to:

1. Tax Crimes
2. Environmental Crimes
3. Fraud
4. Illegal drug activity
5. Gambling
6. Bribery
7. Corruption

The goal of placing this illegal money is to get this illegally obtained money into a financial system. This is accomplished by changing the currency, transporting large amounts of cash, and making numerous cash deposits.

The goal of layering is simply to conceal the money, obtained through criminal activity. This is done in a number of ways including wire transfers, withdrawals of cash, and cash deposits into other accounts.

The goal of integration is to create an environment that makes the money to appear to have come from a legitimate enterprise. This can be accomplished by creating fictitious loans, showing inflated sales from legitimate businesses and disguising ownership of various assets.

To conduct any money laundering investigation, you must have some idea of what constitutes a financial investigation. Part of this understanding requires one to understand several terms.

1. Asset: Money or anything that can be turned into money.
2. Liability: An obligation or claim against an asset. If you have a car payment, the bank has a claim against your car.
3. Net worth: This is what you've got after you subtract the liabilities from the assets.
4. Income: Money you earn, or steal.
5. Expenses: Costs of living or doing business, i.e. food, rent, gas, etc.

Just knowing a few concepts will help you to analyze financial documents. And, like everything else, you need a plan. Once you get your hands on the financial records, look at the:

a. date
b. payee
c. who made the deposits
d. review the records for patterns
e. review the records for unusual deposits or payments
f. analyze money flow among multiple accounts

One very simple exercise is to see if the person is living beyond their means. One simply has to look at the case of former CIA employee Aldrich Ames, who was charged with spying and was directly responsible for sending at least 10 men to their deaths. Ames tipped his hand by calling attention to himself by his unexplained wealth. Simply put, he couldn't explain where all his money was coming from, and, in the process, left a huge paper trail for investigators.

As a GS 14, making maybe $50,000 a year, Ames bought a home in VA for $540,000 in cash. He drove a new Jaguar, which he paid $50,000 in cash for; ran up phone bills in Italy of over $5,000 a month, and made cash deposits to his bank account in excess of $1.5 million. In short, he did not layer the money, and, had an integration problem.

So, how do we get a snapshot of whether someone is living beyond their means?

Well, for starters, we can look at:

1. Mortgage a-nd rent payments
2. Car payments
3. Insurance payments
4. Food
5. Gasoline credit card
6. Utilities
7. Day care
8. Donations to churches, etc.
9. Personal loan payments
10. Alimony and/or child support
11. Credit card bills
12. Taxes

You get the picture. You'll want to see what someone's expenses are and determine if their income matches their lifestyle. "But remember, most financial institutions are big and impersonal. And the bad guys are looking to take advantage of that."[4] Getting all the information you need to conduct this evaluation won't be easy.

FINCEN Form **104** (Formerly Form 4789) (Eff. December 2003) Department of the Treasury FinCEN	**Currency Transaction Report** ▶ Previous editions will not be accepted after August 31, 2004. ▶ Please type or print. *(Complete all parts that apply--See Instructions)*	OMB No. 1506-0004

1   Check all box(es) that apply: **a** ☐ Amends prior report   **b** ☐ Multiple persons   **c** ☐ Multiple transactions

Part I	**Person(s) Involved in Transaction(s)**

Section A--Person(s) on Whose Behalf Transaction(s) Is Conducted

2 Individual's last name or entity's name	**3** First name	**4** Middle initial

5 Doing business as (DBA)	**6** SSN or EIN

7 Address (number, street, and apt. or suite no.)	**8** Date of birth MM / DD / YYYY

9 City	**10** State	**11** ZIP code	**12** Country code (if not U.S.)	**13** Occupation, profession, or business

14 If an individual, describe method used to verify identity: **a** ☐ Driver's license/State I.D.   **b** ☐ Passport   **c** ☐ Alien registration

d ☐ Other _____   **e** ☐ Issued by: _____   **f** Number: _____

Section B--Individual(s) Conducting Transaction(s) (if other than above).

If Section B is left blank or incomplete, check the box(es) below to indicate the reason(s)

a ☐ Armored Car Service   **b** ☐ Mail Deposit or Shipment   **c** ☐ Night Deposit or Automated Teller Machine   **d** ☐ Multiple Transactions   **e** ☐ Conducted On Own Behalf

15 Individual's last name	**16** First name	**17** Middle initial

18 Address (number, street, and apt. or suite no.)	**19** SSN

20 City	**21** State	**22** ZIP code	**23** Country code (If not U.S.)	**24** Date of birth MM / DD / YYYY

25 If an individual, describe method used to verify identity: **a** ☐ Driver's license/State I.D.   **b** ☐ Passport   **c** ☐ Alien registration

d ☐ Other _____   **e** ☐ Issued by: _____   **f** Number: _____

Part II	**Amount and Type of Transaction(s). Check all boxes that apply.**

26   Total cash in $_____ **0**.00   **27**   Total cash out $_____ **0**.00   **28** Date of transaction ___/___/___ MM DD YYYY

26a   Foreign cash in_____ **0**.00 *(see instructions, page 4)*   **27a** Foreign cash out _____ **0**.00 *(see instructions, page 4)*

29 ☐ Foreign Country_____   **30** ☐ Wire Transfer(s)   **31** ☐ Negotiable Instrument(s) Purchased

32 ☐ Negotiable Instrument(s) Cashed   **33** ☐ Currency Exchange(s)   **34** ☐ Deposit(s)/Withdrawal(s)

35 ☐ Account Number(s) Affected (if any):   **36** ☐ Other (specify)

_____   _____

_____   _____

_____   _____

Part III	**Financial Institution Where Transaction(s) Takes Place**

37 Name of financial institution	Enter Regulator or BSA Examiner code number ▶ (see Instructions)

38 Address (number, street, and apt. or suite no.)	**39** EIN or SSN

40 City	**41** State	**42** ZIP code	**43** Routing (MICR) number

Sign ▶ Here	**44** Title of approving official	**45** Signature of approving official	**46** Date of signature MM / DD / YYYY
	47 Type or print preparer's name	**48** Type or print name of person to contact	**49** Telephone number ( ) -

▶ For Paperwork Reduction Act Notice, see page 4.   Cat. No. 37683N   FinCEN Form **104** (Formerly Form 4789) **(Rev. 08-03)**

FinCEN Form 104 (formerly Form 4789) (Eff. 12-03)   Page 2

Multiple Persons
Complete applicable parts below if box 1b on page 1 is checked

Part I   Person(s) Involved in Transaction(s)

Section A--Person(s) on Whose Behalf Transaction(s) Is Conducted

2 Individual's last name or entity's name	3 First name	4 Middle initial

5 Doing business as (DBA)   **6** SSN or EIN

7 Address (number, street, and apt. or suite no.)   **8** Date of birth   ___/___/___   MM DD YYYY

9 City	10 State	11 ZIP code	12 Country code (if not U.S.)	13 Occupation, profession, or business

14 If an individual, describe method used to verify identity: **a** ☐ Driver's license/State I.D.   **b** ☐ Passport   **c** ☐ Alien registration

d ☐ Other_____   **e** Issued by:_____   **f** Number:_____

Section B--Individual(s) Conducting Transaction(s) (if other than above).

15 Individual's last name	16 First name	17 Middle initial

18 Address (number, street, and apt. or suite no.)   **19** SSN

20 City	21 State	22 ZIP code	23 Country code (if not U.S.)	24 Date of birth ___/___/___ MM DD YYYY

25 If an individual, describe method used to verify identity: **a** ☐ Driver's license/State I.D.   **b** ☐ Passport   **c** ☐ Alien registration

d ☐ Other_____   **e** Issued by:_____   **f** Number:_____

Part I   Person(s) Involved in Transaction(s)

Section A--Person(s) on Whose Behalf Transaction(s) Is Conducted

2 Individual's last name or entity's name	3 First name	4 Middle initial

5 Doing business as (DBA)   **6** SSN or EIN

7 Address (number, street, and apt. or suite no.)   **8** Date of birth   ___/___/___   MM DD YYYY

9 City	10 State	11 ZIP code	12 Country code (if not U.S.)	13 Occupation, profession, or business

14 If an individual, describe method used to verify identity: **a** ☐ Driver's license/State I.D.   **b** ☐ Passport   **c** ☐ Alien registration

d ☐ Other_____   **e** Issued by:_____   **f** Number:_____

Section B--Individual(s) Conducting Transaction(s) (if other than above).

15 Individual's last name	16 First name	17 Middle initial

18 Address (number, street, and apt. or suite no.)   **19** SSN

20 City	21 State	22 ZIP code	23 Country code (if not U.S.)	24 Date of birth ___/___/___ MM DD YYYY

25 If an individual, describe method used to verify identity: **a** ☐ Driver's license/State I.D.   **b** ☐ Passport   **c** ☐ Alien registration

d ☐ Other_____   **e** Issued by:_____   **f** Number:_____

Questions for Discussion

1. Do some research and discuss the following:
   A. What is meant by Cyber laundering?
   B. What is meant by Smurfing?
   C. What is a currency transaction report?
2. How might money laundering be used to facilitate drug smuggling and terrorism?
3. How might identity theft be used to facilitate money laundering? Be very specific.
4. Research what the Financial Action Task Force (FATF) is; who is part of it and what do they do?
5. Research the Bank Secrecy Act. What are the provisions of this Act and how might it aid criminal investigators in a money laundering investigation?
6. What are the three stages of money laundering? Define and give an example of each stage.

Work Sheet

Exercises

1. Identify 15 personal things that would be considered an asset for both Mann and Thompson.
2. Identify 10 business related things that would be considered an asset for D & B Environmental.
3. Identify 10 things that would be considered a liability for both Thompson and Mann.
4. Identify 10 things that would be considered a liability for D & B Environmental.
5. Based on his conversation with the auditor, Alan Pinette, identify 10 business-related items Mike Cook should subpoena from D & B Environmental in order conduct a financial analysis on the company. Identify 10 things or items that Cook should subpoena from both Thompson and Mann for furtherance of conducting a financial analysis of both individuals.

Work Sheet

Websites

1. http://www.treasury.gov/resource-center/terrorist-illicit-finance/Pages/Money-Laundering.aspx
2. http://www.interpol.int/Crime-areas/Financial-crime/Money-laundering

Notes

1. Madinger, John. *Money Laundering: A Guide for Criminal Investigators.* 2nd Edition, 1. Taylor & Francis Group.
2. Mathers, Chris. (2004). *Crime School: Money Laundering; True Crime Meets the World of Business and Finance.* 22. Firefly.
3. Madinger, ibid. pg. 40.
4. Mathers, ibid. pg. 126.

Additional Readings

Friedrichs, David. *Trusted Criminals.*

Lasley, James R., Nikos R. Guskos, and Randy A. Seymour. *Criminal Investigation: An Illustrated Case Study Approach.*

Madinger, John. *Money Laundering: A Guide for Criminal Investigators.*

Mathers, Chris. *Crime School: Money Laundering.*

CHAPTER 11
COMPUTER CRIME

"People ask me all the time, 'What keeps you up at night?' And I say, 'Spicy Mexican food, weapons of mass destruction, and cyber attacks.'"

Dutch Ruppersberger

Chapter Objectives

1. Describe how computer crime investigations are conducted.
2. Understand the relationship between investigation and digital forensics.
3. Recognize proper steps for seizing and handling electronic evidence.
4. Understand the requirements of a legally valid search warrant for computers.
5. Understand the concept of managing a multi-agency jurisdictional case.
6. Understand the basic requirements and records needed to conduct a financial audit.
7. Understand the differences between the crimes of making False Statements and the False Claims Act.

In a few minutes, Mike Cook was going to meet with an agent from the Defense Criminal Investigative Service (DCIS). Until yesterday, he hadn't even heard of the agency. Now, he was meeting with someone named Amber Fox from DCIS. Cook had no idea how this meeting was going to go. The last thing he needed, so he thought, was yet another agency and investigator he didn't know joining on his case. And, he had work to do. He didn't have time to deal with another agency and sit through yet another meeting. But he had no choice. If it was one thing Lisa Swanson had always stressed, it was making sure everyone was shown the professional courtesy her agents wanted when they were meeting with their colleagues from other law enforcement agencies. And that was exactly what he was about to do, whether he liked it or not.

Amber Fox was thirty-four years old, of medium height and slender build. She took exceptional pride in her appearance, always professionally dressed in what some might describe as conservative attire. Amber liked to work out but normally not to the extent that caused her to sweat or, more importantly, mess up her hair. She would be more inclined to be seen on an elliptical machine listening to music and reading the latest romantic novel than running on a dirt trail. She'd gotten her Bachelor's degree in criminal justice and had been smart enough, after much prodding from an over-fatherly professor, to get a minor in accounting. After graduation, she wasn't sure what she wanted to do other than be a federal investigator. But she was young. And most federal agencies were looking for older, more mature agents; people with some proven track record of employment. So Amber joined the Peace Corps. After two years of working in South America she knew it was time to come home and get her career started. Because of her time in the Peace Corps, and, her minor in accounting, Amber was hired by the Defense Department's (DoD) Office of Inspector General (OIG) as an auditor. It was here that she learned how to conduct internal audits on large defense contractors in order to ensure efficiency and effectiveness. But her heart was in conducting criminal investigations. So after three years of stellar performance in the audit division, Amber was hired as a special agent with DCIS, which also fell under the purview of the DoD OIG. Since then, she had demonstrated herself to be more than simply competent. She loved her work and her work product showed it. And while she had worked with the FBI, the Office of Health and Human Services, the Postal Inspector's Office of Inspector General, the IRS and even the U.S. Customs Service, she had never had occasion to work with the Bureau of Alcohol, Tobacco and Firearms. For her, this meeting was a first.

"Welcome to ATF," Cook said, extending his hand.

"Thank you," Amber replied.

"So tell me, how did you hear about us investigating D & B?" Cook asked. "And what is DCIS' interest in an attempted bombing and the bombing of an airplane?"

"Latrelle Jackson. He called checking up on D & B. Claimed he had some issues about hazardous waste contracts they had with DoD. As for an interest in the bombing of the airplane, we have virtually no interest. As for the attempted bombing of the company, not much interest there either, except, if they were trying to destroy what we think might be a lot of false documents related to DoD contracts."

"I've never had any occasion to work with DoD, and, I must confess, have virtually no knowledge of DoD contracts. What can you tell me about those contracts?"

"D & B has several contracts with DoD to haul and dispose of hazardous waste. Some of these contracts are very lucrative. I guess Latrelle and his intern did some calculating, based on the records you recovered from the company, and found that some of the numbers with regard to how much waste they claimed to have disposed of on any given day, don't make sense. So he contacted us for some background information. Latrelle also suggested I reach out to you. That's why I'm here. If D & B were falsifying documents and invoices for payment and were illegally disposing of hazardous waste generated by DoD, then DCIS is very interested in this case. And we're going to investigate that portion of it," Amber said, making sure the message to Mike Cook was loud and clear. DCIS was going to be involved in the investigation, with or without his blessing.

"So you're basically interested in the alleged fraudulent documents D & B may have created in connection with DoD contracts?"

"That's right. We can help each other. If you're looking for a motive for the attempted bombing of D & B, and we can prove they falsified documents that generated money for the company, it might help prove the motive you're looking for."

"We're looking at some other theories as well. Including the possibility of some money laundering."

"That's always a possibility too. But the contract fraud, if we can prove they didn't actually dispose of the waste as they said they did, might be easier to prove. Either way, if we can show that they did in fact falsify the records, we have a whole new set of charges we can levy against them."

"Such as?"

"For one, False Statements. You know, Title 18 U.S.C. Section 1001. Each false count carries a penalty of monetary fines and imprisonment of up to five years. And there's the False Claims Act. These are civil penalties. In essence, it provides monetary penalties for knowingly presenting, or causing to be presented a false claim for payment."

"Yes, I know about the False Statement penalties. Not that familiar with the False Claims Act since we have little to no occasion to charge that in our investigations."

"We use it all the time. The DoD is not always singularly focused on making a criminal case. A lot of our work does in fact result in civil penalties. But we certainly conduct both criminal and civil investigations."

"So, what would you like to do now?" Cook asked.

"I'd like to help. We can investigate this together, or separate. That's up to you. But I think we can help each other."

"Maybe we can. If we do this together, everything runs through me," Cook said. I have EPA looking at this, a local detective, who has been with me from the start, an auditor, an insurance investigator, and now you. I have to manage all this from here. I'm not suggesting you run your investigative steps through me, but we have to coordinate all of our efforts."

"That's not going to be a problem," Amber replied.

"Good. Do you know AUSA Carlos Sanchez?"

"The forgetful one," Amber replied.

"That's him. He's assigned to this case. I'll call him and tell him DCIS is joining in the investigation."

"Why not send him an email or a memo," Amber suggested. "If you simply tell him in a phone call, he'll forget."

It was the first time that morning that Mike Cook had occasion to smile.

"Let's try to set something up for tomorrow morning. I want to get everyone here to discuss a game plan and lay out duties and responsibilities. Can you clear your calendar?"

"No. But I will."

The first call Mike Cook made was to AUSA Carlos Sanchez. This meeting would not have the significance it needed if Sanchez were not present. After all, it was Sanchez who ultimately would have to prosecute anyone that might be charged in this case. And it was Sanchez who would issue subpoenas in the case.

Cook made his case to Sanchez, explaining the new developments in the case along with DCIS now joining the investigation. Sanchez said he would clear an hour for the meeting at 11 a.m. the following day. So once Cook had the commitment of the prosecutor, he began making all the required phone calls. He told everyone that it was important and wanted everyone in his office at 11 a.m. for a meeting.

He was asking but the people on the other end of the line knew that it wasn't simply a request. Cook wanted to make sure everyone knew each other, and what role they were going to play in this investigation. And much to his surprise, the next morning, everyone showed up. Having lunch served in the conference room didn't hurt. He knew that the rules of law enforcement, in addition to coming home safely, included never getting wet or going hungry. Free food was always a great motivator to get people to attend a meeting.

At 11 a.m. the next morning, once the introductions were made, Mike Cook wasted no time getting down to business. He hated meetings, and was sure most people seated around the conference room felt the same way. But this meeting was important. And all eyes, especially those of his boss, Lisa Swanson, were on him.

"I want to thank everyone for coming in today, especially on such short notice. As I said yesterday, this team has grown in size since Tony Martin and I found ourselves waist deep in fire debris and gassed documents. And, we're still not exactly sure what we have here. But information is coming to light that suggests Alan Thompson and Eric Mann may have had a hand in blowing up the Twin Engine King Air and attempting to blow up their company, D & B Environmental.

"What I'd like to do is have everyone start with what we know and then see where we're going with this. So far, we know that Alan Thompson and Eric Mann increased the amount of fire insurance on D & B from two to three million dollars about two months prior to the attempted bombing or arson of the company. And, according to Angela Lyle, the office manager of D & B, Alan Thompson removed a personal picture from his office the day prior to the attempted bombing of the company. Is that right John?"

"That's what she told me," John Sherry said. "I have that in my notes. But I'd suggest you get a statement from her to that affect," Sherry said, looking directly at Cook. The old insurance investigator certainly wasn't happy about having been summoned to this meeting.

"I intend to do exactly that. Have they filed any insurance claims yet?"

"Not yet," Sherry replied.

"We also know, or suspect, that D & B was billing the DoD for the transportation and disposal of hazardous waste that appears, anyway, to have been more waste than they could have disposed of on any given day. Latrelle, can you talk more about this?"

"My intern has done a great job looking over many of the invoices and records you recovered. What she found is what appears to be a significant discrepancy in the amount of waste disposed of than what several of the drivers could have disposed of in any given day. We've created a chart that demonstrates what we're talking about," Jackson said as he opened a small folder and handed a copy of the graphed chart he mentioned to each person in the room.

"Everyone has met Amber Fox from DCIS. Amber came in yesterday after learning from Latrelle about the DoD contracts D & B had. Amber, can you tell everyone DCIS' interest in this and what, if anything, you've found?"

"DCIS is interested in any possible contract fraud Mann, Thompson, or D & B may have committed in connection with their DoD contracts. After our meeting yesterday, I ran some checks and found that D & B either had or still has, over a dozen contracts for the removal of hazardous waste from two military facilities in the state. These contracts, over the last two years, are worth over a million dollars.

While a lot of what we do involves far more money than that with regard to contract fraud, we're still very concerned because there might be DoD generated waste out there somewhere. If so, we want to get ahead of that."

"Anything else?"

"Yes. I appreciate the work Latrelle Jackson and his intern have done. But I'd like to have our internal auditor take a hard look at this too. We're going to need to do that if, in fact, they committed some type of contract fraud."

"Latrelle, can you coordinate that with Amber?" Cook asked.

"Of course. This is going to need more of a detailed look than what we've done. Our examination has been rudimentary at best. But we're confident that the data is correct. Someone will have to marry this up to the related DoD contracts."

"Tony, you have anything to add?"

Tony Martin studied everyone in the room for a few moments before speaking. He wanted to make sure he chose his words correctly. In his experience, not all federal agents embraced local detectives being part of their investigation. Then he said, "there's a lot going on here that I'm not that well versed in; illegal disposal of hazardous waste, money laundering, contract fraud, etc. I still think we have to break this down to basics. We have a plane that blew up and a business that someone tried to blow up. There weren't any signs of a break in at D & B when we arrived there and found that bomb on top of the records. As for the plane, we've done almost nothing so far to look into that. I think someone at D & B who isn't involved in all of this knows more than he/she is saying. What I always try to do is flip somebody early on. I still think we need to take a look at that. I'm just not sure who the weak link might be just yet."

"I tend to agree with Tony," Cook said. "This is turning into more than what we had anticipated. I'm always looking for a motive if I'm trying to prove arson and we have a couple of shots of demonstrating that if, we can prove they illegally disposed of hazardous waste and/or submitted false claims and/or statements to the DoD. But I agree that someone knows more than they're saying. Flipping someone would help move our case along."

"Try the office manager," Sherry said without hesitation.

"Why her?" Cook asked.

"She told me about the photo Thompson took out of the office. She ran the office. What secretary worth her salt doesn't know every last thing going on in an office? Secretaries know who is goofing off, who is sleeping with who, when the boss is lying about where he or she is, and so forth. Is her name on any of the invoices?"

"Yes and no," Latrelle replied. "She submitted most all of them. But they were submitted electronically. Here's an example of one," he added as he handed it to Amber Fox to examine.

"That's a DoD invoice alright," Fox said. "But as you said, it was electronically generated. As you can see, there is no signature on the document. So we have to demonstrate that she generated the invoice."

"How can we do that?" Cook asked.

"For one thing, I'd want to get my hands on the company's computers sooner than later," Fox replied. "We'll have to conduct computer forensics and of course, look at which terminal was used to generate the

INVOICE

NAME OF CARRIER			INVOICE or B/L NO.		DATE
SHIPPER: (COMPLETE NAME AND ADDRESS)			CONSIGNEE:		

No. of Pkgs.	(★) HM	Description of Shipment	Gross Weight	Purchase Order No.
		TOTAL		

(★) HM   Mark with "★" to designate Hazardous Materials as defined by the Department of Transportation (DOT) Regulations governing the transportation of hazardous materials. Label in accordance with regulations.

invoices. We'll also examine the metadata logs, and schedules of the person who was responsible for the terminal to see if they were actually there at the time."

"Anything else?"

"There is the potential for a good bit of circumstantial evidence that we can get from the terminal. We can try to identify the user profile where the document was found. That should help us narrow down the author, as long as the profile wasn't used by multiple users. And if the invoice was sent via email as an attachment, the email header will contain information about the sender's email address, their IP address, the file path or directory name, where the attachment resided. Once we get inside the computer, we can look for address books, which should give us some additional leads. But we really want to look at the documents, correspondence files, E-mail files, and any spreadsheets that might exist on it."

"So you're talking about getting a search warrant?"

"I am."

"Carlos, what do you think?"

Carlos Sanchez had sat quietly listening to everything being said in the meeting. If there was anyone in the room who had definitely come for the food, it was him. But as he ate and listened, his mind wondered to what he saw as his biggest challenge; waiting to smoke a cigar. But that would have to wait till the meeting was over and he took his real lunch break. Then his second biggest challenge would kick in; trying to mask the smell of the cigar from his wife. So the longer he waited, the less time he'd have to let the odor dissipate.

"I think a search warrant is in order," Sanchez said. "Let's get the company computers and any other records that weren't piled up and gassed. Why don't you and Amber draft up a request and come over to my office tomorrow morning?"

"Amber?" Cook said, looking directly at her.

"I can work on that this afternoon if you'd like."

"What about a potential search date?" Cook asked. "If we get this signed, how does next Tuesday sound? We can meet on Monday and go over the details. See how many people we need."

"That's a bit of a push," Sanchez said. "Let's get the warrant signed first. Then we can decide the day to execute it."

"I agree," Lisa Swanson interjected. "We're going to need to get the Computer Analysis and Response Team (CART team) ready. We need to give them time to gear up for this."

"Why do we need a CART team for one or two computers?" Sherry asked.

"Because electronic evidence is very fragile," Pinette interjected. "It can be altered, damaged, or even destroyed if not handled or seized properly."

"Alan's right," Amber Fox added. "And there may be more than just one or two computers involved. I want to make sure we get our hands on her cell phone if it's used for company business. And, any portable tablets, such as an iPad."

Mike Cook took a moment to digest what Sanchez and Lisa Swanson had just said. It was clear to him that perhaps he was rushing the process just a bit.

"Okay," Cook said. "I may have gotten ahead of myself. Let's revisit the date of executing the warrant after we actually get the warrant signed."

Everyone agreed on the flexible timetable and that the details and logistics of executing the warrant still needed to be worked out.

"What about interviewing Angela Lyle?" Cook asked.

"I'd do that as soon as possible. You might want to include what she has to say in the warrant request," Sanchez offered.

Then Cook said to Sanchez, "Tony and I will get that done in short order." He then looked directly at Latrelle Jackson and asked, "Can you go with us? You can focus in on the environmental questions."

Both Tony and Latrelle nodded in agreement. They would go with Mike Cook and conduct the interview with Angela Lyle.

Sanchez listened carefully then said, "When you talk to her, make sure you ask her who shared the office with her. And find out if the computer is physically locked, and if so, who has access to it. One of the things we've run into recently is that now, many people can access company files from home. Ask her if D & B's files can be accessed from someplace other than the business, say through a network program."

"Maybe I should talk to the head of our CART team first, get some ideas from them as to what other questions to ask before interviewing Lyle again," Cook said.

"That's probably a very good idea," Lisa Swanson said. "This technology is constantly changing. I can barely keep up myself, and I'm not that old."

"What about looking into the airplane a bit more," Tony asked.

"I thought I'd ride up Friday and check on the facility that handled the maintenance on the plane. Can you go with me?"

"I can as of now. Depends what else happens in town between now and then. I don't have the luxury of just working on one or two cases at a time," Tony replied with a smirk on his face. It was his way of letting everyone know that he had more on his plate than simply this one case.

"What about the foreman?" Sanchez asked. "Why don't we subpoena him before the grand jury?"

"That's a good idea. Can you get me a grand jury subpoena for him? I'll serve it when I interview Angela Lyle."

"Tomorrow, when you come by the office," Sanchez replied.

"What about getting records for our auditor, Alan?" Cook asked.

Alan Pinette, like Sanchez before, had just sat there, not saying a word. Now it was his time to talk.

"I need a bunch of records. For instance, I need bank statements, cancelled checks, deposit tickets, credit and debit memos, Forms 1099, 1089, or back-up withholding documents. I also need loan ledger sheets, any loan applications the owners and/or the company made, credit reports, credit card statements, financial statements, etc."

"You and Mike draft a subpoena request and have it on my desk as soon as possible," Sanchez said. "I take it you have some account numbers and institutions to serve the subpoena on?"

"We have some to get us started," Pinette replied.

"I can help get some of that information," Fox added. "I'll check with the contracting office and see where payments were being made. That will help."

"Thanks," Cook replied.

The meeting ended shortly after noon. Everyone knew their assignments and the time constraints placed upon them. For this case to proceed on schedule everyone would have to do their job without offering a host of excuses as to why they couldn't complete their task in a timely manner. This wasn't college where some professor, as some were apt to do, had put them on team projects to present something to the class.It seemed there was always some drama with one or more of the students assigned to the team who couldn't, for some petty reason, get their part of the project done in time. The excuses were plentiful; break-ups, car problems, spats with roommates, problems at work, and so on. There was, of course, the occasional legitimate excuse. But Mike knew back then, that most excuses centered around nothing more than people not being prepared or managing their time properly. For this plan to work as agreed upon by everyone in the meeting, each member of this investigation team would have to give their responsibility a high priority or explain to everyone on the team why the investigation couldn't proceed as planned. That wasn't something Mike Cook was going to want to hear. There would be no time for petty excuses.

Mike Cook and Tony Martin wasted no time themselves getting back into the investigation. They were eager to take a run at Angela Lyle. Only this time, instead of interviewing her at the office, they'd knock on her door that evening. They had no intention of telling her in advance they were coming to see her. And this time, they'd have Latrelle Jackson with them; someone who actually understood the environmental business. Cook was confident that Amber Fox would handle the other phase of the investigation, the one dealing with the possible fraudulent invoices submitted to DoD, in quick and efficient manner. At first, he had been reluctant to have yet another investigator join the investigation. Now, he was beginning to see just how beneficial it was to have other people involved who brought with them an area of expertise that neither he nor Tony Martin had.

The three men waited until just after dark to surprise Angela Lyle. They hoped that by catching her at home, she would be more inclined to share inside information about D & B's operation, and exactly what it was, that Alan Thompson and Eric Mann did. And, they wanted to learn more about this so called photograph that Thompson had allegedly removed from his office the day prior to someone attempted to blow the place up. They also wanted to get her to admit that it was she who generated the invoices for D & B that were ultimately submitted to the DoD for payment. They would let her know that they were aware some of the invoices were fraudulent. By doing so, they hoped that Lyle would see that protecting Mann and/or Thompson was not in her best interest.

And so, it was just after eight in the evening and already growing dark when the three men, Mike Cook, Tony Martin, and Latrelle Jackson drove up to Angela Lyle's home. It was a small, modest home in a residential neighborhood. And although it was a residential neighborhood, the homes were on large lots providing each homeowner with some breathing space. Angela Lyle would either tell them more than she already had, or, would demand to talk to a lawyer. It was going to be Mike Cook's job to convince her to talk to them. They wanted her cooperation and were prepared to deal for it.

When they approached the front door, they saw that it was ajar. Mike knocked several times, hard, so that whoever was inside, would know that someone was trying to get their attention. But there was no answer. He could hear music coming from inside, so he knocked again. But the result was the same: no answer. Still, the door was cracked open.

"What do you think Tony?" Cook asked.

"It's dark inside, but the front door is ajar and there is music coming from inside. I don't like this."

"Me either," Cook said.

Tony Martin pulled a flashlight from his car and shined it through the window. Nothing.

"Latrelle; stay here. Tony and I will check the back."

Latrelle nodded in agreement. The two men, using Tony's flashlight, the only light available, walked to the rear of the house. When they shone the light through the back window they saw the last thing they expected to see that night. There are some days in life that are perfect—when fantasy is indistinguishable from reality. For Mike Cook, this was NOT one of those days. Nor was it for Angela Lyle. Mike Cook could see her lying face down on the floor in a pool of blood. Angela Lyle, the office manager of D & B Environmental and the one person he and Tony Martin had hoped to convince to cooperate in their investigation, was dead.

© LZ Image/Shutterstock.com

A Brief Discussion about Computer Crime, and Managing Task Force Investigations

Years ago, actually not that long ago, when your author started in this business, there were no computers, well, none to speak of anyway. The few that did exist were mostly owned by, and used in support of, the federal government. They were so large, that you'd need a modest size home to fit one into. Today, we all carry with us a smart phone. And that smart phone that you carry in your pocket or purse, is more powerful than all the onboard computers that ferried all the American astronauts to the moon. That's right, that smart phone in your pocket can do more than everything the astronauts had available to them when they journeyed to the moon and back. And years ago, when your author was new to this profession, bank robbers used guns and ski masks when they robbed a bank. Today, they use computers. And when your author started in this profession, there was virtually no such crime known as "identity theft." Today, identity theft is one of the fastest growing crimes in the country.

There are entire courses, and rightfully so, dedicated to the subject of computer crime. For the purposes of this chapter and our discussion of criminal investigation, let's focus on some of the very basic issues involving the use of computers to facilitate a variety of crimes. I'll leave the more in-depth conversation about computer crime for the advanced courses on this subject.

Most federal agencies have what is known as a Computer Analysis and Response Team (CART). One of the more well known is the FBI's such team. Almost every significant search today by law enforcement requires a member or members of a CART team to participate in the planning and execution of computer search warrants. This team provides assistance to FBI field offices, and other law enforcement agencies when involved in a joint multi-agency investigation, in the search and seizure of computer evidence. They also conduct forensic examinations of seized digital media. Most federal agencies have such teams and provide similar services to their field agents. Even large police departments now realize that the potential for harm caused by and through the use of computers, requires them to have specialized personnel trained to deal with *Cyber-crime*. Simply put, *Cyber-crime* is any crime that involves a computer or network. There are various types of computer crimes including:

1. *Computer as the target.* Here the criminal tries to access the computer in order to change a criminal history, modify information such as a driver's license, steal information such as credit card data, or even access a university's registrar's office in order to change a grade. Unleashing a virus that will harm a network or disrupt communications, usually as an attachment to email, also falls under this category.

   One of the best examples of a crime in which the computer is the target can be found in the book *The Cuckoo's Egg* by Cliff Stoll. This book recounts the true story of a hacker from Germany, who infiltrated a number of computers in the United States. Many of the systems infiltrated were from the military, universities, and government contractors. The hacker attempted to locate and steal national security information to sell to foreign governments.[1] On the commercial scene, *Kingpin*, by Kevin Poulson, describes the successful hunt for one of the largest identity thieves ever identified by federal law enforcement.

2. *Computer as a means of communication.* This refers to the fact that cyber criminals often use computers, including digital devices such as tablets and smart phones, as a means of communication. E-mails, text messages, and social media are used by criminals to discuss criminal conduct, and can also be used to communicate with victims. Computers also keep large amounts of data on Internet that can be very valuable in an investigation.

3. *Computer as storage device.* Computers store massive amounts of data. This includes documents created on the computer, records of network activity, and attachments to e-mails. It also includes information that was placed on the computer and not completely deleted that can be recovered by effective computer forensic techniques. Smart phones store massive amounts of useful data such as phone records, contacts, text messages, photos, and records of Internet browsing.

In our story, the latter two uses are the focus of the investigation, particularly for Amber Fox. Special Agent Fox knows that while the computer is not essentially needed for the crime of submitting false invoices to occur, the use of the computer relates to the criminal act itself. Simply put, this technology aids in helping the crime move along faster by allowing for large amounts of information to be processed and difficult to detect. Two such crimes that also fall under this category include money laundering and child pornography. Suffice to say, that with regard to money laundering, the use of the computer has added an entirely new dimension to dealing with this type of crime. As indicated in the previous chapter, in only a matter of seconds, and with the simple click of a mouse, criminals can instantly transmit millions of dollars to offshore accounts through personal computers.

The law used to prosecute computer criminals in the United States is the wire fraud statute,[2] which prohibits the use of communication wires in interstate or international commerce to commit fraud. "This law requires intent to defraud the victim out of money or property and use of interstate or international wires during the commission of a crime. The problem with this law is that it was not written for computer crimes. Not every crime committed with a computer is done intentionally to commit a fraud, and not all computer crimes cross state or international lines."[3]

Over the years, Congress has passed additional laws including, in 1984, the Computer Fraud and Abuse Act (CFAA). Since its original passage, the Act has been amended a number of times. "The CFAA, 18 U.S.C. 1030, protects computers in which there is a federal interest—federal computers, bank computers, and computers used in or affecting interstate and foreign commerce. (Because of the nature of Internet communications, virtually every computer connected to the Internet is a "protected computer" under the CFAA.) It shields them from trespassing, threats, damage, espionage, and from being corruptly used as instruments of fraud."[4]

It is also important to remember that much evidence that is relevant to a computer crime investigation is not on the computer itself. Records of Internet communications are transmitted to Internet Service Providers (ISPs), such as Verizon and Comcast, or to application providers such as Google or Apple. Access to these records requires specialized warrants and court orders issued under the Electronic Communications Privacy Act (ECPA).

As noted earlier, we'll leave the more detailed discussion concerning computer crimes and the use of computers to facilitate crimes to a more advanced discussion on the topic. Many pundits believe it's not if the United States experiences a cyber attack, but when. People new to the profession of law enforcement will no doubt be trained as to how to deal with a stand-alone computer believed to have been a tool of a crime and, if found by a first responder. In fact, there are a variety of policies and procedures, and they vary from agency to agency. For the purposes of our discussion here, students should understand that if they, as a first responder, come across a computer that is believed to have been part of a crime, they should never attempt to search the computer for evidence. Instead, if the computer is on, photograph the front and back of the computer as well as the surrounding area. "Computer crime evidence, referred to as digital evidence, must be handled carefully to preserve the integrity of the physical device as well as the data that it contains."[5] After that, make sure you've been properly trained and are acting in accordance with your agency policies and procedures. If you haven't been so trained, request support from someone in your agency that has. As stated earlier, many major federal, state, and local law enforcement agencies have units that specialize in computer search and seizure. The time to involve these units is during the search planning process. It is important to ensure that a computer search warrant properly describes the use of the computer in the commission of the crime, to ensure that all relevant evidence is within the scope of the warrant. Keep in mind, that, "each piece of equipment related to the specific computer crime has its own method of collection. The items are unique in size and relevance to the scene."[6]

One can only imagine what a skillful and determined computer hacker could do to the infrastructure of this country were they able to hack into our utility systems and our banking system. Imagine, interrupting our power and water supply for days or weeks. Without power, our food supplies begin to dwindle. Imagine no running water. Then imagine working by candlelight as we try to live like those in the 1800s. Computer crime is more than someone simply hacking into your computer and stealing your money. On a much grander scale, computer crime can cripple our life as we know it.

© iQoncept/Shutterstock.com

As you recall from one of our previous chapters, under the Fourth Amendment, an application for a valid warrant must establish probable cause that a crime has been committed, and that evidence of the crime will be found in the place to be searched. This is not always an easy task when dealing with computers. Investigators don't always know the type of computer that was used to facilitate a crime. When drafting a search warrant for computer evidence, young investigators should not hesitate to seek expert advice and counsel from those far more knowledgeable than they are regarding computers. If your department or agency does not have specialists trained in helping with this, especially since the technology is constantly changing, know that outside help is available from computer manufacturers and, from state universities. Don't be afraid to seek help. I've never met an investigator that knew it all. I have, however, met a number of them that thought they did, in fact, know it all.

Another emerging section within law enforcement deals with monitoring chat rooms and social networking. Again, your author is dating himself. When I worked in this profession computers did not exist. And when they started coming into play, chat rooms and social networking were virtually unheard of. Today, they are commonplace. And while millions enjoy posting photos of themselves on line in any variety of manner, or letting everyone they know that they are "going for a run," or are bored, this activity is basically harmless. Sadly, this, along with texting, is becoming, in large part, the way we as Americans relate to and/or communicate with each other. More sadly, this technology has provided a forum for pedophiles to lure children into illicit relationships. Police departments now commonly use "sting" operations whereby officers pose as children in order to lure these pedophiles out into the open. Howard W. Cox, a former federal computer crimes prosecutor, also notes that criminal investigators should be cautious in their personal use of social media. "There have been a number of high profile cases where inappropriate social media comments about their cases by law enforcement and prosecutors have resulted in the dismissal of charges or reversal of convictions. As a prosecutor, I avoided Facebook, Twitter, and blogging in any form."

I remember when I first started my career as a young police office in south Florida. One of the common beliefs among officers and detectives back then was that any really good case that was developed would result in the FBI coming in and taking it away from us once all the hard and dirty work was done. And, of course, they'd take the credit for it. A few years later, when I joined federal law enforcement, I worked alongside a number of FBI agents very early in my career. Since both offices were considered small Resident Office's, we got to know each other rather well. And yes, there were a few occasions when the FBI did in fact exercise their authority and take over a federal or local investigation. The fact of the matter is, the FBI has broad jurisdiction in a number of crimes, and, they are within their right to do so. However, as my career progressed, which included a stint in headquarters, I witnessed a major transformation, not only in the FBI, but in most every federal and state agency. People started to realize that they had to work together. The FBI, as did other law enforcement agencies, realized that they did not have the expertise to handle all matters all the time. There is not only safety in numbers, there is the ability to accomplish far more with many than one can accomplish alone.

As a young ATF agent, we were all competing with one another, and, the agency personnel department, to investigate certain complex crimes in order to get a promotion. As such, we all were looking to be the lead investigator on a variety of cases. On one occasion, I was tasked with being part of a medium-size team, about 10 agents, to investigate a large arson case. At the time, I was leading the office in case production. I was on what baseball analysts might call, a "good hitting streak." I was making a name for myself. But I wasn't the lead agent on this particular case. So, I didn't give it my all. I was more concerned about a couple of other cases that I was responsible for. So, my irritation of having to spend time on this particular case, when I could be investigating my own cases, showed. A few days later, my supervisor walked over to my desk and without hesitation, said, "Come get a cup of coffee with me." By the look on his face, I knew I wasn't getting a commendation. It was clear from his look and tone, that he was not happy.

We took the elevator down to the bottom floor where there was a small snack bar that we frequented each morning, and mid-day in the afternoon. I sensed that something was coming and it wasn't going to be good. I was right.

"I want you to know that I realize that you're a fine investigator. A good one actually; when you work alone that is. But you're not a team player. If the case isn't yours you make it clear that you want nothing to do with it. That's not a reputation you want for yourself," my boss said to me.

I had no idea that was some people's perception. Sure, I wanted to work my own cases, but I had no idea that I was developing a reputation for being less than a total team player. Fortunately, I was young and it was still early in my career. There was time to change. And change I did. From that moment on, I embraced every joint investigation, multi-agency task force operation and effort that came my way. Sure, there were agencies I preferred not to work with any more than I had to. But this more because of the local personalities involved. Still, as time went on, I realized just how important "cooperation" among the agencies was necessary to accomplish our mission.

Multi-agency task forces are not a recent phenomenon. They've been around for a number of decades. Today, especially after 9/11, and very often, under the leadership of the FBI, agency partnerships are tackling a number of high profile criminal enterprises. For instance, the FBI's Washington Field

Office, *Joint Terrorism Task Force (JTTF)*, "brings together representatives of 34 local, state, and federal agencies that respond to all terrorism leads, develop and investigate cases, provide support for special events, and proactively identify threats and trends that may impact the region, the nation, and the world.

"The task force—dedicated to protecting the national capital region from terrorist attack—develops intelligence on and conducts investigations of international terrorists and domestic terrorists such as white supremacist organizations, lone wolves, black separatists, animal and eco-terrorist groups, anti-abortion and pro-life extremists, anarchists, and violent special interest groups. It also investigates bomb threats, whether they come by mail, phone, or the Internet."[7]

The FBI has a JTTF in almost every field office in the country. The FBI also manages task forces dealing with gangs and violent crime. While 9/11 certainly brought on the need for more cooperation among agencies, the sniper attacks on the nation's capitol in October 2002 kicked the need up even more.

The sniper's victims were shot with a high-powered rifle from long distances, leaving no eyewitnesses and very little information for law enforcement. The shootings spanned eight local jurisdictions, and involved more than a thousand investigators from local and state agencies, as well as members of the Federal Bureau of Investigation (FBI); Bureau of Alcohol, Tobacco, Firearms and Explosives (ATF); the U.S. Marshals Service; the U.S. Secret Service and other federal law enforcement agencies. The result was what some believe is the largest multijurisdictional, multi-agency investigation in our country's history—an investigation that can serve as a case study of cooperation among local, state, and federal law enforcement.

While the chief executives most affected by the sniper case—and those under their command—developed ad hoc protocols for working together, other agencies now have in this report the comprehensive information to help them anticipate and resolve many obstacles to future collaboration.

"Law enforcement agencies at every level of government must learn from the sniper investigation team's successful approaches, and address the many issues it identified that require a thoughtful and thorough strategy for performing a complex, high-profile investigation in the future—a strategy that can be tailored to the unique needs and resources of the agencies' communities."[8]

So how do we decide who is in charge of these multi-agency investigations? "If the investigation is limited to one jurisdiction, the answer is obvious—the chief, sheriff, or other top local law enforcement executive of that jurisdiction. But if the investigation crosses jurisdictional or state lines, or involves law enforcement agencies from other levels of government, the answer may not be so self-evident. Determining who is in charge will also influence where the task force will be located. Attempting to answer one without considering the other may create significant problems."[9]

There is no substitute for fostering relationships with other law enforcement agencies. This is crucial to promoting and fostering communication and coordinating resources. A pre-existing relationship can engender a basic level of trust and can help facilitate meshing of resources. In our fictional story, Mike Cook is realizing that he needs to coordinate the services and expertise from several individuals outside his agency and even law enforcement in order to investigate this crime. In the real world, one simply needs to watch the national news on any given night when some national tragedy has occurred to see the multiple agencies working together to resolve whatever crime has just occurred.

During the D.C. Sniper case, Michael Bouchard, ATF Special Agent in Charge, and who is now retired, was one of the three principle leaders of this multi-agency task force. In regard to the many lessons learned from this operation, Bouchard said, "Before September 11, federal agencies and local law enforcement worked together halfheartedly. This investigation [the D.C. Sniper Case] is an example of how law enforcement will be done in the future."[10] Bouchard is right; September 11, and the D.C. Sniper case was a wake-up call for federal and state agencies to share resources and work together.

Model Subpoena Language for Use in Financial Subpoena's

Financial Institution Records
. . . to bring with you and produce:

The following documents for all accounts bearing the signatory authority of (names) and/or in the name(s) of (names), and/or bearing the account number(s) (account numbers), for the period _____ to _____ including, but not limited to:

1. All documents pertaining to all open or closed checking, savings, or other deposit or checking accounts in the name of or under signature authority of any of the named parties or entities including, but not limited to:

   A. Signature cards
   B. Corporate board authorization minutes or partnership resolutions
   C. Bank statements
   D. Canceled checks
   E. Deposit tickets
   F. Items deposited
   G. Credit and debit memos
   H. Forms 1099, 1089, or back-up withholding documents.

2. All documents pertaining to open or closed bank loans or mortgage documents, reflecting loans made to or cosigned by any of the named parties or entities including, but not limited to:

   A. Loan applications
   B. Corporate board authorization minutes or partnership resolutions
   C. Loan ledger sheets
   D. Documents (checks, debit memos, cash in tickets, wires in, etc.) reflecting the means by which loan repayments were made
   E. Documents (bank checks, credit memos, cash out tickets, wires out, etc.) reflecting disbursement of the loan proceeds.
   F. Loan correspondence files including, but not limited to:

      1) Letters to the bank
      2) Letters from the bank
      3) Notes, memoranda, etc. to the file

   G. Collateral agreements and documents
   H. Credit reports
   I. Financial statements
   J. Notes or other instruments reflecting the obligation to pay
   K. Real estate mortgages, chattel mortgages, or other security instruments for loans
   L. Forms 1099, 1089, or back-up withholding documents
   M. Loan amortization statements

Continued

3. All documents pertaining to CDs purchased or redeemed by any of the named parties or entities including, but not limited to:

    A. Copies of the certificates

    B. Corporate board authorization minutes or partnership resolutions

    C. Documents (checks, debit memos, cash in tickets, wires in, etc.) reflecting the means by which the CD was purchased

    D. Documents (bank checks, credit memos, cash out tickets, wires out, etc.) reflecting disbursement of the proceeds of any negotiated CD

    E. Records reflecting interest earned, withdrawn or reinvested

    F. Records reflecting roll-overs

    G. Forms 1099, 1089, or back-up withholding documents

*This is a partial list of the language, adapted from US Department of Justice, *Financial Investigations Checklist,* U.S. Department of Justice, Washington, D.C., June 1998.

Questions for Discussion

1. While he didn't have pre-existing relationships with any of the team members, is Mike Cook doing enough now to foster those relationships. Discuss both pro and con. What is he doing to foster the relationships? What can he be doing better?
2. What is cyber-crime? What are the three ways that computers can be used in cyber-crime?
3. Why is an understanding of chat rooms and social networking important to law enforcement?
4. What are some of the advantages of forming task forces to investigate crimes?

Work Sheet

Exercises

1. Research the following cases and provide a briefing.
   a. United States of America v. Mark L. Simons 206 F. 3d 392 (4th Cir., February 28, 2000)
   b. Trulock v. Freeh, 275 F.3d 391 (4th Cir. 2001)

2. Research three different task forces around the country dealing with cyber-crime that include non-law-enforcement members on the team and provide details as to who the members of the group are.

3. Research and provide an overview of the Electronic Communications Privacy Act "ECPA", (18 U.S.C. SS 2701–11).

4. Identify five types of computerized files that might be of interest to an investigator.

5. Prepare a Search Warrant for the computer and related items at D & B Environmental. Assume you have probable cause. Identify the items you want to search for.

6. Prepare a subpoena for financial records related to D & B Environmental. Identify the items you want from the financial institution.

Work Sheet

Websites

1. https://www.fbi.gov/about-us/investigate/cyber.

Notes

1. Lasley, James R., Nikos R. Guskos, and Randy A. Seymour. *Criminal Investigation: An Illustrated Case Study Approach*. pg. 452. Pearson Publishing.
2. Title 18 USC 1343, www.justice.gov.
3. Lasley, et al., ibid. pg. 461.
4. Charles Doyle, Senior Specialist in American Public Law. (2014). *Cybercrime: An Overview of the Federal Computer Fraud and Abuse Statute and Related Federal Criminal Laws*. Congressional Research Service, 15 October.
5. Secret service. 2010. Guidelines for Seizing Electronic Evidence.
6. Lasley, et al., ibid. pg. 459.
7. https://www.fbi.gov/washingtondc/about-us/our-partnerships/partners.
8. Murphy, Gerard R., Chuck Wexler, with Heather J. Davies, and Martha Plotkin. (2004). Managing a Multi-jurisdictional case: Identifying the Lessons Learned from the Sniper Investigation. *A Report Prepared by the Police Executive Research Forum for the Office of Justice Programs U.S. Department of Justice*, October.
9. Ibid. pg. 20.
10. Ibid. pg. 16.

Additional Readings

Becker, Ronald F. and Aric W. Dutelle. *Criminal Investigation*. 4th Edition.

Computer Crime & Intellectual Property Section. (2009). *Searching & Seizing Computers and Obtaining Electronic Evidence in Criminal Investigations*. 3rd Edition. Criminal Division, Department of Justice, August.

Computer Crime & Intellectual Property Section. (2010). *Prosecuting Computer Crimes*. 2nd Edition. Criminal Division, Department of Justice, November.

Koppel, Ted. (2015). Interviewed. AARP Bulletin, October.

Lasley, James R., Nikos R. Guskos, and Randy A. Seymour. *Criminal Investigation: An Illustrated Case Study Approach*. Pearson Publishing.

Managing a Multi-jurisdictional case: Identifying the Lessons Learned from the Sniper Investigation. *A Report Prepared by the Police Executive Research Forum for the Office of Justice Programs U.S. Department of Justice*, October.

Murphy, Gerard R., Chuck Wexler with Heather J. Davies and Martha Plotkin. (2004).

Osterburg, James W. and Richard H. Ward. *Criminal Investigation*. 7th Edition.

Swanson, C., N. Chamelin, L. Territo, and R. W. Taylor. *Criminal Investigation*. 10th Edition.

CHAPTER 12
DEATH INVESTIGATION

"If you're that obsessed with someone, why would you kill her? Humans are full of contradictions."

Ai Yazawa

"The first thing we do, let's kill all the lawyers."

William Shakespeare, King Henry VI, Part 2

© Stokkete/Shutterstock.com

Chapter Objectives

1. Become familiar with the methods and evidence involved in death investigation.
2. Become familiar with the methods used in estimating the time of death.
3. Understand the duties and responsibilities of the responding officer.
4. Understand why people kill.
5. Understand the difference between homicide and murder.
6. Become familiar with the theories of Murder Typologies & Interrogation Strategies.
7. Understand the difference between Justified and Excusable Homicides.

Recommended Reading

1. *Murder in Greenwich,* by Mark Furhman.
2. *Murder: A Family Affair,* by Ernie Dorling.
3. *The Onion Field,* by Joseph Wambaugh.
4. *In Cold Blood,* by Truman Capote.
5. *The Blooding,* by Joseph Wambaugh.
6. *In his Garden: The Anatomy of a Murderer,* by Leo Damore.

The three men looked at the body of Angela Lyle lying on the floor in the kitchen. Tony Martin crouched down so he could examine the body. He checked her pulse: nothing. There was no heartbeat. No respiration. While he did not have the authority to pronounce death, he knew she was dead. And so did Cook and Jackson. After a quick check of the house for other victims or suspects, Tony Martin bent down over the body of Lyle. *Rigor mortis* had not yet begun. But there was blood everywhere around her. Martin knew that the bloodstain patterns would have to be documented and collected and that an interpretation of the patterns would be a critical piece of evidence in understanding the sequence of events surrounding the crime. It was the first time Latrelle Jackson had actually been to a murder scene. It wasn't often that EPA agents found themselves at the scene of a homicide. For Mike Cook, he had certainly seen his share of dead bodies as both a Marine and during his three years as a police officer before joining ATF. For Tony Martin, he too had seen his share of homicides, all as a cop and now detective. Still, none of them had reached a point where they were immune from experiencing the darkness of it all. So, for three men standing in the kitchen next to the body of Angela Lyle; well, it gave them all a strange chill. Cook and Martin knew Angela Lyle. This was not a situation where any of the three men would need to demonstrate their best efforts at *objectification*. For a few brief moments there was silence among everyone in the room. It was Tony Martin who first broke that silence.

"This changes everything," Tony said. "I need everyone to take a few steps back and not touch a thing until we can photograph every inch of this place." Tony looked at both men and added, "I need your help protecting this crime scene until I can get some units out here along with our crime lab." As a detective, Tony Martin was not normally the first officer on the scene of a homicide. He had been the first responder on several murder scenes as a patrol officer and he knew very well that he had to follow a strict set of departmental guidelines to not only protect the crime scene, but himself, and anyone else who was present with him. The responsibility to immediately protect the scene from having any evidence contaminated or lost was now his. And Mike Cook and Latrelle Jackson were ready to help.

"Anything you need," Mike replied. "I will need to call Lisa and AUSA Sanchez as soon as I can. We should also let Sara Howard know. She may want to coordinate with your lab folks."

"Let me talk to Lieutenant Van Pelt. I'm sure he'll be happy to get all the help he can. But right now, this is a homicide. I've got to do this by the numbers. And that includes getting a *Mincey Warrant* to conduct the crime scene search."

"A Mincey Warrant," Latrelle said.

"Yes. From what I understand, Angela was the sole resident of this house. We'll have to confirm that and then speak with our prosecutor for a determination on whether we will need a warrant to process the scene. If she was the only person with a privacy interest in the premises, we should be able to proceed without a warrant. But we may not be able to confirm that tonight. So right now, since there are no real exigent circumstances here, and there is nothing here to indicate that the evidence would be lost or destroyed during the time it would take to get a warrant, I think we should get one. In the meantime, Latrelle, would you please grab a notebook and start a crime scene security log. I want everyone who comes in and out of this crime scene logged in. I'll have an officer take over as soon as I can get one assigned."

"No problem," Latrelle replied.

Tony said, "It looks like the crime scene is compact. We should be able to contain it until we get some help. Mike, if you can take some notes for me, I'd appreciate it."

"Absolutely," Mike said as he took out his notebook from his jacket pocket and began taking notes.

"Start by making a note that here are two glasses of red wine on the table. One glass empty. One glass half full."

"Got it. And the bottle is corked and half full."

"That's the idea. Leave nothing out."

"Make a note too, that all the lights in the house except for this kitchen light over the stove were off. Once the crime scene unit completes videoing everything, we'll also need to examine the locks on the windows and doors to see if they were tampered with."

"Got it."

"Let's see what's in the refrigerator too. And get a photo of what's inside. Make sure to include the freezer, kitchen cabinets, oven, and medicine cabinets. And take a snapshot of the thermostat. I want to make sure the temperature inside the house is recorded."

In under 30 minutes, the house and surrounding area was lit up like a movie scene. Yellow tape was being placed around the house and its curtilage which was now surrounded by both marked and unmarked police cars, an ambulance, a vehicle from the coroner's office, along with a vehicle from the crime scene investigative team. A patrol officer was assigned to keep a log of everyone entering and leaving the crime scene. Lt. Ed Van Pelt was already taking command of the scene and giving orders to everyone involved in the investigation. The crime scene unit was in the process of taking video and overall pictures of the scene and body before anything was removed or manipulated. Once this was completed, the medical examiner would examine the body.

"Any guess as to the cause and time of death?" Van Pelt asked the medical examiner.

"Time of death; not yet," Kimiko said. "But I think I'll have a rough idea in a few minutes." Kimiko Matsui was born in the United States; the child of Japanese parents who had emigrated to the states in the 1970s. Her parents had tried several times to have children and when they finally did, they thought long about giving their daughter a more traditional American girl's name. Instead, they chose to preserve a bit of their heritage by naming their daughter Kimiko, which in Asian means, "child without equal." After graduating with a Master's degree in forensic science from the University of New Haven, in Connecticut, Kimiko realized that she was not done with her education and went on to medical school where she graduated at the top of her class from the University of North Carolina school of medicine. As a certified pathologist and the medical examiner, Kimiko had proven her parents right in picking that name for her; for with regard to identifying manner, cause and time and death, she was virtually without equal. And, it would be Kimiko who would be the ultimate authority on determining the manner and cause of death.

Latrelle Jackson whispered to Mike Cook, "I've never worked on a murder case before. How do they estimate the time of death?"

Latrelle's whisper wasn't quite low enough. Kimiko heard her ask Mike Cook the question.

Without stopping what she was doing, Kimiko, still examining the body of Angela Lyle, and not making eye contact with Latrelle Jackson, said in a low voice, "after death, the body starts to cool down to whatever the outside or room temperature is. When someone dies, the body temperature usually starts to drop from its normal 98.6 degrees by a factor of about 1.5 degrees for each hour for about the first 12 hours. Then one degree per hour after until it reaches what we call the ambient temperature, which is the temperature of the environment the body is actually in. Then, after about 30 hours, it starts to go up again because of the heat generated by decomposition. But this varies by room or outside temperature, so you need to know weather conditions. We call this *algor mortis*."

"*Algor mortis*?"

"It's basic physics. The body's loss of heat is based on the fact that the body will reach the temperature of the surrounding environment it's in. Which, is why you're going to want to note the temperature inside the house right now."

"That sounds simple enough," Jackson said.

Now, her eyes shifting focus to Jackson, Kimiko said, "There's a bit more to it; algor mortis is only a piece of the puzzle. After a person dies, the muscles of the body initially become flaccid. Somewhere between six to eight hours, the muscles become more stiff and the joints freeze. This is called *rigor mortis*. The body is flaccid for about six or eight hours after death, then a hardness begins to set in around the jaw area in front of the ear. It then spreads throughout the body for a period of time, and then the body goes limp again."

"Thank you," Latrelle said.

"We should be able to determine the PMI pretty easily here. The body temperature is still high. She hasn't been dead long."

"PMI?"

"Postmortem interval or PMI refers to the time that has elapsed since a person has died. The interval starts with the last known time the victim was alive and ends when they are discovered dead."

"What about cause of death?" Van Pelt asked.

"I'm guessing *blunt force trauma*."

"What's telling you that?" Tony Martin asked.

"I don't see any entry or exit wounds. It wasn't a gunshot. No knife marks either. There is quite an abrasion, a laceration and skull fracture on her head. Look here," she said pointing her finger to Angela Lyle's bloody scalp. "See this? There is extensive damage to the top and back of the head. Blunt force trauma. That's my initial guess. I'll know more once I conduct an autopsy."

"Anything else?"

"Livor mortis, or what you commonly refer to as postmortem lividity has started to set in."

"Postmortem lividity?" Jackson asked.

"Yes. Look here," Kimiko said pointing at the body of Angela Lyle. "See this reddish, purplish-blue discoloration of the skin? That's due to the blood settling in the lowest level of the body. Lividity can be evident within 30 minutes of death and it becomes fixed after approximately 8–12 hours, but this is variable and dependent on the pre-mortem condition of the body and environmental factors. The lividity in this victim is not fixed yet. Please note the time of this observation. There are no signs of lividity on the top or side surfaces of the body which tells me that it is likely that the body wasn't moved after her death even though the lividity is not fixed. The lividity as well as the blood pool surrounding her and blood flows from her wounds are consistent with her position. There are no signs of lividity on the top or side surfaces of the body which tells me that the body wasn't moved after her death. She was killed right here."

Van Pelt turned his attention to Mike Cook. "What brought you three here tonight?" he asked.

"We were going to interview her about her relationship with the company. We were confident she had falsified some documents associated with the billings for the disposal of hazardous waste. She had no idea we were coming. We wanted to catch her off guard."

"You think this is tied into your investigation?" Van Pelt asked.

"It has to be," Cook replied. "I don't believe in coincidence. This happened too close to our learning about her having told John Sherry, the insurance investigator, about a picture Alan Thompson had taken out of his office the day prior to the bombing attempt on D & B. My guess, is that someone learned she had told Sherry about this and wasn't happy."

"That someone being Thompson?"

"That would be my first guess."

"Tony; what are your thoughts on this?"

"Same as Mike's. This is far too coincidental."

"Explain," Van Pelt ordered.

"Look at the crime scene. It's random and sloppy. This is typical of an argument or conflict murder. The body was left in the open to be found. I'm guessing in the same position in which she was killed. There is no weapon here either. These types of murders, such as an argument or conflict killing, usually results from a verbal dispute or from some personal conflict between the victim and the killer. Her purse is still here with credit cards and some cash in it. This wasn't well planned. And I'm betting she knew her killer."

Kimiko interrupted the conversation, removed her plastic gloves and said, "She's probably been dead about two hours but we'll know more definitively after the autopsy and with the investigative information you uncover. You guys should have tried to surprise her a little earlier."

"Okay Tony, you have the ticket on this murder," Van Pelt said. "Remember, while this might look like it's connected to D & B, and/or Thompson, investigate this like any other homicide. Get into Lyle's past. Conduct a complete victimology work up of the victim. Go over this place closely. Look to see what might be missing. If this doesn't involve your suspects at D & B, you're going to want to make sure you've covered all your bases. I've got two officers conducting a canvas of the neighborhood right now. With these over-sized lots, I wouldn't be surprised if the canvas comes up empty. But let's hope for the best. Maybe somebody saw something," Van Pelt added.

Van Pelt knew that canvassing, as tactic in this case to search for witnesses and surveillance video evidence, would be almost futile. Still, it was not a tactic he could, or would even consider, not employing. Van Pelt also knew that every crime scene told a story. In this case, the story had a lot of holes in it. No sign of forced entry and nothing appeared to have been stolen. But the story wasn't without some information. The crime scene was well contained. And, it would appear from initial observations, that Angela might have actually known her killer.

And just like that, Detective Tony Martin was assigned to lead the investigation into the murder of Angela Lyle. And with it came the responsibility of recording the crime scene, coordinating the collection and preservation of the evidence, ascertaining the motive for the crime, and questioning witnesses and suspects, if one were later identified. He directed the crime scene technicians as to how he wanted the body photographed, which included close ups of her head injury along with a full-body shot. Martin also directed the crime scene technicians as to what he wanted photographed and what items and evidence he wanted included in the crime scene sketch.

"We're clear now. I'd like to bag the body and take her downtown," Kimiko said.

Martin nodded. "Okay," was all he said.

Angela Lyle was placed inside of a black plastic bag and rolled out of her home and into the back of a van where she would be transported to the medical examiner's office. Cook, Martin, and Jackson stayed behind and assisted the department's forensic team in gathering what little evidence there was inside Angela Lyle's home. And, of course, that same two hours proved Lt. Van Pelt right; the canvas of the neighborhood revealed nothing of value. No one saw or heard anything unusual and none of the surrounding homes had video surveillance of the street.

For two more hours the crime scene team gathered what evidence they could, although there was very little. They were able to gather blood samples, of course. They took photographs. They dusted and lifted fingerprints from several surfaces and objects contextually relevant to the scene. They swabbed certain areas for DNA. What they didn't find, was any sign of a break-in. Nor did they find anything that appeared, at least on the surface, to be the weapon that might have delivered the blow to Angela Lyle's head. It would be a few days before they would be able to get the results of any questioned fingerprints that were recovered. There did not appear to have been anything of major value stolen from the house. In fact, Angela's purse with just over a hundred and twenty dollars inside it, was still in the living room. The team did, however, seize her computer, iPad, and cell phone and electronic storage devices. They also searched the apartment for information that would assist them with the victimology workup on Angela. They needed to develop as much investigative information as they could while they were at the scene. Martin knew that once the scene was released, they might not have another opportunity to gather this information. Before the phone was placed into inventory, Tony Martin examined it closely.

"Anything on that phone?" Mike asked.

"Luckily, she didn't password protect it. It shows two calls earlier today from John Thomas, the foreman," Tony said.

"Text messages?" Mike asked.

"One, from Eric Mann. It says, 'don't say anything until we can talk.'"

"What do you think that means?" Mike asked.

"Not sure. But we certainly want to talk to Mann. The sooner the better."

"Does the phone contain anyone identified as to who to call in case of an emergency?"

"Two people actually. Looks like a possible family member, a George Lyle, and woman named Brandi Gardner."

It was almost midnight when Tony Martin sat down in the small conference room in the detective division and called both George Lyle and Brandi Gardner. In both instances, he got a recorded voice telling him to leave a message. Martin then poured both Mike Cook and Latrelle Jackson a cup of coffee. All three men knew they weren't going home anytime soon.

"I've called Lisa Swanson and Amber Fox," Mike said. "Amber will be here by 8 a.m. Lisa wants you to know that whatever you need to just let us know."

"Just tell me what you need me to do," Latrelle added. "This is a bit new to me, but I'm a quick learner."

"We need to consider some things right out of the gate," Tony said. "I know we all think that this is tied into D & B. But like Lt. Van Pelt said, we need to look at this from every angle since it might not be related."

"What do you suggest?" Mike asked.

"We need to do a complete victimology work up on Angela Lyle."

"What do you mean by a victimology work up?" Latrelle asked.

"We need to know why she was targeted for this crime. Find out if she was known, personally, to whoever did this. Why was she the target? Let's find out what her personal relationship was with everyone who worked at D & B. I want to learn about her work habits, her romantic affairs, and her employment history. I want to know who her friends are, who her enemies might be, her financial background, where she went to school, and who her doctors are. I want to retrace the past 48 hours of her life. I want to go through her Facebook and other social media pages. And when we're doing this, I want you to keep in mind something that's drilled into us when we go to homicide training; that is, everyone lives three lives."

"Three lives," Mike said, with a smirk on his face.

"That's right, three lives. Everyone has a professional life, a personal life or private life; and a sexual life. The private life people lead is usually shared with only a few close friends. We have to find those friends and talk to them. And remember, the three lives people lead don't always match up to what people might think. We need to dig into every facet of her life."

"Okay, what else?" Latrelle asked.

"There was no evidence of forced entry. That might suggest she knew her attacker. This could be domestic related."

"But she wasn't married," Latrelle said.

Tony said, "That's true. But she could have had a boyfriend, or she could have been having an affair. We need to get into her personal lifestyle—daily routines, habits, and activities. We need to compile a complete list of family members with contact information. I want to talk to all her co-workers, get her financial history, check her spending, credit card use, and so forth."

Cook said, "You have any support here to help get this going?"

"We do. They'll be here in a few hours. This will get priority."

"What do you want Latrelle and me to do in the meantime?"

"We need to go see Thomas. Talk to him. Find out what you can about their relationship. But first, let's do some background on him and come up with an interview strategy. We don't want to go in cold. Based on the nature of his text, he and/or Thomas may be involved in this, and we might only get one shot at interviewing him. I'm going to go to the autopsy this morning. Let's meet here at noon and regroup."

"What about Amber? She'll be here at 8 a.m."

"She can go to the autopsy with me. That is, if she's up to it. As far as I'm concerned, she's either all in this case or she isn't."

Cook and Jackson looked at each other and nodded in agreement. Amber Fox was late coming to the investigation. And this case had just taken a whole new turn. The team could use her help, but it would have to extend far beyond that of simply tracking some fraudulent invoices related to DoD contracts.

"Do you have any reason to believe this isn't connected to D & B?" Latrelle asked.

"No, I don't," Tony said. "But I don't want to draw any conclusions right now. People kill for various reasons. It runs the gamut. I've seen people kill for financial gain. They kill for sexual gratification, self protection and various emotional factors. There are sex-connected homicides and of course, people kill in self defense."

"Well, I think we can rule out this being a sexual gratification type killing," Mike Cook said.

"I agree. She was single. I certainly want to look at any existing insurance policies she has. But my guess is we can rule out financial gain too," replied Martin.

"By eliminating some of the reasons, it will us help us focus on why she was killed, and maybe by whom."

It was about 5 a.m. when Mike Cook called AUSA Carlos Sanchez and told him that Angela Lyle had been murdered. The last thing Cook wanted now, was a jurisdictional tug of war between the feds and the local police. Sanchez told Cook that he would see to it that this was a joint investigation, even though a potential federal witness had just been murdered. Sanchez was confident that the local district attorney (DA) would understand. If he/she didn't, federal authorities would indeed take charge of the case. But both Cook and Sanchez wanted to avoid that. The final decision would depend on what the local D.A.'s response would be to the murder of Angela Lyle.

At 9 a.m., Detective Tony Martin, much to his pleasant surprise, was standing next to Special Agent Amber Fox inside the county medical examiner's office. They were both looking at the naked body of Angela Lyle lying on a stainless steel table. On the side wall was a hose and bucket. At one end of the table was a drainage tray. An adjustable fluorescent light hung from the side wall and over the table to provide light for Kimiko Matsui who was getting ready to perform the autopsy on Angela. A small microphone was attached to her smock. This would allow her to record the process and any findings she might have during the procedure. At 9:08 that morning, the technicians at the medical examiner's office began to cut and saw and disembowel the body of Angela Lyle while Kimiko Matsui documented her findings.

Kimiko spoke distinctly and without reservation. "File number 766654," she said into the microphone. "The body is that of Angela Lyle, a Caucasian female. Reported age, 43. Height, 5' 5". Weight 128 pounds with light blond hair, and blue eyes. There is a tattoo of a rose on her left ankle."

Kimiko continued with the technical findings of her autopsy. When she was finished, she concluded that there was a large rounded break and bruising on Angela's face along with some pieces of scalp and skull missing. Kimiko's final report would, of course, include details of her findings related to all of the internal organs she would remove from Lyle's body; none of which were of value to contradict her conclusion that Lyle had died from a violent blow to the head. When she was finished with her autopsy, she handed over evidence to Tony Martin which included fibers and hair from Angela's clothing and body surfaces, the clothing itself, vaginal swabs and smears, rectal swabs and smears, oral swabs and smears, fingernail clippings, jewelry, samples of head hair, eyelashes, and eyebrows, as well as fingerprints.

As autopsies go, this one was pretty straight forward. Kimiko removed her smock and told Tony Martin and Amber Fox that her report would show that Angela Lyle had been struck with a violent blow across the back of the head.

"Weapon?" Tony asked.

"Not sure. You find something, I'll try to marry it up. "

"Anything else?"

"Not sure she struggled much. I didn't find any defensive wounds. It was almost as if she was struck by surprise."

Martin nodded. "Got it," he said.

A Brief Discussion on Death Investigation

Murder is one of the most feared crimes of all. If a serial killer is active, it can completely immobilize a community, and drain the resources of the various law enforcement agencies tasked with stopping the killer. As James Osterburg and Richard Ward point out in their bestselling text, *Criminal Investigation, a Method for Reconstructing the Past*, "murder is a word that is associated with fear, fascination, and curiosity."[1] On a side note, I sometimes, find it more beneficial to learn how to do something right by witnessing or leaning how something was done wrong, or learning from one's mistakes. The best book I've found that demonstrates how NOT to conduct a death or homicide investigation is *Murder in Greenwich* by Mark Furhman, which, is listed at the beginning of this chapter under Recommended Reading. However, for the purposes of this chapter let's consider a few things:

First, in an introductory course on criminal investigation it is important to have a discussion on death investigation. However, one of the things that I find so many textbooks trying to do, is push this subject to limits not normally conducive to students being introduced to the concepts of criminal investigation. In other words, we, as professors (and authors) sometimes try to overload our students with too much information that they may not be ready for. The purpose of this chapter is not to provide all the information necessary to cause one to think they might become a homicide investigator. While there are certainly exceptions to almost everything, most homicide investigators are older, more seasoned, and well trained. They have spent years honing their skills to be in a position of responsibility associated with conducting an investigation into someone's death. Instead, our goal with this chapter, is to highlight those issues associated with death investigation that will promote analytical thinking related to death investigations. More specialized training on this subject awaits those of you who continue in this profession and demonstrate the skills necessary to be good investigators.

A homicide is simply the killing of one human being by another. And all homicides are not criminal. Some are actually *justifiable* or *excusable*. For instance, a police officer killing a suspect in the line of duty or, someone killing in self defense would be classified as justifiable. Killing someone by accident without any evidence of gross negligence and without intent to injure, such as a killing a hunter who one might mistake as a deer, could, be classified as an excusable homicide. It would, however, all depend on the circumstances of the case. It would all be in the details and evidence.

Murder on the other hand, is the unlawful killing of another human being with *malice aforethought* (premeditation). However, any investigation into the world of violent crime, such as homicide, suicide, and sex offenses, carries with it some standard procedures of analysis and reconstruction. Homicide involves both the study of victimology and suspectology. In our story, you heard Detective Tony Martin telling Special Agents Mike Cook and Latrelle Jackson, exactly what he wanted to do in order to look into conducting the victimology on Angela Lyle. So, why conduct a victimology assessment on the victim? As Tony Martin told Mike Cook and Latrelle Jackson, conducting a *victimology* aids investigators in discovering why a person was targeted, whether they were known to the offender or not, or, if the victim was simply in the wrong place at the wrong time. At a minimum, investigators conducting a victimology profile or investigation should consider look for:

1. Physical traits
2. Marital status
3. Personal lifestyle
4. Occupation
5. Education
6. Medical/Mental history
7. Criminal justice system history
8. Last known activities, including establishing a timeline of events
9. Map of travel prior to offense
10. Friends and enemies.
11. Telephone records
12. E-mail traffic
13. Romantic affairs

Homicides should be investigated quickly because information and evidence will often lose its freshness and become tainted in short order. There are times when a preliminary walk-through will tell you that the death is by natural or accidental causes. In our story, we learn that Lyle's death was not accidental. However, as a general rule, *you should treat all apparent death scenes as homicides at first.* A suicide can, of course, also be accidental or intentional. The most common accidental deaths involve misuse of firearms and drugs. The most common suicides involve firearms, chemical asphyxiation, overdosing, and hanging and jumping (although sexual asphyxiation is usually classified as accidental). The special case of drowning is equally likely to be either accidental or intentional. With suicides, a note, if one is found or, left behind for loved ones, should be treated as a *questioned document*. Questioned documents are those documents whose origin is unknown and might potentially be disputed in a court of law. With regard to suicide notes, investigators should be suspicious of the origin of the note and the authorship.

When looking at potential suicides such as hanging, carbon monoxide, slashing wrists, firearms and drug overdoses, investigators should look, and investigate, the stressors in one's life, such as the death of a spouse, divorce, marital difficulties, serious illness or disease, being fired at work and, yes, even retirement.

When looking at possible suicides, investigators should also consider conducting what is referred to as a "*psychological autopsy.*" This term, first coined in 1977 by the Los Angeles Medical Examiner's Office, focuses on the manner and circumstances of those deaths suspected to be a suicide. When conducting a psychological autopsy, investigators look at:

1. The alcohol and drug history of the deceased, including dealing with stress, their medical history, and recent stressors in the victim's life including their military history, employment history, educational history, and sexual history.
2. Interpersonal relationships, writings by the deceased, books, and music owned by the deceased. Web sites visited, phone calls made, and hobbies.
3. Reactions from family members, friends, co-workers, and enemies about the victim's death and early warning signs exhibited.
4. The intention of the deceased in their own demise.
5. Fantasies, dreams, thoughts, premonitions, fears, or phobias the deceased may have had.
6. Timeline of events leading up the day of the deceased death.

Homicide investigation

The U.S. does a good job of tracking dead people and determining criminal causes of death. According to recent FBI statistics, there are about 35 homicides in this country every day. In 2012, there were just under 13,000 homicides. Homicide is a crime with a pretty high clearance rate. Almost 65% of all homicides are solved by arrest of the perpetrator. For our purposes, the LAW of homicide needs to be clearly understood. As Osterburg and Ward point out, "Criminal homicide is the unlawful taking of a human life."[1] However, there are two kinds of criminal homicide: murder, which, as stated earlier, is the unlawful killing of another human being with malice aforethought and manslaughter, which is the unlawful killing of another without intent. The degrees of homicide vary from state to state. But some similarities do exist. Such as:

- First degree, often referred to as cold-blooded murder, requires proof of premeditation, deliberation, and malice. Here, the murder is well planned in advance.
- Second degree, normally requires proof of malice aforethought and intent to do bodily harm.
- Voluntary manslaughter usually occurs during the heat of passion. Most statures require proof of provocation allowing the accused no time to cool off. Killing in self-defense is a common defense to a charge of voluntary manslaughter.
- Involuntary manslaughter is most often associated with accidents. Proof that the offender demonstrated a reckless disregard of the consequences must usually be shown. Often, defense attorneys will try to prove insanity as a defense to this charge.

Investigators should treat all cases of death, at first, as a homicide; even suspected suicides. Subtle homicides can slip through the cracks if foul play is not considered and the scene is not documented appropriately. Examine the crime scene for evidence of passion, provocation, and signs of struggle. Analyze the wound patterns, and try to reconstruct what happened from the fingerprints, bloodstains, and ballistics.

Of course, the support of laboratory personnel will be needed for that. And remember, each crime scene helps tell the story. No small item should be overlooked. Record the temperature of the house if the body is inside. Note the temperature if the body is found outdoors. Look for things taken and NOT taken from the crime scene. The crime scene is like a puzzle. Investigators should strive to put the puzzle together. Once they do, it will often create a picture as to what occurred and in what sequence. Remember, the facts derived from the physical evidence and the analysis of the scene drive the theory, not the other way around.

Early in our story, Detective Martin tells Cook and Jackson that he wants to obtain a Mincey Warrant to conduct a crime scene search of the premises where Angela Lyle was found. In 1978, the U.S. Supreme Court ruled that the police can conduct a warrantless search of the crime scene for additional victims or if a killer is still on the premises. And, the police may seize any evidence that is in plain view during the course of this legitimate search. However, the court ruled that the Fourth Amendment does not justify a warrantless search simply because of the seriousness of the offense, in this case, a homicide. The only exception to this rule is if obtaining a warrant would mean that the evidence would be lost, destroyed, or removed in the time necessary to obtain a warrant. And since most every crime scene merits probable cause, obtaining a Mincey Warrant is usually quite easy to do.

In our fictional story, the medical examiner, Kimiko Matsui, explains to Latrelle Jackson, albeit briefly, how rigor mortis assists in determining the time of death. Although dependent on the state of the body prior to death and environmental factors, the de-compositional changes surrounding the onset and regression of rigor mortis follow a general timeline. The following illustrates:

- stiffness in jaw—6 hours after death
- stiffness in upper torso—12 hours after death
- stiffness in whole body—18 hours after death
- limpness returns to body—36 hours after death

Forensic or medical examiners will also look for things such as the contents of the victim's stomach, and insect infestation, to aid in determining time of death. **Forensic entomology**, a relatively new area of study in determining the PMI, is the study of insects as they relate to a criminal investigation. Insect activity, which students will learn more about in advanced courses on homicide investigation, aid medical examiners and forensic examiners in determining PMI based on the type and development of insects and their larvae that are found on or within a decomposed body.

So, why is it that people kill? In our story, Detective Martin explains a few of the reasons people kill; for instance love. Some sociologists prefer the term, "emotional factors." We kill for financial gain; sexual gratification (think serial killers); we kill for self-protection; the removal of an inconvenience or impediment (think witness against us), and of course, there are completely motiveless crimes, such as the Washington D.C. snipers a few years ago who killed just because they wanted to. But kill we do. And finding out why someone was killed is a piece of the puzzle the investigator must look for.

Over the many years of teaching, I've found that students have always been intrigued by the study of serial killers. The fact of the matter is, that the number of investigators in this country focusing their time and energy on serial murders is exceptionally small. Investigators are more apt to be involved in a homicide investigation similar to the one in our story; that is, one body.

As noted several times throughout this text, it is the intent of this author to create a leaning platform to encourage critical and analytical thinking with regard to conducting a criminal investigation. As our story develops, the reader should see how our investigative team is relying on various experts to help with solving the puzzle of the various crimes surfacing throughout this investigation. That is why, if one becomes a good and competent investigator, they should be able to investigate a small theft, burglary, sexual assault, homicide, and yes, even be part of a team that searches for serial killers. Simply put, a good investigator should be able to investigate just about anything, once he/she knows or understands the elements to any particular offense.

While this course, and this text, is not designed to make any student a qualified homicide investigator, no academic discussion of killings would be complete without some brief mention of mass shootings. Students should understand that there are basically two kinds of mass murder. One results from a crime spree spread out over a period of time. The second, is when multiple deaths occur in one, (usually random) shooting incident. Unfortunately, the United States is experiencing a rise in the latter type of shootings. These events, which now seem to grace our television screens on an almost weekly basis, are most often committed by those who have great difficulty coping with society's norms. And while there is some evidence to show that these shootings most often end with the perpetrator shot and killed by the police, it nonetheless, is becoming, what appears to be, an accepted part of our culture. The commonly accepted definition of mass killings includes at least four people shot dead in a public place. And while this definition might exclude some of the more recent shootings in this country, it still suggests that the United States is seeing an increase in this type of criminal activity. University of Alabama professor Adam Lankford, who has completed a study on mass shootings suggests that killing former colleagues, schoolmates, or groups of strangers not only serves as an act of revenge but as a way of forcing the world to be aware of the killer's inner torment. "They fantasize about going out in a blaze of glory. In the United States, fame is revered as an end unto itself, even when the notoriety is negative."[2]

We do seem to be a country caught up in celebrity worship. While mass murderers seem to want revenge and notoriety, serial killers, who are usually male, (although there are exceptions) are more often motivated by a sexual or aggressive drive to exert power and control over their victims through killing.

With that in mind, a short discussion of serial killers should help students understand the complexities involved in dealing with such cases. Without re-inventing the wheel, I rely on a colleague of mine, Richard Walter, who I've had the privilege of teaching a number of cold case seminars with at the Henry Lee School of Criminal Justice and Forensic Sciences in New Haven, Connecticut. Richard is one of the foremost authorities on serial killings and has helped police departments around the world solve some of the most complex murder cases one might ever encounter. He is, indeed, one of the foremost authorities on this subject that you will ever meet.

Murder Typologies & Interrogation Strategies
(Obtained with permission from Richard Walter)

Power-Assertive (PA):

Characteristics—Rape is planned whereas murder is not. Offender uses aggression and demands to justify his manhood, uses intimidation to maintain a machismo appearance. He targets his own age group and leaves an organized crime scene. He will bring the weapon to the scene and leaves with it. He will also set boundaries to his actions (i.e., he won't entirely remove the head). No mutilation of the body, but may see signs of beating, cutting, strangling.

Who is he? He's domineering. He takes pride in his image as a man and is likely to be well built. He may drive a pick-up truck or sports vehicle. He's antisocial and a school dropout. If he has a military record, it is likely poor. He'll brag about his crime in a bar for glory points. He has a phobia of being labeled a "pervert". He'll use weapon such as guns, knives, and ropes.

Power Reassurance (PR):

Characteristics—The offender lives in scripted fantasy world and feels threatened if reality breaks into the fantasy. He acts out fantasies for verbal reassurance from victim. Rape is planned whereas murder is not. Murder is typically a result of a failed rape which leads to overkill and postmortem mutilation. Sexual activity usually occurs postmortem. You would often see wounds to the breasts and groin/thigh areas. The body may have insertions. He avoids women in his own age group and targets those older or younger and chooses familiar locations. He commits attacks during nightly hours and leaves a disorganized crime scene.

Who is he? He's a loner and a "weirdo". Likely to conduct stalker activities prior to the attack. He is concerned about his sexual competence and seeks reassurance and the need to justify his power. If he has a military record, the offender was likely a passive soldier who took orders well. Weapon of choice may be clothing, fists, and knives.

Anger-Retaliatory (AR):

Characteristics—Rape and murder are planned. Typically, the offender commits the attack in a familiar location. The crime is driven by a need to seek revenge against a woman of power or a substitute through anger, sparking a burst of violence. He targets women in the same age group or slightly older. It is a frenzied attack. He leaves a disorganized scene.

Who is he? He's impulsive, self-centered, and pathologically attached to women. He usually has superficial relationships and becomes estranged from marriage or has a history of domestic abuse. If he has a military record, it may show discharge for behavioral issues. Attacks in areas where he's familiar.

Anger-Excitation (AE):

Characteristics—Rape and murder are planned. It is sadistic in nature. The extended torture and killing can be ritualistic. Satisfaction stems from inflicting terror and pain rather than the death itself. It is a crime of luxury. The body may be disposed in an unfamiliar location. A con or ruse may be used to lure the victim. May see signs of cutting, bruising, and ligature marks.

Who is he? He may appear as an average person, conducting a normal life. He's likely well-educated and financially stable. He can separate a normal lifestyle from his criminal activities. He seeks domination and mastery. There may be sexual or non-sexual emotions. The fantasy fuels the ritualistic attack. He's methodical in his actions.

In a follow up interview with Richard Walter as an addendum to his Murder Typologies and Interrogation Strategies, he added, "although an understanding of the crime continuum through the arrangement of the four sub-types (aka DNA of crime) it is pertinent and relevant for general learning in a variety of disciplines, it should not be assumed that they can be applied in everyday work without further specialization and training. In particular, caution and restraint should be applied in the areas of interviewing and interrogation . . . the logical extension of sub-type analysis. Here, without further achievement and definition within a field, an inappropriate training in interviewing and interrogation could/would unwittingly cause confusion, misdirection and dismal results. Again, the wise reader [young student] will wait until the need and/or professional services call for this type of specific training. Otherwise, the impetuous abuser of the skill may quickly find the unseen thorn from walking amongst the dead rosebushes.

"For a proper development, it would seem prudent for the reader's [students] to consider the bifurcated elements of the power and anger continuums. Accordingly, once they identify a type within one of their friends, relatives, enemies or character's on television, they could try to imagine that person having a secret which you would like to reveal. Given some thought, what approach and questions should be posed at the interview? For example, would you pose the same approach and question to various characters from foreign politicians to entertainers or to sports figures.

"Finally, given further education and training, the reader, or student, will learn that each discipline may need to learn different techniques and strategies to achieve the right results.

"In the information game, it is not the answer, but the question which is often the most important and relevant sequence of the issue."[3]

For the purposes of this course, students should know that there are any number of books designed to help investigators understand the do's and don'ts of a homicide investigation. Indeed, several traditional textbooks go into much more detail related to this subject. But this is not a typical textbook. No entry level college course in basic criminal investigation is going to make anyone an instant candidate to become a homicide investigator. What students should understand is the basic concepts relating to the subject of death investigation such as, the legal definition of homicide, the difference between murder and manslaughter; why people kill, the responsibilities of first responders to a murder scene, the importance of the crime scene investigation, and what methodology is used to determine the time of death. Understanding the concepts of victimology and the characteristics and murder typologies, will go a long way to establishing the building blocks of someday becoming a homicide investigator. However, investigators should keep in mind, that there are no absolutes regarding the murder typologies mentioned above. Nor, are there any absolutes regarding the concepts of victimology. These are simply tools. And while they are usually good tools to utilize, I'm tempted to keep in mind the words of one science professor who, many years ago said, "when dealing with living, breathing things, there are no constants."

Another thing to keep in mind is that "every homicide investigation should start at the body. Then it should move out from the body to encompass the surrounding crime scene. The body is the nucleus of the homicide investigation. The body will not lie. The body holds the facts that will lead to the suspect. It is your best witness."[4] I've been telling students for years, it's the one time I believe the dead are actually talking to you. It's up to you to figure out what the deceased is saying.

No detail, no matter how small one might think it is at the time, should not go unnoticed or undocumented. The smallest detail could easily be the key to solving the puzzle associated with a death investigation. Keep in mind, that most good investigators, and most students, when either dealing with the complexities of a crime such as homicide, or in this case, the challenges of answering questions in the exercises below, are most often right. It's just that some are more right than others.

Questions for Discussion

1. What is the legal definition of homicide?
2. What is meant by objectification?
3. Explain the legal differences between murder and manslaughter.
4. What is the difference between justifiable and excusable homicide?
5. What are the most common motives for committing murder?
6. What is the purpose of reconstructing the crime scene?
7. What must Detective Tony Martin establish to prove that Angela Lyle was the victim of a homicide?
8. What is rigor mortis, or postmortem lividity?
9. What is the purpose of an autopsy?
10. What is meant algor mortis?
11. Why does Tony Martin want to know what is in Angela Lyle's refrigerator?
12. Do some research and provide five examples of the type of killings that might involve a charge of 2nd degree homicide.
13. What factors are considered in determining PMI?
14. What is the goal of conducting a victimology work up?
15. Explain the different motivations for killing, for mass murderers, and serial killers.

Work Sheet

Exercises

1. Identify a list of 20 questions related to the death of Angela Lyle that Mike Cook and Tony Martin would want to ask of the following people:

   a. D & B Environmental foreman John Thomas.

   b. Alan Thompson

   c. Eric Mann

2. On Angela Lyle's telephone, Detective Martin found two names to be contacted in case of an emergency (ICE); that of George Lyle and Brandi Gardner. Develop 25 questions for both Lyle and Gardner related to their relationship with Angela and her death. Do not include the name, address and phone number of either George Lyle or Gardner as part of your 25 questions.

3. Conduct a victimology on yourself for the last 48 hours. Create a timeline. Be as honest as you can about your activities in the past 48 hours. Be prepared to discuss. That is what the investigators will be looking to do in the event you are a victim of a crime.

Work Sheet

Notes

1. Osterburg, James W. and Richard H. Ward. *Criminal Investigation: A Method for Reconstructing the Past*. 7th Edition, 372.
2. Adam Lankford, University of Alabama. (2015). *The Week*, 11 September.
3. Interview with Richard Walter. (2015). 12 October.
4. Mark Fuhrman. *Murder in Greenwich*. 95.

Additional Readings

Douglas, John E., Ann W. Burgess, Allen G. Burgess, and Robert K. Ressler. *Crime Classification Manual: A Standard System for Investigating and Classifying Violent Crimes*.

Keppel, R. D. and R. Walter. (1999). Profiling killers: A revised classification model for understanding sexual Murder. *International Journal of Offender Therapy and Comparative Criminology* 43(4).

Lasley, James R. and Nikos R. Guskos with Randy A. Seymour. *Criminal Investigation: An Illustrated Case Study Approach*.

Di Maio, Vincent J. and Susanna E. Dana. (1998). *Handbook of Forensic Pathology*. 21–22. Austin, TX: Landes Biosceince.

Mincey v. Arizona 437 U.S. 385 (1978).

Osterburg, James W. and Richard H. Ward. *Criminal Investigation: A Method for Reconstructing the Past*. 7th Edition.

Ronald F. Becker and Aric W. Dutelle. *Criminal Investigation*. 4th Edition.

Shneidman, Edwin S. (1994). The psychological autopsy. *American Psychologist* 49(1):75–76, January. http://dx.doi.org/10.1037/0003-066X.49.1.75.

Spitz, Werner U. M.D. and Daniel J. Spitz, M.D. *Medicolegal Investigation of Death, Guidelines for the Application of Pathology of Crime Investigation*. 4th Edition.

Thomas O'Connor, Dr. Austin Peay State University.

Walter, Richard. Scholar in Residence, Oklahoma State University.

https://www.fbi.gov/about-us/cjis/ucr/crime-in-the-u.s/2012/crime-in-the-u.s.-2012/offenses-known-to-law-enforcement/expanded-homicide/expandhomicidemain.

CHAPTER 13
CONSPIRACY AND ORGANIZED CRIME

"Organized crime conspiracy crimes are the most elusive and painstaking investigations that law enforcement agencies encounter."

Thomas E. Baker
Intelligence-Led Policing
Leadership, Strategies & Tactics

"It's no secret that organized crime in America takes in over forty billion dollars a year.
     This is quite a profitable sum, especially when one considers that the Mafia spends very little for office supplies."

Woody Allen

"(Of Organized Crime) We're Bigger than U.S. Steel"

Meyer Lanskey

Chapter Objectives

1. Describe what constitutes organized crime.
2. Understand the definition of conspiracy.
3. Identify the tools and techniques used to investigate conspiracy and organized crime.
4. Understand the provisions of the RICO Act.
5. Understand what enterprise crime is.
6. Become familiar with the various types of organized crime groups.

Recommended Reading

1. *Takedown: The Fall of the Last Mafia Empire*, by Rick Cowan and Douglas Century.
2. *Wise Guy: Life in a Mafia Family*, by Nicholas Pileggi.

Figure 13.1 Meyer Lansky being escorted by federal agents after indictment.

Mike Cook and Latrelle Jackson knocked on John Thomas' farm house door just after 6 a.m. It was still dark outside but they were sure someone was inside and awake since the house was lit up. Thomas answered the door fully dressed and ready to leave the house for work. He was surprised to see Mike Cook at that early hour of the morning.

"Mr. Thomas," Cook began. "Sorry to bother you so early in the morning. This is Special Agent Latrelle Jackson of the Environmental Protection Agency. We have some bad news. Can we come inside?"

"What's this all about?"

"It's about Angela Lyle. She's been murdered."

"Murdered? What do you mean? I spoke to her last night!"

"We know. That's why we want to talk to you. Can we please come in?"

Thomas invited the two men inside. "Please, have a seat," Thomas said pointing to chairs at the kitchen table. "What happened?"

"She was killed last night. Can you tell us where you were last night between the hours of 5 and 8 p.m.?" Cook asked.

"I was home."

"Can anyone verify that?"

"My wife can. But she's asleep. What's going on here?"

"It seemed you were the last person to speak to her, at least according to her cell phone. In fact, the cell phone records show that you talk to her a lot."

"We were friends," Thomas replied.

"Just friends?" Cook asked.

"This is very difficult for me right now."

"I can understand that. But how can we talk about it so that you'll be more comfortable?"

Thomas didn't respond. He simply stood in his kitchen with his head held low.

Mike Cook said, "Mr. Thomas, we're looking for any help we can get regarding Angela's murder. You talked to her shortly before she was killed. And you talked to her a good bit. We also know that you two worked together. I would think you'd want to help find out what really happened."

"I have no idea what happened."

"Well, we also know that not all the hazardous waste that was picked up from various places made its way to any approved disposal facility. So we're looking for your help. This is a good time for you to get on the right side of this. Let us help you."

"We had a brief affair," Thomas said. "But we ended it recently."

"When did you end it?"

"Right after someone tried to blow the plant up."

"Why then?"

"I told her we were both in over our heads."

"What do you mean by that?"

"Angela was very smart. She was good with the numbers. She could do things with the books and the balance sheet that most people had no idea of. She could hide money with the best of them. And that's what they had her do. She managed the books and doctored the numbers."

"What about the invoices and manifests related to the waste?" Latrelle asked.

"That too," Thomas replied.

"She told you all of this?" Cook asked.

"She did. We'd talk about it."

"Did she say who she was doing it for?"

"Thompson and Mann. That's who she was doing it for."

"Do you know why?"

"Money. We all did it for the money."

"What do you mean by all?"

"I did it too. I didn't realize it at first. They told me it wasn't a problem. I had no idea exactly what I was doing. I thought it was a way to simply make a little extra money."

"What is it exactly that you did?"

"I let them bury a bunch of this stuff on my farm. They told me they contracted with people all the time to bury this stuff. That it wasn't harmful. So I said okay."

Latrelle asked, "Where is this stuff buried?"

Thomas turned and pointed out the kitchen window. "There. Just beyond those trees. We carved out about ten acres for them. They buried a bunch of waste out there."

"Where exactly?"

"There. Where the corn is growing."

"You're growing corn on top of the waste dump?" Latrelle asked.

"Yes. Last year's crop was the best ever. This year's should even be better."

For a brief moment, Mike Cook and Latrelle Jackson were speechless. The two investigators' eyes shifted as they stared at each other. Jackson ran his hand across the cheeks of his face feeling the stubble of a beard that had not been shaved in the past 24 hours. Mike Cook knew that in a situation such as this, where a witness and potential suspect to a large conspiracy was talking, dead silence could prove to be disastrous. Cook had to keep the conversation going.

"When did this happen?"

"About a year and half ago."

"And who asked you to do this?"

"Eric Mann. Said it wasn't a problem if we buried it."

"And he paid you?"

"Five thousand dollars," Thomas replied.

"You ever talk to Alan Thompson about this?"

"Not really. Dealt mostly with Mann. Thompson did thank me once for helping out the company. But that was all he said."

"Any idea who might have wanted to kill Angela?"

"Had to be Mann and or Thompson. I think she might have started seeing Mann around the time we broke it off."

"What makes you say that?"

"Just a hunch. Things were going south for us before someone tried to blow the plant up. After that, when I told her I suspected Mann and Thompson of being involved, she said I was crazy. She defended Mann a bit too much."

"Did she offer any idea as to who might have tried to blow the plant up?" Cook asked.

"Not really. Thought it might have been a competitor. But she was convinced Mann and Thompson had nothing to do with it."

"And you? What do you think?"

"What is going on here?" Sandy Thomas asked as she walked into the kitchen wearing a robe.

Cook introduced himself along with Latrelle Jackson.

"Sorry to be here so early Mrs. Thomas. We needed to ask your husband some questions about D & B Engineering and Angela Lyle," Cook said.

"Angela was killed last night," Thomas told his wife.

"Killed. How?"

"Medical examiner is still working on that," Cook replied.

"John, does this have anything to do with someone trying to blow the plant up?"

"I don't know," Thomas replied.

"This is awful. You two look like you can use some coffee," Sandy said. "Please sit down."

She served them coffee and cinnamon rolls that she had warmed in the oven. It was a gesture that Mike Cook appreciated more than Sandy could have imagined.

"So, John, tell me; any idea who might want to kill Angela?" Cook asked.

"She got along with everyone as far as I could tell. But I think she knew too much about D & B illegally disposing of the waste."

"So you're saying Thompson and Mann?"

"I'm not saying anything other than she knew a lot about the things the company shouldn't have been doing."

"What do you mean by things the company shouldn't have been doing and illegally disposing of waste?" asked Sandy.

Latrelle Jackson said, "The waste buried on your farm is illegal. It's an environmental hazard. It's going to have to be dug up."

"Does that mean we have to give the money back?" Sandy asked.

Latrelle and Mike looked at each other again, both men dumbfounded by the question. Mike ran his hands through his hair and said, "No. You don't have to give the money back."

"Any other ideas what they were doing with the waste?"

"I know they were taking a lot of it to Mann's brother-in-laws place about a hundred miles from here; just over the state line."

"What place is that?" Latrelle demanded.

"Crane Environmental. They have a license to dispose of a lot of the waste D &B wasn't authorized to destroy."

"And Crane is owned by Mann's brother-in-law?" Jackson asked.

"That's what Angela told me."

"Do you know the brother-in-law's name?"

"Ralph Browning, I think."

"What do you know about the plane that Mann owned; the one that was blown up?" Cook asked.

"Not much. He'd use it for company business. Sometimes he'd lease it out. Or so I heard. Really never talked to him much about it."

"Can we walk outside. I'd like you to show me exactly where the waste is buried. What section of the farm is it in?" Latrelle asked.

The three men walked outside just as the sun was starting to rise casting a golden shadow on Thomas' corn field. As they entered the corn field, Cook and Jackson could see that the area Thomas was showing them, where he claimed the waste was buried, was adjacent to a river.

"Where does this river go?" Jackson asked.

"About 15 miles south of here where it meets another river."

"Isn't that the river that supplies water for three counties south of here?"

"I think so," Thomas replied. "Why?"

Cook and Jackson just stared at each other; neither wanting to think about the answer to Thomas' question.

"Did you actually drive the waste out here yourself?" Mike asked.

"Me, no."

"Well who did?"

"It was usually Sammy."

"Sammy Collins?"

"Yeah, that's him. He drove all the waste out here to the farm."

"We interviewed him right after they tried to blow D & B up."

"I know. He didn't tell you anything. Eric Mann was paying him extra to drive the trucks out here. I think he's paying him a bit more to keep his mouth shut too."

"And how about you John; is he paying you to keep your mouth shut too?"

"Nope. Just said the government was going to try and make something out of nothing. That he and Alan Thompson would try and find out who was trying to put them out of business."

It was nearly 1 p.m. by the time Tony Martin and Amber Fox met Mike Cook and Latrelle Jackson at Martin's office. Martin had a numb ache in his shoulders. He attributed it to the lack of sleep in the past 24 hours. He didn't complain however. He knew that Cook and Jackson had been up all night too. Only Amber Fox appeared rested and refreshed. Tony Martin felt obligated to apologize for his appearance and the fact that they all needed a shower. Amber smiled, and said, "This isn't my first time working with guys who have been up all night."

Cook and Jackson spent the first 30-minutes briefing Tony and Amber as to what John Thomas had told them.

"Where is Thomas now?" Martin asked.

"Work. I told him to go in as if he knew nothing. And to not tell anyone we'd been out to see him," Cook replied.

"Think he'll keep his mouth shut?" Tony asked.

"I do. He knows he's in trouble regarding burying the waste on his property."

"What are we going to do about him?" Martin asked.

"He's a wealth of information. I'd like to get him immunity on the environmental violations. Latrelle, what are your thoughts on that?"

"I have no problem with it. Get Sanchez to okay it quickly. Because we have to dig that land up, and soon. And we'll need a warrant for that."

"Will Thomas give us his consent to search his farm?" Tony asked.

"I think he will. So we can move quickly," Latrelle replied. "But let's get a search warrant anyway. A consent-to-search can be revoked at anytime. And, it opens us up to attack by the defense if we go to trial."

Mike nodded in agreement.

"I'll get to work on it today," Latrelle said.

"Do you think he had anything to do with Angela's murder?" Tony asked.

"I don't think so. He admitted to having an affair with her but that she was breaking it off around the time someone tried to blow up D & B. I think he was relieved that the affair was ending."

"Will he testify?"

"He's not going to have a choice."

Mike Cook looked at Amber and said, "Any thoughts on this?"

"Yes. Crane Environmental comes up in our preliminary inquiry into D & B's contracts. It seems D & B was using Crane to dispose of some of the waste they were picking up and transporting. At least that's what their invoices say."

"Your theory?"

"Depending on the waste we find at Thomas' farm, we might be able to show that Mann and Thompson conspired with Ralph Browning and Crane to falsify invoices showing that Crane properly disposed of the waste.

"Sounds good."

"Will it be possible to trace some of the waste we find on that farm?" Amber asked.

"It's possible. We'll just have to see what we dig up," Latrelle replied.

"What about the murder of Angela Lyle?" Mike Cook asked.

Tony Martin gave everyone in the room a detailed account of what the medical examiner had found. "We have no weapon," Tony said. "And right now, my gut tells me it has something to do with Mann and Thompson. Mike, I think you and I go out to D & B now and see these two guys. Amber, can you get everything you can on Crane Environmental. I want to know the value of all the contracts they had with D & B or directly with the DoD. Latrelle, can you go see Sanchez and tell him what we want to do with John Thomas. Also, what's your move regarding the farm?"

"After I see Sanchez and talk about immunity for Thomas and see if a consent search will suffice, I'm going to contact our National Enforcement Investigations Center in Denver and talk to our folks about getting an environmental team down here to dig up the 10 acres of Thomas' farm."

"How many of our agents and support personnel are we going to need for this search?" Mike asked.

"Almost none other than a patrol presence to protect the scene 24/7 once we start the search."

Mike Cook said, "I don't understand."

"Our guys will come in with a team of scientists and engineers. They'll dig up the land, gather the samples, document the chain of custody and run the tests for us. Once they start, that section of land will be deemed a hazardous site. All of us who enter it will have to undergo a de-contamination process. Don't worry, these guys know what they're doing. And we're going to have to get the water tested ASAP. That could open a whole new can of worms for us. I suggest everyone brief their supervisors. Depending on what the water tests show, this will change everything. I've seen this before. Tell the bosses to get ready for a media frenzy. Tony, can you arrange to have a patrol unit sit on this site at the end of each day until the team starts back up in the morning?"

"That shouldn't be a problem," Tony replied.

"This is just great," Mike said, rubbing his hands over his face and eyes. "Ask Sanchez if we can get Thomas in front of a grand jury sooner than later. I want his testimony locked in ASAP. And tell him we might have a RICO case here."

"A RICO case?" asked Tony Martin who sounded puzzled.

"Yes, RICO; also known as Racketeer Influenced and Corrupt Organizations Act. This has been around since 1970. We've used it a number of times."

"Isn't that specifically designed for organized crime?" Tony asked.

"Initially, that was no doubt the intent. But since then, the RICO statutes have been used in a variety of criminal investigations involving ongoing criminal conspiracies and organized crime activity. And the definition of organized crime has changed. If this case doesn't involve a major conspiracy and a criminal organization, I don't know what does. So Latrelle, please tell Sanchez I'll be in touch soon to lay out why I think RICO applies here."

"Will do," Latrelle said. "But how will that actually help us?"

"We can use the asset forfeiture provision of RICO to seize assets. The theory behind this is simply to take the profit out of committing crime. We know that many criminal enterprises mirror legitimate businesses. Obviously, the big difference here is that they generate money from illegal activity. If we can prove a RICO violation, we seize many of their assets. That means their business, homes, cars, and so forth."

Tony Martin simply wanted to lay down on a bed for a few moments to clear his head. But that would have to wait. Angela Lyle had suffered a violent death. And finding her killer was now his sole priority. If working with the feds to see who was illegally disposing of hazardous waste and trying to blow things up would help him find her killer, then so be it. Because right now, he had little else to go on.

Tony said to Mike Cook, "Let's get going. I want to see what Mann and Thompson have to say about this."

"So do I Mike; so do I."

A Brief Discussion about Conspiracy and Organized Crime

"The famous police administrator, O.W. Wilson, advocated war as the primary threat to society. Second to war is crime—the supreme threat. Organized crime is a form of warfare against global societies and attacks their basic institutions."[1]

The common law definition defines criminal conspiracy as: (1) two or more persons, and (2) an agreement to violate the criminal law. Basically, a criminal conspiracy exists when two or more people agree to commit almost any unlawful act, then take some action toward its completion. The action taken need not itself be a crime, but it must indicate that those involved in the conspiracy knew of the plan and intended to break the law, or, what is referred to as, the *underlying crime*. For instance, you agree to drive an underage person to the local liquor store for the purpose of purchasing beer for a double keg party someone in the dorm is throwing, knowing that the person buying the beer is underage, and, has a fake driver's license to show that he or she is old enough to buy the alcohol. You, driving that person to the liquor store, is not a crime in itself, that is, the act of simply driving an automobile. However, because you drove that person to the liquor store, and he or she bought the alcohol using false identification, you, even though you sat in the car, are guilty of the conspiracy. A pretty simplistic example, yes. But you get the idea.

Let's see if we can kick it up a notch. One person may be charged with and convicted of both conspiracy and the underlying crime based on the same circumstances. For example, Andy, Dan, and Alice plan a bank robbery. They (1) visit the bank first to assess security, (2) pool their money and buy a gun together, and (3) write a demand letter. All three can be charged with conspiracy to commit robbery, regardless of whether the robbery itself is actually attempted or completed.[2] There is no limit to the number of people who can participate in a conspiracy. And, individuals can be guilty of conspiracy even if they don't know each other. Under federal conspiracy laws, a conspiracy to commit a federal crime happens whenever there is an agreement to commit a specific federal crime between two or more people, and at least one of those people makes some overt act to further the conspiracy.[3] Students should keep in mind that this overt act, in itself, need not be a crime. Agreeing to rob a bank with two or more individuals, and one of the people with whom the agreement is made purchases ski masks, satisfies the overt act requirement.

"The mens rea (subjective mental element requirement) consists of two parts: (1) the defendant must actually possess the intent to commit the crime of conspiracy, and (2) co-conspirators must intend to complete the criminal act or objective. Under common law, the requirement for conspiracy is in place when conspirators reach the criminal agreement."[4]

As Thomas E. Baker points out in his excellent book, *Organized Crime Conspiracies*, "the essence of the conspiracy statute is simple—criminal agreement."[5] Baker also points out, that, "co-conspirators are liable for the criminal acts of other criminal conspiracy members. The *Vicarious Liability Principle* holds them accountable."[6] The vicarious liability principle holds a person liable for the actions of another person who, or when, they are engaged in some form of joint or collective activity. In other words, you're accountable for the actions of others when you join in a conspiracy.

Baker also argues that to ideally prosecute someone in a conspiracy, investigators would be well served to, "have one member of the conspiracy withdraw and testify against the co-conspirators. Or, give the conspirator immunity to testify against the others."[7]

Organized crime comes in many forms. No doubt, most everyone has seen a variety of Hollywood movies including *Scarface, Goodfellas,* the *Godfather* trilogy, or the television show *The Sopranos,* to get a feel for how organized crime is perceived in many circles. But organized crime comes in many forms. There are Asian gangs that smuggle humans to the United States for the sole purpose of prostitution. Russian gangs, (which tend to operate in larger cities such as New York, Boston, Chicago, Philadelphia and Miami) are engaging, among other things, in credit card fraud and extortion. Organized Chinese gangs, known as the Triad, are engaging in money laundering, prostitution, extortion, and drugs. There are Mexican and Columbian drug cartels; there is the Yakuza in Japan whose internal structure is very similar to what we refer to as the Italian mafia in this country. And, there are motorcycle gangs in this country that fit the definition of organized crime, and, who specialize in crimes associated with extortion, murder for hire, and both drug and arms trafficking. And these are just a few of the organized crime groups operating throughout the United States and the world.

There are many definitions of organized crime. One that I find most applicable suggests that:

> "Organized crime is crime committed by criminal organizations whose existence has continuity over time and across crimes, and that use systematic violence and corruption to facilitate their criminal activities. These criminal organizations have varying capacities to inflict economic, physical, psychological, and societal harm. The greater their capacity to harm, the greater the danger they pose to society."[8]

Organized crime groups engage in a wide variety of criminal enterprises including money laundering, insurance fraud, computer crime, terrorist activities, arms trafficking, trafficking in people, and illegal drug trafficking. Many of these organized crime groups, identified above, have, within their organization, or, on their payroll, people whose job it is to simply protect them. These people include lawyers, bankers, and legitimate business people. Some of these people also include judges and financial advisors. And yes, police officers; many of whom have been charged and convicted of providing inside information to organized criminal groups.

There has been some movement by criminologists to redefine the definition of organized crime to include the term enterprise crime. Enterprise crime, according to James Osterburg and Richard Ward in their book, *Criminal Investigation, A method for reconstructing the past,* includes, "a much broader range of criminal activity than what is commonly thought of as traditional organized crime; it is characterized by criminal networks and illegal relationships, and more recently, by other primary goals of individuals involved in enterprise criminality."[9]

What we're seeing is a rapid growth in what is referred to as transnational criminal organizations. These organizations seek to exploit financial markets. As Osterburg and Ward point out, "enterprise criminals differ from traditional law breakers in several ways. They represent a greater economic threat to society, are much more difficult to investigate and bring to trial and conviction, and are usually self-perpetuating."[10] Simply put, by self-perpetuating, these criminal groups can go on for indefinite periods of time, regardless of changes in the organizations structural hierarchy. In other words, if they lose some soldiers, or the head of the organization, others will step in to replace them.

Investigating these types of organizations are literally, the most challenging of crimes for law enforcement to investigate. These groups exist to "make money." And, it is essential that they reinvest their illegal money into legitimate businesses. As discussed in Chapter 10, knowing how to investigate money laundering is an essential tool for today's investigator. But investigators should always keep in mind, that the primary motivator in organized crime is fear. Fear garners respect. Without dominating through fear and often bloodshed, the organized crime boss will realize little to no respect. Violence is an essential factor in virtually every organized criminal empire. Without it, the organization is simply not a significant factor in the world of organized crime.

Another pathway to investigating these types of organizations, is gathering intelligence. Identify your target. Discover how the organization is structured. Determine what crime(s) are they most engaged in. Where might they be vulnerable? Collect information through sources and informants, newspaper articles, public records, and Internet sources. As discussed in Chapter 5, informants should be cultivated and used whenever possible. And, as noted in Chapter 5, informants who have been arrested are often looking for some "prison time" relief. Members of organized crime who are arrested on RICO charges face very long sentences. RICO offers law enforcement a number of investigative tools. Often, people faced with such long sentences are apt to help law enforcement in return for some sort of reduced prison sentence. "In many cases, the threat of a RICO indictment can force defendants to plead guilty to lesser charges, in part because the seizure of assets would make it difficult to pay a defense attorney. Despite its harsh provisions, a RICO-related charge is considered easy to prove in court, as it focuses on patterns of behavior as opposed to criminal acts."[11]

Surveillance and undercover operations are still yet more tools in the investigators' arsenal in their attempt to fight organized crime. "Surveillances and undercover operations offer opportunities to learn about suspect activities and relationships."[12] There are a variety of types of surveillance activities law enforcement might engage in. Some include, foot surveillance, vehicle surveillance, one and two person surveillances. Other types of surveillance include using a mail cover to learn what mail the target is receiving. A mail cover is traditionally authorized for 30 days and usually requested by U.S. Postal inspectors or other law enforcement agencies based on an application that they have reasonable grounds to suspect someone of having committed a felony or having engaged in a violation a federal statue. While people might tend to use the mail much less frequently these days, with the quick and easy access to the Internet through a variety of devices, many of which fit into the palm of one's hand, what one receives in the mail, can, and does occasionally consist of valuable information about the target of an investigation. Keep in mind, this is just one of a number of "surveillance" techniques available to investigators. A more detailed discussion of the various surveillance techniques available to law enforcement is better found in Thomas E. Baker's excellent book, *Organized Crime Conspiracies, Investigator Strategies & Tactics*. What is more important than using a mail cover as a surveillance technique, is using electronic and media devices as a surveillance tool and method. Again, a strong background in computer technology will aid investigators in a range of surveillance activity from monitoring one's location to tracking money through various banks and other financial institutions.

The employment of trained and competent analysts is also an invaluable tool in the fight against organized crime.

One brief note on the subject of asset forfeiture. Students should be aware of the federal governments asset forfeiture provisions as it's a valuable law enforcement tool if one is able to use it. There are two types of forfeiture actions; criminal and civil. A criminal forfeiture action must be judicial, that is, the property subject to forfeiture is actually identified or named in the same indictment that charges the defendant in a criminal violation. A civil forfeiture is an action against property. The link at the end of this chapter provides more information on the topic of asset forfeiture.

The following are the standard instructions given by a judge to jurors in a trial where defendants are charged with conspiracy to commit arson.

8.2 CONSPIRACY TO COMMIT ARSON (18 U.S.C. § 81)

The defendant is charged in [Count _____ of] the indictment with conspiracy to commit arson in violation of Section 81 of Title 18 of the United States Code. In order for the defendant to be found guilty of that charge, the government must prove each of the following elements beyond a reasonable doubt:

First, beginning on or about [*date*], and ending on or about [*date*], there was an agreement between two or more persons to commit arson; and

Second, the defendant became a member of the conspiracy knowing of its object and intending to help accomplish it.

As used in this instruction "arson" is the intentional setting of a fire to or burning [*specify building*] located on [*specify place of federal jurisdiction*], which is wrongful and without justification.

A conspiracy is a kind of criminal partnership—an agreement of two or more persons to commit one or more crimes. The crime of conspiracy is the agreement to do something unlawful; it does not matter whether the crime agreed upon was committed.

For a conspiracy to have existed, it is not necessary that the conspirators made a formal agreement or that they agreed on every detail of the conspiracy. It is not enough, however, that they simply met, discussed matters of common interest, acted in similar ways, or perhaps helped one another. You must find that there was a plan to commit arson.

One becomes a member of a conspiracy by willfully participating in the unlawful plan with the intent to advance or further some object or purpose of the conspiracy, even though the person does not have full knowledge of all the details of the conspiracy. Furthermore, one who willfully joins an existing conspiracy is as responsible for it as the originators. On the other hand, one who has no knowledge of a conspiracy, but happens to act in a way which furthers some object or purpose of the conspiracy, does not thereby become a conspirator. Similarly, a person does not become a conspirator merely by associating with one or more persons who are conspirators, nor merely by knowing that a conspiracy exists.

[If you decide that the defendant is guilty, you must then decide whether the government has proved beyond a reasonable doubt that [the building was regularly used by people as a place in which to live and sleep] [a person's life was placed in jeopardy].]

Questions for Discussion

1. What is an underlying crime?
2. What is enterprise crime?
3. What is RICO?
4. What are the provisions of the RICO Act? Do some research. How does this act help investigators? What are the underlying crimes associated with RICO? How might the asset forfeiture provisions of RICO aid investigators?
5. Define conspiracy.
6. Define organized crime.
7. What is meant by asset forfeiture? (Do some independent research.)

Work Sheet

Exercises

1. Write up a report of interview for John Thomas.
2. Prepare a one-page briefing paper supporting an argument to include RICO violations in this ongoing investigation.
3. Identify a list of 20 questions that should be asked to Mann and Thompson directly related to questioning them about the death of Angela Lyle. Remember, name, address, phone number, do not count as part of the 20 questions.
4. Prepare a list of 15 questions to ask the character Sammy Collins. Remember, name, address, and phone number don't count.

Work Sheet

Websites

1. https://www.fbi.gov/about-us/investigate/white_collar/asset-forfeiture.

Notes

1. Thomas E. Baker. *Organized Crime Conspiracies: Investigator Strategies & Tactics*, pg. 91.
2. http://criminal.findlaw.com/criminal-charges/conspiracy.html.
3. https://www.whitecollarcrimeresources.com/federal-conspiracy-charges.html.
4. Baker, ibid. pg. 33.
5. Ibid. pg. 34.
6. Ibid. pg. 35.
7. Ibid. pg. 191.
8. James O. Finckenauer and Yuri A. Voronin. (2001). The Threat of Russian Organized Crime, National Institute of Justice, pg. 2. June.
9. Ward, pg. 593.
10. Ibid. pg. 593.
11. Sanders, Alain and Painton, Priscilla (August 21, 1989). Law: Showdown at Gucci. *Time*. Retrieved September 30, 2009.
12. Baker, ibid. pg. 91.

References

http://www3.ce9.uscourts.gov/jury-instructions/node/457.
https://www.fbi.gov/about-us/investigate/white_collar/asset-forfeiture.

CHAPTER 14
CASE SUMMARY

© Rawpixel.com/Shutterstock.com

"The general public might think that by the time the suspect in a major investigation is arrested, the work of the investigators end, but in reality, it gets more intense."

Joseph Wambaugh, Fire Lover

Chapter Objectives

1. Understand the statutes involving:

   A. Federal mail fraud, (U.S. Code Title 18, Section 1341)
   B. Importation, Manufacture, Distribution and storage of Explosive Materials (18 U.S. Code Chapter 40)
   C. Arson, (U.S. Code Title 18, Chapter 5)
   D. Money Laundering, (U.S. Code, Title 18, Sections 1956 & 1957)
   E. False Claims, (U.S. Code, Title 31, Section 3729)
   F. Illegal disposal of hazardous waste, (42 U.S.C. 6928(d) (2) (A)
   G. False statements; (U.S. Code, Title 18, Section 1001)

2. Gain an understanding of the evidence necessary to charge:

    A. Money Laundering
    B. Arson
    C. False Claims
    D. Illegal disposal of hazardous waste.
    E. False Statements
    F. Murder

Mike Cook awoke early that morning. It was unusually cool for that time of year. He took his breakfast of tomato juice, dry toast, and coffee at his small kitchen table in his apartment before driving to the office. It had been eight weeks since Angela Lyle's death. What had begun with a simple telephone call to investigate the destruction of a small private airplane and the attempted arson of a business, blossomed into a task force investigating a host of state and federal crimes, including murder. Mike Cook had no way of knowing that the early morning wake-up call he'd received from detective Tony Martin would result in him having to deal with a cast of investigators from other agencies, lawyers, and support personnel, who were now filing into the ATF conference room to review where everyone was at with regard to their part in this investigation. And now, as he entered the large conference room, he saw, sitting in the back against the wall and not at the table, his boss, Lisa Swanson. Lisa looked up, smiled briefly, and took a sip of her coffee.In instances like these, Lisa found that it was best to let the lead case agent run things. She was there to observe and offer whatever help and guidance she could, if and when it was requested. Lisa was of the opinion that it was her job to make sure her agents had whatever they needed to do their job; not to get in the way of it.

Mike Cook sat at the head of the table in the windowless conference room. The room was designed that way based on a bureaucratic theory that not being able to look out of a window would keep people's minds from wandering off topic. To his immediate right was Detective Tony Martin. To his immediate left was AUSA Carlos Sanchez. To Sanchez's left sat Latrelle Jackson and Amber Fox. Seated around the rest of the table for this first all hands meeting of what Cook and Martin privately and jokingly referred to as the "cast of thousands task force" were the other participants who played an active role in this investigation.

Mike started the meeting by welcoming everyone and giving an overview of the time line of events leading up to this meeting.

"Let me begin by telling everyone that Tony Martin and I tried talking to both Eric Mann and Alan Thompson. As soon as they learned that Angela Lyle had been murdered and that they were suspected of having illegally disposed of hazardous waste, both men requested an attorney. Of course, that immediately ended our effort to get any more information out of them.

"We also interviewed Sammy Collins, a truck driver for D & B who, we learned, had driven the illegal waste to John Thomas' farm and helped bury it on the property. According to Collins, who was convinced to cooperate as soon as he realized he faced a potentially long prison sentence, he was approached by Alan Thompson to transport the waste to the farm. Collins also claimed that he was paid about $100 for every extra trip he made, which, was in addition to his regular salary. Collins also claims that he made about 100 trips to the farm unloading the waste from one of the D & B's dump trucks. Collins testimony has been secured by AUSA Sanchez, who has agreed to grant him immunity from prosecution for his cooperation.

"Six weeks ago, we executed a search warrant at John Thomas' farm. As many of you know, this search took almost five full days to complete. With the help of The Environmental Protection Agency's National Enforcement Investigations Center in Denver, we dug up approximately ten acres of land on Thomas' farm. The search revealed a large variety of hazardous waste that had been illegally buried there. Rachael Flynn is here with us from Denver. Rachael, can you tell us what you learned?"

Rachael Flynn enjoyed a well respected reputation in scientific circles. Based in Denver with EPA's NEI, she had worked her entire career there after graduating with her Master's Degree in forensic science at Michigan State University. Rachael rose quickly through the ranks becoming a team supervisor in five years. "As some of you know," Rachael began, "one of our objectives related to this search was to gather the facts related to what, if any exposures were, or are, dangerous or safe. And, if the exposures are dangerous, to determine what is causing the environmental problem. Using a team of forensic scientists and engineers from our NEI center, we spent five days digging up approximately ten acres of land on the farm belonging to John Thomas. We uncovered approximately 600 cans of toxic waste in fifty gallon drums, much of which had seeped into the ground.

"We took samples from the ground, air, and from the water from the adjacent river next to the farm. As you might know, toxic waste can, and is, often very difficult to see, taste, or smell. And, is often difficult at best to prove and investigate. This is not the case here. We were able to identify many of the drums we dug up as the stickers were still on many of them. And, using a variety of scientific tests, which, I will not bore everyone with here in this meeting, we were able to prove that most of the drums contained waste that is classified by EPA as hazardous.

"We also took samples from the water immediately adjacent to the farm where the waste was buried, as well as one mile, three miles, and five miles downstream. From those sites, our analysis did not show any measurable pollutants in the water that could be attributed to the waste recovered from Thomas' farm. In other words, the good news here is that the water was not contaminated. We got to it early because my experience tells me that it was only a matter of time before that happened. For now, the water is fine. But there is ground contamination. What is important, is that this was not an unintentional contamination. We can show that this was a deliberate contamination attributed directly to illegal waste-hauling practices.

"I have a complete report here of the tests that were conducted, the methodology that was used, the people involved, and, the chain of custody for all the materials we removed and tested."

"And what happened to the waste that you didn't test?" AUSA Sanchez asked.

"We had it transported to an approved facility for destruction," replied Latrelle Jackson. "I have the reports on that."

Mike Cook said, "Thank you Rachael. Let's follow up on that a little. Latrelle, can you tell us what you found out about Crane Environmental?"

Latrelle said, "While Rachael and her team were conducting the search of Thomas' farm, EPA and DCIS executed a search warrant on Crane Environmental. During the search, Ralph Browning refused to answer any of our questions. We seized computers, along with several boxes of company records. Along with the records Mike and Tony seized from the day of the attempt to blow up D & B Environmental, Amber and I were able to find over forty-two instances where waste was shown to have been legally disposed of at Crane, it was in fact, buried on the John Thomas' farm. We can prove that the documents in the possession of both D & B and Crane showing the proper and legal disposal of the waste are false."

Mike Cook said, "Amber, anything to add to that?"

"Yes. In addition to the forty-two false documents, I was able to trace eight of those back to contracts D & B had with the Department of Defense to haul and dispose of waste. In each of those eight instances, electronic documents show that D & B certified to the DoD that the waste was legally hauled and disposed of at Crane Environmental. We know this is not the case since those containers or drums, were dug up on Thomas' farm by Rachael and her team. DoD subsequently transferred funds to D & B to satisfy payment in connection with those contracts. It will be difficult to prove that either Alan Thompson or Eric Mann actually sent the electronic documents. In fact, we think, based on what we know about who handled most all of the office invoicing and payments that it was sent by Angela Lyle. Our techs are working with EPA's techs to determine who the electronic signature belongs to."

"Where did the money get sent?" AUSA Sanchez asked.

Alan Pinette said, "I can show that the money went directly into the account of D & B for each of those invoices."

"So D & B did get the money?" Sanchez said.

"For the invoices with DoD that Amber is talking about, yes."

"And was Crane paid any money for these eight DoD contracts?" Sanchez asked.

"Not that I can find in their financial records," Pinette replied. "Working with DoD and their auditors, we can show that the D & B did receive the money from DoD for those eight contracts. We can also show that they, D & B that is, submitted false written or electronic statements to a government agency, in this case, the DoD, and that this false statement is a material fact that influenced the outcome of that agency's actions. The action here is that the government paid the claim and suffered a loss. We can also show that D & B submitted false statements to the DoD that the waste in question was legally disposed of at Crane Environmental when, in fact, it was buried on John Thomas' farm."

"Did your financial analysis of D & B indicate anything else?" Mike asked.

"I went over so many stacks of papers that it made the Dead Sea Scrolls look like a Harlequin novel," Pinette said, not realizing he was adding some levity to the discussion when everyone in the room gave out a small laugh. It was as if his statement caught them by surprise. Without smiling himself, Pinette said, "from what I've been able to learn so far, based on the financial records I've been able to examine, it looks like D & B made approximately $2.3 million in the last 16 months, stemming from both government and civilian contracts to haul and dispose of waste that may have been disposed of illegally. That does not include about $3 million dollars of billable invoices for what may be associated with the legitimate disposal of waste. I can, as I said, show about $2.3 million in what they billed for the waste associated with various contracts that were falsely billed to private parties. About $1.2 million of $2.3 million is directly related to DoD contracts."

"Do you know where that $2.3 million is?" asked Mike Cook.

"I'm not sure. I haven't found any other bank accounts with either Mann or Thompson's name on them. I even checked the financials of Angela Lyle. There was very little there. She was, however, being paid extremely well. In fact, her salary, starting this past year, jumped about fifty percent. She must have been doing something right for them to have given her such a huge raise. But I did find about $500,000 in rental fees from the airplane that was blown up. The money showed up in a separate account belonging to Mann. Apparently, they rented that plane out a good bit."

"That's not true," Mike Cook said. "Tony and I reviewed the flight logs recovered from the plane. It didn't show very much in the way of other operators using the plane. We also checked with the maintenance facility that worked on the plane. The plane wasn't used that much. In fact, there were less than 40 hours of flying time on the plane in the last 18 months. At least according to the flight and maintenance logs. So I don't know how they could have generated a half a million dollars in rental fees from leasing out the plane over that period of time."

"They could have been using the plane to launder some of the money," Pinette said.

"Carlos, does the illegal disposal of hazardous waste qualify as an underlying offense for money laundering?" Mike asked.

"I believe it does," Sanchez explained. "There was a case in 2013 where the defendant engaged in a fraud scheme to sell renewable fuel to brokers and oil companies, when in fact, his company produced no fuel at all and did not have a facility capable of producing bio-diesel fuel. He was convicted of wire fraud, money laundering, and violating the Clean Air Act. So yes, I think it qualifies. I'll have to do some more research, but yes, I think this environmental crime qualifies as the substantive offense."

Mike Cook then turned his attention to Tony Martin, the detective he'd become exceptionally close to in the past three months, working together almost every single day. Cook did not make a move or decision impacting on the case without consulting with him. If there ever was a true partnership between the feds and local police, this was a textbook example of it.

"Tony, what can you tell us about the murder of Angela Lyle?"

Tony Martin paused, albeit briefly, and glanced around the long conference table. In the past four months, he had not met any of these people other than a brief meeting with Mike Cook. Then, without further hesitation, he said, "As most of you know, Angela was killed by a striking blow to the head. All of the blood recovered from the crime scene belonged to Angela. This is not a surprise since our theory is that she was struck by surprise and, that she knew her attacker.

"We have not found a murder weapon as of yet. Our persons of interest are both Mann and Thompson. We're still working on establishing an affair that we believe she was having with Mann. Mike and I talked to a Brandi Gardner. We found her contact information on Angela's cell phone. According to Ms. Gardner, who was one of Angela's best friends, Angela had been pre-occupied a good bit prior to being killed. Gardner claims that Angela had been seeing a married man at D & B but was breaking the relationship off because she had started an affair with her boss. Gardner didn't want to press her friend about it but told her it wasn't a very good idea. That apparently didn't sit well with Angela so she dropped the subject. Brandi had this conversation with Angela about two weeks prior to her being killed. So I don't think the relationship was very old. And, that seems to gel with what John Thomas said.So we are confident that Mann and Angela were in fact seeing each other, just not for very long."

Tony Martin took a huge gulp from his coffee and said, "We checked everything; nothing connects either man to her killing; not yet. We do know that Angela's name appears on most all of the invoices and paperwork associated with D & B. We'd like to bring both Mann and Thompson in for questioning but they both have lawyers and have refused to answer any of our questions."

Pamela Sullivan, the local prosecutor whose job it would be to prosecute the murderer of Angela Lyle was new to the team. In fact, it was the first time she met with most everyone in the room, including Carlos Sanchez, although she had spoken to him several times. The fact that Pamela had opted to become a prosecutor was a surprise to friends and family alike after graduating from the Harvard School of Law. There was far more money to be made after graduating from an Ivy League law school than ending up in the world of assistant district attorneys.

"Sorry to interrupt," Pamela said. "But what Tony is saying is true. Both men have lawyers and right now they're refusing to cooperate in any part of this investigation, including the attempt to blow up their airplane, the illegal disposal of hazardous waste, and of course, the murder of Angela Lyle. As far as the murder of Lyle goes, we have nothing to connect either man to her murder. We don't have enough probable cause to bring them in, or, get a warrant for their car or home."

"Thank you Pamela," Tony said. "There is no indication that the two of them, Mann and Angela, that is, traveled anywhere together. We ran everything, his credit cards, hers; neither shows any lodging or out of town expenses in the past six months that are out of the ordinary. I believe she started an affair with John Thomas shortly after being hired at D & B, then, after she got involved in hiding money and altering invoices for Mann and Thompson, she started an affair with Mann. That put our foreman, John Thomas, out of the picture.

"A canvas of the area did reveal that Mann's car had been seen at Angela's house on several occasions. However, no one saw his car there the night of the murder. Nor is there any evidence that Thompson was there that night. Doesn't mean they weren't, just means no one saw them or their cars there that night. There is nothing we've been able to find that puts Mann or Thompson in her home that night although Mann's prints are in the house."

"Are you saying all your leads have gone cold?" Sanchez asked.

"With regard to Angela's murder, right now, it seems that way. However, we do know or highly suspect some things about the killer."

"Such as?" Sanchez asked.

"First, we believe the suspect knew Angela Lyle. Second, the suspect felt very comfortable in Angela's home. Third, the suspect had a personal attachment to Angela."

"How did you come up with this?" Sanchez asked.

"I simply tried profiling the killer without any suspects in mind," Tony said. "Based on the crime scene, and the evidence, I tried to come up with a profile of someone without putting a face on them. Granted, it was not easy to do, suspecting that Mann and/or Thompson had something to do with this. But I examined the crime scene and asked how the murder was committed. The killer, or killers, left quickly. They didn't do anything to cover up the crime. That was a choice he or they made. So what was going through the killers mind? To get away quickly and cover his/her tracks is my best guess. The next question I want to try and answer is why did the killer do this?"

Sanchez stood up, took of his suit jacket and hung it on the back of his chair. "Were either of Mann or Thompson's fingerprints on the wine glasses in the kitchen?"

"No," Tony replied. "If either of them were there, they didn't touch the wine glasses. Makes me think whoever she might have been expecting, went there to kill her. It wasn't just the spur of the moment thing. But because the killer left so quickly, I don't think our suspect is anyone who had done this before. And as far as the wine is concerned, she hadn't had that much of it; her blood alcohol levels were negligible."

"Angela's behavior was no doubt a bit strange," Amber Fox interjected. First, she starts an affair with a married man, the foreman, John Thomas. Then, knowing that Thomas is letting D & B bury waste on his property, she apparently has little reservation about participating in the crime by dummying up invoices and so forth for her bosses, Mann and Thompson. Then, after the attempt to blow up D & B fails, Mann starts showing her some attention. And he too, is married. The question is, why would he show her so much attention? My guess; she knew too much and Mann started the affair to keep her quiet. Sure, she was good with the numbers and helped cover up the false invoices and the dumping of waste, but it doesn't appear she was getting a lot of money for it."

"Not that I've been able to find," Pinette responded. "But then I've only had a cursory look at her financials. I didn't see much out of the ordinary there. But like I said, she got a very healthy raise this past year. Her salary jumped from $50,000 a year to just over $80,000. That's a lot of money for a secretary or office manager in a business the size of D & B."

"What about John Thomas?" Lisa Swanson asked from the back of the room. "Is it possible that John Thomas killed her for breaking off the relationship? And, that Thomas is simply coming clean on the environmental crimes to point the murder finger at either Mann and/or Thompson?"

"That is certainly possible," Tony replied. "But we can't put Thomas there the night of the murder either. And he readily admitted to being in the house where most of their affair took place. So finding his prints in there, which we did, in the kitchen, living room, and bedroom, is explained away. But yes, he too, could be a person of interest. But he's cooperating. And, I think he's scared."

"Has anyone pushed Thomas' wife about the affair or where he was the night of the murder?" Lisa asked.

"Not since that morning when we confronted him in his kitchen and she came downstairs," Mike replied.

"Maybe it's time to lean on her," Lisa offered.

"It's certainly worth a go at her," Tony said quickly. "But like I said, we ran virtually everything. However they were going about this affair, they kept it off their phone, both in calls and text messages. And, there was nothing about it on their e-mail."

"Are you sure they were having an affair?" Lisa asked.

"According to John Thomas, yes. And according to her best friend, Brandi Gardner, she was starting to see her boss. Said he owned an airplane. Was going to take her flying. The plane is Mann's. He has a pilot's license. Nothing points to Thompson having much to do with the plane unless it's related to business. And only then, Mann is at the controls. So if you're asking if we have pictures of them in bed together, the answer is no. Do I think they were starting an affair, yes I do?"

Mike Cook felt Tony's frustration with Lisa's questions and felt it would be best for all concerned if he refocused the meeting on a new subject. He glanced around the room and saw John Sherry sitting patiently at the opposite end of the conference table. "John, what can you tell us about the Mann and Thompson's insurance."

"Well," Sherry began. "There is not much new to report that you don't already know. Thompson and Mann increased their insurance on D & B from two million to three million dollars several weeks before someone tried to blow the place up. The day prior to someone trying to blow them up or burn them down, however you want to call it, Thompson removed a very sentimental photo from his office. According to the late Angela Lyle, this picture had been in his office for well over a year. Quite coincidental that he removed it the day prior to someone trying to destroy the place. But since it didn't burn down, they haven't submitted a claim for anything on the business. And after finding the illegally dumped waste on the farm, we've taken steps to cancel their policy. However, Mann did have the plane insured for $1,800,000. Three weeks ago he filed a claim for the entire amount of the policy. And, he mailed a signed copy of the claim to our national headquarters. We do not, at this time, intend to pay the claim, especially after hearing that the plane may have been used in a money laundering scheme. However, we do plan to call him in for a deposition on this claim. Other than that, I don't have much to add."

"And who has a copy of this claim?"

"Our home office. It's been logged in."

"Can we maintain a chain of custody on that document?"

"Of course, we can. We've done this before," Sherry said sarcastically. "We know this could end up as evidence associated with a charge relating to mail fraud."

"I'll need the name of the person who received the claim."

"Not a problem."

"When do you plan to conduct that deposition?" Sanchez asked.

"Sometime in the next two weeks."

"And who will be conducting that?"

"Our in house counsel. I'll also be there."

"And if Mann refuses to give a deposition?" Sanchez asked.

"Then we automatically deny the claim."

"You'll keep us informed?" asked Mike Cook.

"Of course," replied Sherry.

Lieutenant Tom Gonzalez from the fire department was the next to speak. He told the group gathered in the conference room that he responded to both the fire of the airplane and the attempted bombing/ arson of D & B Environmental.

"What we found at the site of the airplane fire," Gonzalez began, "was a rudimentary explosive device consisting of a wind up clock, some batteries and matches placed on top of a five gallon gas can. The device ignited the matches which, of course, caused the gasoline to explode."

"The lab did in fact identify the liquid as gasoline," Mike Cook added.

"The device found at D & B appears to be the exact type of device used to destroy the aircraft," Gonzalez added. "As you know, the device, which was set to go at 3 a.m., failed. It's my understanding, that the records recovered from the scene, were also saturated in gasoline."

"That's correct," Cook said.

Gonzalez concluded his short briefing explaining what he and his department did at the scene of the aircraft fire, how they secured the scene, what they found, and the fact that the fire was indeed deliberately set. Gonzalez would, if necessary, be able to testify to issues involving chain of custody and the fact that the fire was not accidental.

Mike Cook said, "as everyone has heard, we know that the fire of the aircraft was deliberately set. There was a deliberate attempt to destroy D & B Environmental along with virtually all of its company records. We know that Eric Mann and Alan Thompson increased the insurance on D & B about a month prior to someone trying to blow it up. We know that Thompson took out a sentimental photo from his office the day prior to the attempt on D & B. We know that Mann's flight logs reveal far less use of the aircraft than what he was reporting with regard to leasing the plane out. And, that this plane was used to hide money made from the illegal disposal of hazardous waste. We know that D & B dumped approximately 100 dump truck loads of waste onto John Thomas' farm. And, we know that Ralph Browning, of Crane Environmental was in possession of false documents associated with D & B and DoD contracts. We also know that the late Angela Lyle was apparently responsible for actually submitting many if not all of these invoices and demands for payment. And, that she was having an affair with both John Thomas and later, Eric Mann.

"My question is, do we have enough to arrest anyone now, and if so, on what charges?"

There was a brief moment of silence in the room. Mike Cook then said, "Where do we go from here?"

Box 14.1 Environmental Crimes Bulletin, U.S. Environmental Protection Agency, Office of Criminal Enforcement, Forensics and Training, February 2013.

Maryland 'Clean Green Fuel' Owner of Sentenced to Over 12 Years in Prison for Scheme to Violate EPA Regulations and Sell $9 Million in Fraudulent Renewable Fuel Credits— On February 22, 2013, RODNEY R. HAILEY, of Perry Hall, Maryland, was sentenced in federal district court for the District of Maryland to 151 months in prison followed by three years of supervised release in connection with a scheme in which he sold $9 million in renewable fuel credits which he falsely claimed were produced by his company, Clean Green Fuel, LLC. Hailey's sentence was enhanced when the judge learned that he obstructed justice by concealing, selling and spending assets that were protected by court order. Hailey was also ordered to pay restitution of $42,196,089 to over 20 companies, and forfeit $9.1 million in proceeds of the fraud including cars, jewelry, his home and bank accounts already seized by the government in partial satisfaction of such $9.1 million judgment. Hailey was convicted on June 25, 2012, of eight counts of wire fraud, 32 counts of money laundering and two counts of violating the Clean Air Act. He has been detained since the guilty verdict. According to evidence presented at the six day trial, Hailey owned Clean Green Fuel, LLC, located in the Baltimore area. Hailey registered Clean Green Fuel with the EPA as a producer of bio-diesel fuel, a motor vehicle fuel derived from renewable resources. In order to encourage the production of renewable fuel and lessen the nation's dependence on foreign oil, all oil companies that market petroleum in the U.S. are required to produce a given quantity of renewable fuel or to purchase credits, called renewable identification numbers (RINs), from producers of renewable fuels to satisfy their renewable fuel requirements. Between March 2009 and December 2010, Hailey engaged in a massive fraud scheme, selling over 35 million RINs (representing 23 million gallons of bio-diesel fuel) to brokers and oil companies, when in fact Clean Green Fuel had produced no fuel at all and Hailey did not have a facility capable of producing bio-diesel fuel. Federal law enforcement agents investigated the scheme after a Baltimore County police detective working with Maryland's federal financial crimes task force received a report about a large number of luxury cars parked in front of Hailey's house. The financial crimes task force contacted the EPA's Criminal Investigation Division and initiated a criminal investigation. Two civil inspectors from EPA's Air Enforcement Division visited Clean Green's headquarters on July 22, 2010, to inspect Hailey's bio-diesel production facility, in response to a complaint alleging that Clean Green had been selling false RINs. Hailey was not able to provide an exact location for the biodiesel fuel production facility, nor any records to support claims that Clean Green Fuel had produced biodiesel fuel. When asked to explain his method of production, Hailey falsely stated that he paid employees and contractors to recover waste vegetable oil from 2,700 restaurants in the "Delmarva" area and bring it to his production facility where he converted it to bio-diesel fuel. Hailey claimed that only the drivers who picked up the oil knew the names of the restaurants, and Hailey could not provide the names of the drivers. Hailey made over $9.1 million from selling the false RINs. The loss to the traders and major energy companies who purchased Hailey's false RINs is over $40 million, but the loss also extends to small bio-diesel companies which, as a result of Hailey's scheme, were unable to sell their RINs and have been forced out of business. Hailey used the proceeds of the scheme to purchase luxury vehicles, including BMWs, Ferraris, Bentleys, a Mercedes Benz, a Rolls Royce Phantom, a Lamborghini, a Maserati and others, as well as real estate and more than $80,000 in diamond jewelry. In all of these transactions, Hailey generally used cash or checks drawn on accounts he controlled to make the purchase, including a check for $645,330.15 to buy his home in Perry Hall. The case was investigated by the Maryland Financial Crimes Task Force which included EPA's Criminal Investigation Division, the U.S. Marshals Service, the Baltimore County Police Department and IRS—Criminal Investigation; the U.S. Postal Inspection Service, and EPA Office of Inspector General—Office of Investigations.

Questions for Discussion

1. In our fictional story, AUSA Carlos Sanchez talks about a case involving a defendant who was charged with money laundering in connection with an EPA offense. This case, detailed in Box 14.1, provides an overview of this case. Do you think this case provides a precedent for an EPA offense serving as an underlying offense for a charge of money laundering? Defend your position.

2. At the end our fictional story Mike Cook asks the group seated around the conference table, "where do we go from here?" Determine what, if any, charges might be brought against anyone in our story. Be sure to lay out the evidence for each of these charges in order to satisfy the elements to the offense(s) being charged.

    a. Who are your witnesses? What will each person testify to?

3. What additional work or evidence must be done/collected to add additional charges to anyone involved in our story? What additional leads/investigative work must be done to bring charges against anyone for the murder of Angela Lyle?

4. Is there enough evidence to charge anyone with the murder of Angela Lyle? If so, who? What is the evidence? If not, what additional evidence do you think you need to collect? Use the statutes associated with murder, manslaughter, etc. in the state in which you are currently in to determine the elements of the offense.

Work Sheet

Exercise

1. Research the state statute relating to arson in the state you are in. What are the elements to the offense of arson if charged under that state law? List all the facts relevant to charging Mann and/or Thompson with arson under that state arson statute.

2. List all the facts relevant to charging Mann and Thompson with the arson/bombing of the aircraft and the attempted arson/bombing of D & B Environmental. Include in your answer, a short synopsis of who will testify to what in connection with these offenses.

3. List all the facts relevant to charging Mann, Thompson and Ralph Browning with providing False Claims to the U.S. Government. Include in your answer, a short synopsis of who will testify to what in connection with this offense.

4. List all the facts relevant to charging people in this fictional story with mail fraud. Who might be charged with this offense?

5. List all the facts relevant to charging people in this fictional story with money laundering. What evidence exists to support this charge?

6. List all the facts relevant to charging Mann and/or Thompson with the illegal disposal of hazardous waste.

7. List all the facts relevant to charging any of the characters in our fictional story with False Statements under 18 U.S.C. Section 1001.

8. List all the facts relevant to charging any of the characters in our fictional story with any computer related crimes.

Work Sheet

Websites

1. http://www2.epa.gov/enforcement/criminal-provisions-resource-conservation-and-recovery-act-rcra#one
2. http://www.justice.gov/usam/criminal-resource-manual-2101-money-laundering-overview
3. http://www.justice.gov/sites/default/files/civil/legacy/2011/04/22/C-FRAUDS_FCA_Primer.pdf
4. http://www.justice.gov/usam/criminal-resource-manual-940-18-usc-section-1341-elements-mail-fraud
5. http://www.justice.gov/usam/criminal-resource-manual-1437-federal-explosives-statutes-18-usc-841-848
6. http://www.justice.gov/usam/criminal-resource-manual-903-false-statements-concealment-18-usc-1001

ABOUT THE AUTHOR

Ernie Dorling has been involved in law enforcement for over 25 years. After leaving the Marine Corps in 1975, he joined the Hollywood, FL police department. In 1978, he became a Special Agent with the Bureau of Alcohol, Tobacco and Firearms in the Georgia field office. In 1986, Ernie joined the Defense Criminal Investigative Service (DCIS). During his time with DCIS, he was posted in Atlanta, Georgia; Wiesbaden, Germany; Washington D.C.; and finally, he was the Resident Agent in Charge of the Hartford, CT office until his retirement in 2001.

Immediately after retiring, Ernie Dorling began teaching criminal justice at Tunxis Community College in Farmington, CT. In 2004, he joined the criminal justice department at the Henry Lee School of Criminal Justice and Forensic Sciences at the University of New Haven in CT. During his tenure at UNH, he has focused his teaching on criminal investigation and white-collar crime investigation. In addition to his academic responsibilities, Ernie has participated in teaching a number of cold case seminars to police officers from around the country.

Ernie Dorling holds a Bachelor's of Science Degree in Criminal Justice from Nova University in Fort Lauderdale, FL. He went on to complete his Master's Degree in Public Administration from Troy State University in Alabama. He has also completed post-graduate work at the University of Connecticut.

Ernie Dorling has appeared on radio and local and national television shows discussing a variety of criminal justice issues. He is also the author of several professional and academic journal articles dealing with criminal justice issues and police executive leadership.

CPSIA information can be obtained
at www.ICGtesting.com
Printed in the USA
LVOW02s0228270117
522356LV00002B/9/P